AF830705

CIMA

Managerial Paper P7

FINANCIAL ACCOUNTING AND TAX PRINCIPLES

For exams in 2009

Practice & Revision Kit

In this January 2009 new edition

- We discuss the **best strategies** for revising and taking your CIMA exams
- We show you how to be well prepared for the **2009 exams**
- We give you **lots of great guidance** on tackling questions
- We show you how you can **build your own exams**
- We provide you with **three** mock exams including the **November 2008 exam**

BPP's **i-Pass** product also supports this paper.

BPP LEARNING MEDIA

First edition 2005
Fifth edition January 2009

ISBN 9780 7517 6551 9
(previous ISBN 9780 7517 5191 8)

British Library Cataloguing-in-Publication Data
A catalogue record for this book
is available from the British Library

Published by

BPP Learning Media Ltd
BPP House, Aldine Place
London W12 8AA

www.bpp.com/learningmedia

Printed in the United Kingdom

We are grateful to the Chartered Institute of Management Accountants for permission to reproduce past examination questions. The answers to past examination questions have been prepared by BPP Learning Media Ltd.

Your learning materials, published by BPP Learning Media Ltd, are printed on paper sourced from sustainable, managed forests.

Contents

Question index

The exam format for Paper P7 changed from the May 2007 sitting onwards. Section A is worth a total of 40 marks and the paper has one Section C question worth 30 marks.

Because of this change, we have included amended versions of the questions set in the CIMA exams for 2005 and 2006 that reflect the change in mark allocation from May 2007.

Planning your question practice

Our guidance from page xxiv shows you how to organise your question practice, either by attempting questions from each syllabus area or by **building your own exams** – tackling questions as a series of practice exams.

Exam guidance

You can find additional guidance on a number of questions in this kit on BPP's website: www.bpp.com/cima/extra-questions-guidance

Topic index

Listed below are the key Paper P7 syllabus topics and the numbers of the questions in this kit covering those topics.

If you need to concentrate your practice and revision on certain topics or if you want to attempt all available questions that refer to a particular subject, you will find this index useful.

Syllabus topic	Question numbers
Balance sheet	23, 24, 25, 26, 27, 28(b), 29
Baumol model	40, 45(f)
Cash flow forecast	46
Cash flow statement	7, 8, 9(a), 10(a), 11(a), 12(a), 13(b)
Company taxation	34, 38(d), (f)
Construction contracts	14, 15, 17, 22(c)
Contingencies	19, 20, 21, 22
Deferred tax	35, 38(a), (b), (c), (e)
Discounts	43
Discontinued operations	21(c), (g), (h), 30
Economic Order Quantity (EOQ)	42, 44
Employee tax	31
Events after the balance sheet date	19, 20
External audit	2, 4
Factoring	42
IAS 1	5, 6
IAS 8	5
IAS 12	35, 38
Income statement	23, 24, 25, 26, 27, 28(b), 29
Indirect taxation	33, 36(b), (g)
Intangible assets	14, 15, 16
International tax	32
Inventories	14, 15, 16(b)
Impairment of assets	14, 15, 16(d), (e)
Leasing	20, 21, 22(b), (d), (f)
Miller Orr model	40, 44, 45(f)
Non-current assets	14, 15, 16(c)
Operating cycle	44, 45
Overdraft	39, 41
Provisions	19, 20, 21, 22(a)
Regulatory framework	1, 3
Related parties	20, 21(d), 22(h)
Research and development	14, 16(a), 22(e)
Revenue recognition	20, 22(g)
Share capital transactions	18
Short-term deposits	39, 40, 41

Syllabus topic	Question numbers
Sources of finance	40, 41
Statement of changes in equity	23, 24, 26(a), 29
Withholding tax	36(f), 37
Working capital	42, 43, 44, 45, 46

Using your BPP Learning Media Practice and Revision Kit

Tackling revision and the exam

You can significantly improve your chances of passing by tackling revision and the exam in the right ways. Our advice is based on recent feedback from CIMA examiners. You may be surprised to know that much examiner advice is the same whatever the exam, and the reasons why many students fail don't vary much between subjects and exam levels.

- We look at the dos and don'ts of revising for, and taking, CIMA exams. Making the most of your revision time can make a big, big difference to how well-prepared you are for the exam
- We focus on Paper P7; we discuss revising the syllabus, what to do (and what not to do) in the exam, how to approach different types of question and ways of obtaining easy marks

Selecting questions

We provide signposts to help you plan your revision.

- A full **question index**
- A **topic index** listing all the questions that cover key topics, so that you can locate the questions that provide practice on these topics, and see the different ways in which they might be examined
- A **BPP question plan** highlighting the most important questions and explaining why you should attempt them
- **Build your own exams**, showing you how you can practise questions in a series of exams

Making the most of question practice

At BPP we realise that you need more than just questions and model answers to get the most from your question practice.

- Our **Top tips** provide essential advice on tackling questions, presenting answers and the key points that answers need to include
- We show you how you can pick up **Easy marks** on questions, as we know that picking up all readily available marks often can make the difference between passing and failing
- We summarise **Examiner's comments** to show you how students who sat the exam coped with the questions
- We refer to the **BPP 2008 Study Text** for detailed coverage of the topics covered in each question

Attempting mock exams

There are three mock exams that provide practice at coping with the pressures of the exam day. We strongly recommend that you attempt them under exam conditions. **Mock exams 1 and 2** reflect the question styles and syllabus coverage of the exam; **Mock exam 3** is the actual November 2008 exam. To help you get the most out of doing these exams, we not only provide help with each answer, but also guidance on how you should have approached the whole exam.

How to revise

☑ Plan your revision

At the start of your revision period, you should draw up a **timetable** to plan how long you will spend on each subject and how you will revise each area. You need to consider the total time you have available and also the time that will be required to revise for other exams you're taking.

☑ Practise Practise Practise

The **more exam-standard questions** you do, the **more likely you are to pass** the exam. Practising full questions will mean that you'll get used to the time pressure of the exam. When the time is up, you should note where you've got to and then try to complete the question, giving yourself practice everything that the question tests.

☑ Revise enough

Make sure that your revision covers the breadth of the syllabus, as in most papers most topics could be examined in a compulsory question. However it is true that some topics are **key** – they often appear in compulsory questions or are a particular interest of the examiner – and you need to spend sufficient time revising these. Make sure you know the **basics** – the fundamental calculations, proformas and report layouts.

☑ Deal with your difficulties

Difficult areas are topics you find dull and pointless, or subjects that you found problematic when you were studying them. You mustn't become negative about these topics; instead you should build up your knowledge by reading the **Passcards** and using the **Quick quiz** questions in the Study Text to test yourself. When practising questions in the Kit, go back to the Text if you're struggling.

☑ Learn from your mistakes

Having completed a question you must try to look at your answer critically. Always read the **Top tips** guidance in the answers; it's there to help you. Look at **Easy marks** to see how you could have quickly gained credit on the questions that you've done. As you go through the Kit, it's worth noting any traps you've fallen into, and key points in the **Top tips** or **Examiner's comments** sections, and referring to these notes in the days before the exam. Aim to learn at least one new point from each question you attempt, a technical point perhaps or a point on style or approach.

☑ Read the examiners' guidance

We refer throughout this Kit to **Examiner's comments**; these are available on CIMA's website. As well as highlighting weaknesses, examiners' reports often provide clues to future questions, as many examiners will quickly test again areas where problems have arisen. CIMA's website also contains articles that are relevant to this paper, which you should read.

☑ Complete all three mock exams

You should attempt the **Mock exams** at the end of the Kit under **strict exam conditions** to gain experience of selecting questions, managing your time and producing answers.

How NOT to revise

☒ Revise selectively

Examiners are well aware that some students try to forecast the contents of exams, and only revise those areas that they think will be examined. Examiners try to prevent this by doing the unexpected, for example setting the same topic in successive sittings or setting topics in compulsory questions that have previously only been examined in optional questions. Remember you have little choice of questions in most CIMA exams.

☒ Spend all the revision period reading

You cannot pass the exam just by learning the contents of Passcards, Course Notes or Study Texts. You have to develop your **application skills** by practising questions.

☒ Audit the answers

This means reading the answers and guidance without having attempted the questions. Auditing the answers gives you **false reassurance** that you would have tackled the questions in the best way and made the points that our answers do. The feedback we give in our answers will mean more to you if you've attempted the questions and thought through the issues.

☒ Practise some types of question, but not others

Although you may find the numerical parts of certain papers challenging, you shouldn't just practise calculations. These papers will also contain written elements, and you therefore need to spend time practising written question parts as well.

☒ Get bogged down

Don't spend a lot of time worrying about all the minute detail of certain topic areas, and leave yourself insufficient time to cover the rest of the syllabus. Remember that a key skill in the exam is the ability to **concentrate on what's important** and this applies to your revision as well.

☒ Overdo studying

Studying for too long without interruption will mean your studying becomes less effective. A five minute break each hour will help. You should also make sure that you are leading a **healthy lifestyle** (proper meals, good sleep and some times when you're not studying).

How to PASS your exams

☑ Prepare for the day

Make sure you set at least one alarm (or get an alarm call), and allow plenty of time to get to the exam hall. You should have your route planned in advance and should listen on the radio for potential travel problems. You should check the night before to see that you have pens, pencils, erasers, watch, calculator with spare batteries, also exam documentation and evidence of identity.

☑ Select the right questions

You should select the optional questions you feel you can answer **best**, basing your selection on the topics covered, the requirements of the question, how easy it will be to apply the requirements and the availability of easy marks.

☑ Plan your three hours

You need to make sure that you will be answering the correct number of questions, and that you spend the right length of time on each question – this will be determined by the number of marks available. Each mark carries with it a **time allocation** of **1.8 minutes**. A 25 mark question therefore should be selected, completed and checked in 45 minutes. With some papers, it's better to do certain types of question first or last.

☑ Read the questions carefully

To score well, you must follow the requirements of the question, understanding what aspects of the subject area are being covered, and the tasks you will have to carry out. Make sure you are aware of what the **question verbs require**; CIMA provides a table of verbs used together with their meaning as part of the question paper (see p xxi in this Kit). The requirements will also determine what information and examples you should provide. Reading the question scenarios carefully will help you decide what **issues** to discuss, what **techniques** to use, **information** and **examples** to include and how to **organise** your answer.

☑ Plan your answers

Five minutes of planning plus twenty-five minutes of writing is certain to earn you more marks than thirty minutes of writing. Consider when you're planning how your answer should be **structured**, what the **format** should be and **how long** each part should take.

Confirm before you start writing that your plan makes **sense**, covers **all relevant points** and does not include **irrelevant material.**

☑ Show evidence of judgement

Remember that examiners aren't just looking for a display of knowledge; they want to see how well you can **apply** the knowledge you have. Evidence of application and judgement will include writing answers that only contain **relevant** material, using the material in scenarios to **support** what you say, **criticising** the **limitations** and **assumptions** of the techniques you've used and making **reasonable recommendations** that follow from your discussion.

☑ Stay until the end of the exam

Use any spare time to **check and recheck** your script. This includes checking you have filled out the candidate details correctly, you have labelled question parts and workings clearly, you have used headers and underlining effectively and spelling, grammar and arithmetic are correct.

How to FAIL your exams

☒ Don't do enough questions

If you don't attempt sufficient questions on the paper, you are making it harder for yourself to pass the questions that you do attempt. If for example you don't do a 20 mark question, then you will have to score 50 marks out of 80 marks on the rest of the paper, and therefore have to obtain 63% of the marks on the questions you do attempt. Failing to attempt all of the paper is symptomatic of poor time management, poor question selection or failure to revise the whole syllabus.

☒ Include irrelevant material

Markers are given detailed mark guides and will not give credit for irrelevant content. Therefore you should **NOT** braindump into your answer all you know about a broad subject area; the markers will only give credit for what is **relevant**, and you will also be showing that you lack the ability to **judge what's important.** Similarly forcing irrelevant theory into every answer won't gain you marks, nor will providing uncalled for features such as situation analyses, executive summaries and background information.

☒ Fail to use the details in the scenario

General answers or reproductions of old answers that don't refer to what is in the scenario in **this** question won't score enough marks to pass.

☒ Copy out the scenario details

Examiners see **selective** use of the right information as a key skill. If you copy out chunks of the scenario that aren't relevant to the question, or don't use the information to support your own judgements, you won't achieve good marks.

☒ Don't do what the question asks

Failing to provide all the examiner asks for will limit the marks you score. The question part may include two requirements and you should answer **both**, not just the first one. If the requirements specify you should present your work in a certain format (memo, report) there will be marks for doing so, and you will not obtain these marks if you do not use the format specified. You will also decrease your chances by not providing an answer with enough **depth** – producing a single line bullet point list when the examiner asks for a discussion.

☒ Present your work poorly

Markers will only be able to give you credit if they can read your writing. There are also plenty of other things as well that will make it more difficult for markers to reward you. Examples include:

- Not using black or blue ink
- Not showing clearly which question you're attempting
- Scattering question parts from the same question throughout your answer booklet
- Not showing clearly workings or the results of your calculations

Paragraphs that are too long or which lack headers also won't help markers and hence won't help you.

Revising P7

This is a very wide-ranging syllabus, but with not a great deal of depth in some areas. For instance, the tax section of the paper does not use any specific tax regime, so the questions are just 'general'.

The format of the paper allows the examiner to cover a large part of the syllabus, so you cannot afford to neglect any area.

Areas to concentrate on are:

- Financial statements – you will have a compulsory 30-mark question on two out of: income statement, balance sheet, cash flow statement
- Leases and construction contracts
- Taxation and deferred tax
- The IASB *Framework*
- Miller-Orr, Baumol and the EOQ – you are given all these formulae in the exam
- Working capital cycle
- Cash flow forecasts
- Yield to maturity (the examiner is very attached to this)

Question practice

You should use the Passcards and any brief notes you have to revise these topics, but you mustn't spend all your revision time passively reading. Question practice is vital; doing as many questions as you can in full will help develop your ability to analyse scenarios and produce relevant discussion and recommendations. The question plan on page xxiv tells you what questions cover so that you can choose questions covering a variety of topics.

Passing the P7 exam

Displaying the right qualities

The examiners will expect you to display the following qualities.

Qualities required	
Produce neat workings and readable answers	If you produce no workings, the marker can give you no credit for using the right method. If the marker cannot read what you have written they can give you no marks at all.
Carry out standard calculations	You must be able to deal with EOQ, discounts, yield to maturity.
Demonstrate understanding of the basics	Deferred tax and construction contracts can be complex, but you will only get fairly simple questions, so make sure you understand the principles.

Avoiding weaknesses

The examiners have identified weaknesses that occur in many students' answers at every sitting. You will enhance your chances significantly if you ensure you avoid these mistakes:

- Failing to provide what the question verbs require (discussion, evaluation, recommendations) or to write about the topics specified in the question requirements
- Inability to carry out calculations
- Not showing workings in 3-4 mark questions
- Repeating the same material in different parts of answers
- Regurgitation of definitions and lists with no application to the question
- Brain dumping all that is known about a topic (no credit is given for this)
- Failing to answer sufficient questions because of poor time management
- Not answering all parts of optional questions
- Not using the information provided in the question accurately
- Attempting to question spot

Using the reading time

Use the reading time to analyse the adjustments needed in the Section C question and go over the requirements of the Section B questions deciding which parts to answer first.

Tackling questions

Numerical questions

Expect to see numbers throughout the paper. Approach them methodically and show all workings clearly.

Discussion questions

Remember that **depth of discussion** is also important. Discussions will often consist of paragraphs containing 2-3 sentences. Each paragraph should:

- **Make a point**
- **Explain the point** (you must demonstrate **why** the point is important)
- **Illustrate the point** (with material or analysis from the scenario, perhaps an example from real-life)

Gaining the easy marks

The first few marks are always the easiest to gain in any question. This applies particularly to Section B. Spend the same amount of time on each Section B question. This will give you a good chance of scoring marks on each question. Your Section C question carries a lot of marks. Make sure you begin by getting down the format and filling in any numbers which don't require calculation.

Formula to learn

For Paper P7 you are given most of the formulae that you need and they are in the 'Mathematical tables' section at the back of this revision pack.

The formula you *will* need to learn is the formula for the percentage cost of an early settlement discount to the company giving it.

Formula to learn

$$\left[\frac{100}{100-d}\right]^{\frac{365}{t}}-1$$

Where: d is the discount offered (5% = 5 etc.)
t is the reduction in payment period in days

Exam information

Format of the paper

		Number of marks
Section A:	Around 14–18 multiple choice and other objective test questions, 2–4 marks each	40
Section B:	6 compulsory questions, 5 marks each	30
Section C:	1 compulsory question, 30 marks	30
		100

Time allowed: 3 hours plus 20 minutes reading time.

Section A will always contain some multiple choice questions but will not consist solely of multiple choice questions. Section A may contain types of objective test question that are different from those included in the pilot paper. For 3 or 4-mark questions, marks are given for correct workings.

Section B questions will be mainly written discussion, although some calculations may be included. This section will require breadth of syllabus knowledge and also good time management skills.

The **Section C** question will be compulsory and will include **two** of income statement, balance sheet, cash flow statement.

For the papers listed up to November 2006 marks were:

Section A: 50
Section B: 30
Section C: 20

In these papers there was a choice of Section C question.

November 2008

			Marks
Section A			
1	17 objective test questions		40
Section B			
2	(a)	Explain role of SAC and IFRIC	
	(b)	EOQ calculation and discount	
	(c)	Preparation of a cash flow forecast	
	(d)	Calculation of deferred tax provision	
	(e)	Calculation of cash generated from operations	
	(f)	Preparation of cash flow statement	30
Section C			
One compulsory question – 30 marks			
3	Prepare property, plant and equipment note, income statement, statement of changes in equity and balance sheet		30
			100

This paper is Mock exam 3 in this Kit.

May 2008

			Marks
Section A			
1	15 objective test questions		40
Section B			
2	(a)	Explain treatment of expenditure as per *Framework*	
	(b)	Preparation of a cash flow statement	
	(c)	Calculate finance charge of preference shares and show disclosure	
	(d)	Explain benefits and limitations of a JIT purchasing system	
	(e)	Explain the elements of financial statements as per *Framework* giving examples	
	(f)	Corporate income tax calculation	30
Section C			
One compulsory question – 30 marks			
3	Income statement, statement of changes in equity		30

Examiner's comments. There was evidence of a number of well-prepared candidates with a wide range of knowledge, able to tackle most of the sub-questions in questions one and two and prepare a good answer to question three. The answer to question two was generally much better than in the last few diets. Questions 2 (d) and (e) were both relatively well done with quite a few candidates achieving marks on at least one section. However some candidates did not take account of the five mark limit and spent far too long answering these two questions. The overall performance on question three was not as good as it has been in recent examination diets. Unfortunately most students ignored their own comments in part (a) when preparing part (b).

November 2007

			Marks
Section A			
1	15 objective test questions		40
Section B			
2	(a)	Scenario question on IFRS 5	
	(b)	Calculating profits and VAT	
	(c)	Age analysis of receivables	
	(d)	IAS 18 scenario	
	(e)	Explain terms of IAS 24	
	(f)	Evaluate short-term investments	30
Section C			
One compulsory question – 30 marks			
3	Income statement, statement of changes in equity and balance sheet		30
			100

Examiner's comments. There was a good standard of answer being produced by many candidates, but performance overall was disappointing. There seemed to be an increasing number of students that were obviously question spotting and had not prepared for some of the topics on this paper, for example questions 2(c), (e) and (f). Question spotting is not advised in this paper.

May 2007

			Marks
Section A			
1	15 objective test questions		40
Section B			
2	(a)	Calculate corporate income tax	
	(b)	Calculate finance charge and liability relating to lease	
	(c)	Explain purposes of the framework	
	(d)	Treatment of discontinued operation	
	(e)	Calculation based on cost of discount	
	(f)	Advise company on sources of short-term lease	30
Section C			
One compulsory question – 30 marks			
3	Prepare property, plant and equipment note, income statement, statement of changes in equity and balance sheet		30
			100

Examiner's comments. This was the first examination using the new format paper and there seemed to be little impact on the overall pass rates. Question One was generally well done but no one scored full marks. Question Two was generally not so well done. Some candidates were ill-prepared for a question on the purposes of the IASB Framework or one on accepting a discount from a supplier. Question 3 part (b) was well done but many candidates lost marks on part (a).

November 2006

			Marks
Section A			
1	18 objective test questions		50
Section B			
2	(a)	Treatments of gains and impairments on buildings	5
	(b)	Audit report dealing with construction contract	5
	(c)	Adjustments for prior year error and use of provision	5
	(d)	Calculate deferred tax on non-current asset	5
	(e)	Risk and effective yield of investments	5
	(f)	Baumol and Miller Orr	5
Section C			
One question out of two – 20 marks			
3	Income statement, statement of changes in equity and balance sheet		
4	Cash flow statement		20
			100

Examiner's comments. The overall result was generally very pleasing and there was evidence of a number of well-prepared candidates with a wide range of knowledge. However, a number of candidates were obviously question spotting and had not prepared for some of the topics on the paper, for example question 2(b) and 2(e). Question spotting is not advised in this paper as most learning outcomes are covered in each examination.

May 2006

			Marks
Section A			
1	21 objective test questions		50
Section B			
2	(a)	Explain and calculate withholding tax and underlying tax	5
	(b)	Three scenarios on related parties	5
	(c)	Discussion question on development of accounting standards	5
	(d)	Treatment of development costs	5
	(e)	Calculation of finance cost on preference shares	5
	(f)	Preparation of simple income statement	5
Section C			
One question out of two – 20 marks			
3	Cash flow statement		
4	Cash budget		20
			100

Examiner's comments. This was the third paper of the new syllabus and the overall result was generally very pleasing. However a number of candidates had not taken note of the fact that financial statements include cash flow statements. Some candidates had relied on an income statement/balance sheet question and had not revised cash flow statements or cash budgets. Question spotting is not advised in this paper.

November 2005

			Marks
Section A			
1	20 objective test questions		50
Section B			
2	(a)	Explain tax avoidance and tax evasion	5
	(b)	Economic order quality – calculate and advise	5
	(c)	Discontinued operations and provisions – calculate amounts for financial statements	5
	(d)	Identify and explain four qualitative characteristics of financial information from *Framework*	5
	(e)	Non current assets – impairment and valuation	5
	(f)	Explain and calculate yield to maturity	5
Section C			
One question out of two – 20 marks			
3	Income statement, statement of changes in equity and balance sheet		
4	Cash budget and advice on raising funds		20
			100

Examiner's comments. This was the second paper and a good standard of answers was produced by many candidates. Time allocation seemed to be a problem for some candidates with evidence of rushed answers to either question 1 or question 2. Some candidates may have used more time on the Section C question and not spent enough time on the shorter sub-questions as evidenced by lack of workings and questions requiring some calculation being left out to save time.

May 2005

Section A			*Marks*
1	20 objective text questions		50
Section B			
2	(a)	Calculate current and deferred tax balances	
	(b)	Working capital cycle	
	(c)	List and explain 5 elements of financial statements as per *Framework*	
	(d)	Income statement and balance sheet extracts to show construction contract balances	
	(e)	Cash budget	
	(f)	Income statement and balance sheet extracts to show finance lease balances	30
Section C			
One question out of two – 20 marks			
3	Income statement and balance sheet		
4	Cash flow statement – indirect method		20
			100

Examiner's comments. This was the first sitting for this exam and the overall performance was good. Some students appeared to have a problem with time allocation, perhaps rushing through Sections A and B and allocating too much time to Section C. There was a lack of workings for Section A questions, with some questions requiring workings being left out altogether.

If workings are not provided, no marks can be given for a wrong answer. Question 1 carries 50 marks and should receive 50% of the time allocation.

Question 2 was also less well done. Some candidates could not deal with deferred tax, finance leases or construction contracts. Question 3 and 4 were obviously well-prepared and were generally well answered.

Pilot paper

Section A

1 21 objective test questions ranging from 2 to 4 marks each.

Section B – Six short answer questions – 5 marks each

2 Depreciation, change to estimated useful economic life
3 Treatment of decommissioning costs
4 Cash flow forecast
5 Income statement and balance sheet extracts to reflect entries in respect of tax on profits and deferred tax
6 Explain definition of provision as per IAS 37
7 Income statement and balance sheet extracts to show entries for leased asset

Section C – One question out of 2 – 20 marks

8 Income statement, balance sheet and statement of changes in equity
9 Cash flow statement in accordance with IAS 7.

What the examiner means

The table below has been prepared by CIMA to help you interpret exam questions.

Learning objective	Verbs used	Definition	Examples in the Kit
1 Knowledge What you are expected to know	• List • State • Define	• Make a list of • Express, fully or clearly, the details of/facts of • Give the exact meaning of	2 22(g) 36(a)
2 Comprehension What you are expected to understand	• Describe • Distinguish • Explain • Identify • Illustrate	• Communicate the key features • Highlight the differences between • Make clear or intelligible/state the meaning of • Recognise, establish or select after consideration • Use an example to describe or explain something	32 3(a) 3(d) 3(b)
3 Application How you are expected to apply your knowledge	• Apply • Calculate/compute • Demonstrate • Prepare • Reconcile • Solve • Tabulate	• To put to practical use • To ascertain or reckon mathematically • To prove with certainty or to exhibit by practical means • To make or get ready for use • To make or prove consistent/ compatible • Find an answer to • Arrange in a table	38(e) 16(e) 6(b)
4 Analysis How you are expected to analyse the detail of what you have learned	• Analyse • Categorise • Compare and contrast • Construct • Discuss • Interpret • Produce	• Examine in detail the structure of • Place into a defined class or division • Show the similarities and/or differences between • To build up or complete • To examine in detail by argument • To translate into intelligible or familiar terms • To create or bring into existence	 16(a)
5 Evaluation How you are expected to use your learning to evaluate, make decisions or recommendations	• Advise • Evaluate • Recommend	• To counsel, inform or notify • To appraise or assess the value of • To advise on a course of action	45(e)

Exam update

IAS 23 Borrowing Costs

Benchmark treatment

Prior to the revision of IAS 23 the benchmark treatment was to recognise borrowing costs as an expense. **This benchmark/allowed alternative has now been removed**.

IAS 23 revised: capitalisation

Under the revised treatment, all eligible borrowing costs must be **capitalised**.

Only borrowing costs that are **directly attributable** to the acquisition, construction or production of a qualifying asset can be capitalised as part of the cost of that asset. The standard lays out the criteria for determining which borrowing costs are eligible for capitalisation.

Borrowing costs eligible for capitalisation

Those borrowing costs directly attributable to the acquisition, construction or production of a qualifying asset must be identified. These are the borrowing costs that **would have been avoided** had the expenditure on the qualifying asset not been made. This is obviously straightforward where funds have been borrowed for the financing of one particular asset.

Disclosure

The following should be disclosed in the financial statements in relation to borrowing costs.

(a) Amount of borrowing costs **capitalised during the period**

(b) **Capitalisation rate** used to determine the amount of borrowing costs eligible for capitalisation

Useful websites

The websites below provide additional sources of information of relevance to your studies for *Financial Accounting and Tax Principles.*

- BPP — www.bpp.com

  For details of other BPP material for your CIMA studies
- CIMA — www.cimaglobal.com

  The official CIMA website
- *Financial Times* — www.ft.com
- *The Economist* — www.economist.com
- *Wall Street Journal* — www.wsj.com

Using your BPP products

This Kit gives you the question practice and guidance you need in the exam. Our other products can also help you pass:

- **Learning to Learn Accountancy** gives further valuable advice on revision
- **Passcards** provide you with clear topic summaries and exam tips
- **Success CDs** help you revise on the move
- **i-Pass CDs** offer tests of knowledge against the clock
- **Learn Online** is an e-learning resource delivered via the Internet, offering comprehensive tutor support and featuring areas such as study, practice, email service, revision and useful resources

You can purchase these products by visiting www.bpp.com/mybpp.

Planning your question practice

We have already stressed that question practice should be right at the centre of your revision. Whilst you will spend some time looking at your notes and the Paper P7 Passcards, you should spend the majority of your revision time practising questions.

We recommend two ways in which you can practise questions.

- Use **BPP's question plan** to work systematically through the syllabus and attempt key and other questions on a section-by-section basis
- **Build your own exams** – attempt the questions as a series of practice exams

These ways are suggestions and simply following them is no guarantee of success. You or your college may prefer an alternative but equally valid approach.

BPP's question plan

The plan below requires you to devote a **minimum of 45 hours** to revision of Paper P7. Any time you can spend over and above this should only increase your chances of success.

Step 1 **Review your notes** and the chapter summaries in the Paper P7 **Passcards** for each section of the syllabus.

Step 2 **Answer the key questions** for that section. These questions have boxes round the question number in the table below and you should answer them in full. Even if you are short of time you must attempt these questions if you want to pass the exam. You should complete your answers without referring to our solutions.

Step 3 **Attempt the other questions** in that section. For some questions we have suggested that you prepare **answer plans or do the calculations** rather than full solutions. Planning an answer means that you should spend about 30% of the time allowance for the questions brainstorming the question and drawing up a list of points to be included in the answer.

Step 4 **Attempt Mock exams 1, 2 and 3** under strict exam conditions.

Syllabus section	2009 Passcards chapters	Questions in this Kit	Comments	Done ☑
The regulatory framework	1	1, 3	The MCQs are fairly simple here. The Section B questions invite you to spend a lot of time, so *don't do it* – practise answering these question with notes and bullet points.	☐
External audit	2	2, 4	Make sure you know the different types of audit report qualification and be very strict and to the point on the Section B questions.	☐
Financial accounts – presentation	3, 4	5–6	This area is very important – IAS 1 and IAS 8. Do all of the MCQs. Make sure you can write out the formats.	☐
Cash flow statements	8	7, 8	These are good revision for the various components of the cash flow, so do them before attempting the longer questions.	☐
Cash flow statements	8	9–13	These are Section C questions on cash flow statements. This is very likely to come up in Part C. This is not a difficult topic. Do all of these questions and make sure you can produce *net cash flow from operating activities* using both methods.	☐
Non-current assets, inventories and construction contracts	5, 6, 10	14–17	These are fairly complex topics. If you have trouble with the MCQs, go back to the Study Text and revise the area.	☐
Capital transactions and financial instruments	11	18	These MCQs cover most of the important issues in this area. Make sure you understand how to deal with redemption of capital and purchase of own shares.	☐
Accounting standards	7, 9	19-22	These questions cover IAS 10, IAS 24, IAS 37 and IAS 17. These are all important because they are relatively *easy* to learn and apply, so if they come up they will be easy marks. Make sure you can calculate finance lease interest payments using both methods.	☐
Financial statements	3, 4	23-30	Section C will have an accounts preparation question, so practice on these. Make sure you can do all of them.	☐
General principles of taxation	12, 13	31-33	Answer all of these MCQs. There will be more than one question on each topic, so you will get lots of practice.	☐
		36, 37	These are Section B-type questions. Make sure you do not spend more than 9 minutes on each.	☐
Company taxation	14	34, 35	Answer all of these MCQs. Make sure you really understand the adjustments necessary to get from accounting profit to taxable profit and can do it easily.	☐
		38	These are Section B questions on company tax. Deferred tax is the most difficult aspect. Just make sure you understand the basics.	☐

Syllabus section	2009 Passcards chapters	Questions in this Kit	Comments	Done ☑
Short-term finance	16, 17, 18	39-40	Make sure you do these three MCQ questions in the time allocated and look over anything you were unable to deal with.	☐
		41	Try all of these. Learn how to apply Baumol and Miller-Orr. You will be given these formulae in the exam, so there is nothing difficult to remember.	☐
Working capital management	15, 19, 20	42-44	Make sure you can do all of these. Working capital is an important part of the syllabus and it is not difficult. Make sure you can calculate receivables days/payables days etc	☐
		45–46	Do all of these. They are all useful questions and these issues are quite likely to appear in Section B.	☐

Build your own exams

Having revised your notes and the BPP Passcards, you can attempt the questions in the Kit as a series of practice exams. You can organise the questions in the following way:

	Marks
16–20 objective test questions	40
6 Section B questions	30
1 Section C question	30
	100

This Kit contains 19 banks of objective test questions – numbers 1, 2, 5, 7, 14, 15, 18, 19, 20, 31, 32, 33, 34, 35, 39, 40, 42, 43, 44.

For Section A of your exam, do one question from each of these to a total of 40 marks. If you do a 3 or 4-mark question, reduce the number of questions accordingly.

For Section B, do 6 sub-questions from the following questions – 3, 4, 6, 8, 16, 17, 21, 22, 36, 37, 38, 41, 45, 46. Make sure you do at least one question from Part A, one from Part B, one from Part C and one from Part D – see the Question and Answer Checklist.

For Section C, do one of the following: 9, 10, 11, 12, 13, 23, 24, 25, 26, 27, 28, 29, 30.

Also make sure you do the three mock exams, especially mock exam 3, which is the November 2008 paper.

Questions

Extra guidance

Remember you can find additional guidance on a number of questions in this kit on BPP's website: www.bpp.com/cima/extra-question-guidance

Part A: Principles of Regulation of Financial Reporting

Questions 1 to 4 cover Principles of Regulation of Financial Reporting, the subject of Part A of the BPP Study Text for Paper P7.

1 Objective test questions: The regulatory framework 67 mins

1 The process leading to the publication of an International Financial Reporting Standard (IFRS) has a number of stages.

List the THREE stages that normally precede the final issue of an IFRS. **(3 marks)**

11/06

---

2 Guidance on the application and interpretation of International Financial Reporting Standards is provided by:

A The IASB
B The IASC Foundation
C The IFRIC
D The Standards Advisory Council **(2 marks)**

---

3 Which of the following is *not* an advantage of global harmonisation of accounting standards?

A Priority given to different user groups in different countries
B Easier transfer of accounting staff across national borders
C Ability to comply with the requirements of overseas stock exchanges
D Better access to foreign investor funds **(2 marks)**

---

4 The IASB has recently revised and improved a number of standards. One of the major purposes of these revisions has been:

A To make the standards more relevant to developing countries
B To eliminate alternative treatments of items in accounts
C To give preparers of accounts more choice
D To comply with the demands of pressure groups **(2 marks)**

---

5 The International Accounting Standards Board's *Framework for the Preparation and Presentation of Financial Statements* defines five elements of financial statements. Three of the elements are asset, liability and income.

List the other TWO elements. **(2 marks)**

11/06

---

6 Which two of the following, per the *Framework*, are *underlying assumptions* relating to financial statements?

1 The accounts have been prepared on an accruals basis
2 Users are assumed to have sufficient knowledge to be able to understand the financial statements
3 The accounting policies used have been disclosed
4 The business is expected to continue in operation for the foreseeable future
5 The information is free from material error or bias

A 1 and 3
B 2 and 3
C 1 and 4
D 3 and 5 **(2 marks)**

---

7 Which two of the following are not elements of financial statements *per* the *Framework*?

1 Profits
2 Assets
3 Income
4 Equity
5 Losses
6 Expenses

A 2 and 4
B 1 and 5
C 3 and 4
D 5 and 6 **(2 marks)**

8 According to the *Framework*, the income statement measures:

A Financial position
B Performance
C Profitability
D Financial adaptability **(2 marks)**

9 Which two of the following are underlying assumptions in the International Accounting Standards Board's *Framework for the Preparation and Presentation of Financial Statements*?

1 Accruals
2 Relevance
3 Comparability
4 Going concern
5 Reliability

A 1 and 5
B 2 and 5
C 3 and 4
D 1 and 4 **(2 marks)**

Pilot paper

10 The International Accounting Standards Board's *Framework for the Preparation and Presentation of Financial Statements* defines elements of financial statements. In no more than 30 words define an asset. **(2 marks)**

Pilot paper

11 The term GAAP is used to mean

A Generally accepted accounting procedures
B General accounting and audit practice
C Generally agreed accounting practice
D Generally accepted accounting practice **(2 marks)**

5/05

12 Which one of the following is responsible for governance and fundraising in relation to the development of International Accounting Standards?

A International Accounting Standards Board
B International Financial Reporting Interpretations Committee
C International Accounting Standards Committee Foundation Trustees
D Standards Advisory Council **(2 marks)**

5/05

13 Financial statements prepared using International Standards and the International Accounting Standards Board's (IASB *Framework for the Preparation and Presentation of Financial Statements* (Framework) are presumed to apply two of the following four underlying assumptions

1 Relevance
2 Going concern
3 Prudence
4 Accruals

Which two of the above are underlying assumptions according to the IASB's *Framework*?

A 1 and 2 only
B 2 and 3 only
C 3 and 4 only
D 2 and 4 only **(2 marks)**

5/05

---

14 The setting of International Accounting Standards is carried out by co-operation between a number of committees and boards, which include:

1 International Accounting Standards Committee Foundation (IASC Foundation)
2 Standards Advisory Council (SAC)
3 International Financial Reporting Interpretations Committee (IFRIC)

Which of the above reports to, or advises, the International Accounting Standards Board (IASB)?

	Reports to:	*Advises:*
A	1 and 3	2
B	1 and 2	3
C	3	2
D	2	1

(2 marks)

11/05

---

15 The IASB's Framework for the Preparation and Presentation of Financial Statements provides definitions of the elements of financial statements. One of the elements defined by the Framework is 'expenses'.

In no more than **35** words, give the IASB Framework's definition of expenses. **(2 marks)**

5/06

---

16 According to the International Accounting Standards Board's (IASB) *Framework for the Preparation and Presentation of Financial Statements* (Framework), what is the objective of financial statements?

Write your answer in nor more than **35** words. **(2 marks)**

5/07

---

17 Which of the following are functions of the International Accounting Standards Committee Foundation?

1 Issuing International Accounting Standards

2 Approving the annual budget of the International Accounting Standards Committee (IASC) and its committees

3 Enforcing International Accounting Standards

4 Reviewing the strategy of the IASC

5 Publishing an annual report on the activities of the IASC and IASB

A 1, 2 and 5
B 2 and 4
C 1, 3 and 5
D 2, 4 and 5 **(2 marks)**

5/08

---

18 The International Accounting Standards Board's (IASB) *Framework for the Preparation and Presentation of Financial Statements* (Framework), sets out four qualitative characteristics of financial information.

Two of the characteristics are relevance and comparability. List the other TWO characteristics. **(2 marks)**

11/07

(Total = 37 marks)

---

2 Objective test questions: External audit **47 mins**

1 The International Standard on Auditing 701 *Modifications to the Independent Auditor's Report,* classifies modified audit reports into 'matters that do not affect the auditor's opinion' and 'matters that do affect the auditor's opinion'. This latter category is further sub-divided into three categories

List these three categories **(3 marks)**

5/07

---

2 An external auditor gives a qualified audit report that is a 'disclaimer of opinion'.

This means that the auditor

A Has been unable to agree with an accounting treatment used by the directors in relation to a material item.

B Has been prevented from obtaining sufficient appropriate audit evidence.

C Has found extensive errors in the financial statements and concludes that they do not show a true and fair view.

D Has discovered a few immaterial differences that do not affect the auditor's opinion. **(2 marks)**

11/07

---

3 There is a major uncertainty facing Z, a limited liability company. Actions are pending against the company for allegedly supplying faulty goods, causing widespread damage.

The directors have fully described the circumstances of the case in a note to the financial statements.

What form of audit report is appropriate in this case?

A Qualified opinion – limitation on auditors' work
B Disclaimer of opinion
C Unqualified report with an additional explanatory paragraph
D Qualified opinion – disagreement **(2 marks)**

---

4 Which of the following matters are normally covered by the auditors' report?

1 Whether the company has kept proper accounting records

2 Whether the accounts are in agreement with the accounting records

3 Whether the accounts have been prepared in accordance with the relevant legislation and accounting standards

4 Whether other information presented with the financial statements is consistent with them

A 1 and 2 only
B 1, 2 and 3 only
C 3 and 4 only
D All four matters are normally covered **(2 marks)**

---

5 A company's auditors find insufficient evidence to substantiate the company's cash sales, which are material in amount.

What form of qualification of the audit report would normally be appropriate in this situation?

A Qualified opinion – disagreement
B Qualified opinion – limitation on auditors' work
C Disclaimer of opinion
D Qualified opinion – adverse opinion **(2 marks)**

---

6 A company's accounting records were largely destroyed by fire shortly after the balance sheet date. As a result, the financial statements contain a number of figures based on estimates.

What form of qualification of the audit report would be appropriate in this situation?

A Qualified opinion – disagreement
B Qualified opinion – limitations on auditors' work
C Disclaimer of opinion
D Qualified opinion – adverse opinion **(2 marks)**

---

7 An auditor forms the opinion that a company's trade receivables are overstated by a material amount because of the company's failure to provide for a balance due from a company that has ceased trading.

What form of qualification of the audit report would normally be appropriate in this case?

A Qualified opinion – disagreement
B Qualified opinion – limitation on auditors' work
C Disclaimer of opinion
D Qualified opinion – adverse opinion **(2 marks)**

---

8 When carrying out an audit an external auditor must satisfy himself of a number of matters. Which of the following are not one of those matters?

A The accounts have been prepared by a qualified accountant
B Proper accounting records have been kept
C The accounts have been prepared in accordance with local legislation and relevant accounting standards
D The accounts are in agreement with accounting records **(2 marks)**

---

9 If an external auditor does not agree with the directors' treatment of a material item in the accounts, the first action they should take is to:

A Give a qualified opinion of the financial statements.
B Give an unqualified opinion of the financial statements.
C Force the directors to change the treatment of the item in the accounts.
D Persuade the directors to change the treatment of the item in the accounts. **(2 marks)**

11/05

---

10 The external auditor has a duty to report on the truth and fairness of the financial statements and to report any reservations. The auditor is normally given a number of powers by statute to enable the statutory duties to be carried out.

List three powers that are usually granted to the auditor by statute. **(3 marks)**

5/06

---

11 Which one of the powers listed below is unlikely to be granted to the auditor by legislation?

A The right access at all times to the books, records, documents and accounts of the entity

B The right to be notified of, attend and speak at meetings of equity holders

C The right to correct financial statements if the auditor believes the statements do not show a true and fair view

D The right to require officers of the entity to provide whatever information and explanations thought necessary for the performance of the duties of the auditor **(2 marks)**

5/08

---

12 Which one of the following statements would be correct when an independent auditor's report gives an adverse opinion?

A The effect of the disagreement with management is so pervasive that the financial statements are misleading and, in the opinion of the auditor, do not give a true and fair view.

B A disagreement with management over material items needs to be highlighted using an 'except for' statement.

C An opinion cannot be given because insufficient information or access to records has been given to the auditor.

D A disagreement with management over material items means that an unqualified report must be issued. **(2 marks)**

5/08

(Total = 26 marks)

---

3 Section B questions: Regulation **45 mins**

(a) *The Framework for the Preparation and presentation of Financial Statements* (Framework) was first published in 1989 and was adopted by The International Accounting Standards Board (IASB)

Explain the purposes of this framework **(5 marks)**

5/07

(b) *Required*

The International Accounting Standards Board (IASB) *Framework for the Preparation and Presentation of Financial Statements (Framework)* defines the elements of financial statements.

Explain each of the elements, illustrating each with an example. **(5 marks)**

5/08

(c) The IASB's *Framework* identifies four principal qualitative characteristics of financial information.

Required

Identify and explain each of the four principal qualitative characteristics of financial information listed in the IASB's *Framework.* **(5 marks)**

11/05

(d) C is a small developing country which passed legislation to create a recognised professional accounting body two years ago. At the same time as the accounting body was created, new regulations governing financial reporting requirements of entities were passed. However, there are currently no accounting standards in C.

C's government has asked the new professional accounting body to prepare a report setting out the country's options for developing and implementing a set of high quality local accounting standards. The government request also referred to the work of the IASB and its International Financial Reporting Standards.

Required

As an advisor to the professional accounting body, outline three options open to C for the development of a set of high quality local accounting standards. Identify one advantage and one disadvantage of each option. **(5 marks)**

5/06

(e) EK publishes various types of book and occasionally produces films which it sells to major film distributors.

(i) On 31 March 20X7, EK acquired book publishing and film rights to the next book to be written by an internationally acclaimed author, for $1 million. The author has not yet started writing the book but expects to complete it in 20X9.

(ii) Between 1 June and 31 July 20X7, EK spent $500,000 exhibiting its range of products at a major international trade fair. This was the first time EK had attended this type of event. No new orders were taken as a direct result of the event, although EK directors claim to have made valuable contacts that should generate additional sales or additional funding for films in the future. No estimate can be made of additional revenue at present.

(iii) During the year, EK employed an external consultant to redesign EK's corporate logo and to create advertising material to improve EK's corporate image. The total cost of the consultancy was $800,000.

EK's directors want to treat all of the above items of expenditure as assets.

Required

Explain how EK should treat these items of expenditure in its financial statements for the year ended 31 October 20X7 with reference to the International Accounting Standard Board's (IASB) *Framework for the Preparation and Presentation of Financial Statements (Framework)* and relevant International Financial Reporting Standards. **(5 marks)**

5/08

(Total = 25 marks)

4 Section B questions: External audit **27 mins**

(a) Explain the circumstances in which an audit report will express each of the following:

(i) A qualified opinion
(ii) A disclaimer of opinion
(iii) An adverse opinion **(5 marks)**

(b) An auditor, in carrying out his statutory duty, may sometimes find himself to be in conflict with the directors of the company. What statutory rights does he have to assist him in discharging his responsibility to the shareholders? **(5 marks)**

(c) DC is carrying out three different construction contracts. The balances and results for the year to 30 September 2006 were as follows:

Contract	*1*	*2*	*3*
Contract end date	*30 Sept 2010*	*31 Dec 2007*	*30 Sept 2007*
	$m	$m	$m
Profit/(loss) recognised for year	2	2.3	(0.6)
Expected total profit/(loss) on contract	12	5.0	(3.0)

DC's management have included $3.7m profit in the income statement for the year ended 30 September 2006.

No allowance has been made in the income statement for the future loss expected to arise on contract 3, as management consider the loss should be offset against the expected profits on the other two contracts.

EA & Co are DC's external auditors. EA & Co consider that the profit in relation to long term contracts for the year ended 30 September 2006 should be $1.3m, according to IAS 11 *Construction Contracts*. Assume that EA & Co have been unable to persuade DC's management to change their treatment of the long term contract profit/loss.

Required

(i) Explain the objective of an external audit.

(ii) Identify, with reasons, the type of audit report that would be appropriate for EA & Co to use for DC's financial statements for the year ended 30 September 2006. Briefly explain what information should be included in the audit report in relation to the contracts.

Your answer should refer to appropriate International Standards on Auditing (ISA). **(5 marks)**

11/06

(Total = 15 marks)

Part B: Single Company Financial Accounts

Questions 5 to 30 cover Single Company Financial Accounts, the subject of Part B of the BPP Study Text for Paper P7.

5 Objective test questions: Presentation — 43 mins

1 Which, if any, of the following statements about limited liability companies are correct, according to IAS 1?

1 Companies must produce their financial statements within one year after their balance sheet date.

2 The accounting policies adopted by a company must be disclosed by note.

3 The accounting records of a limited liability company must be open to inspection by a member of the company at all times.

A 2 only
B 2 and 3 only
C 1 and 3 only
D None of the statements is correct **(2 marks)**

---

2 Which of the following items can appear in a company's statement of changes in equity, according to IAS 1 *Presentation of financial statements?*

1 Net profit or loss for the period
2 Dividends paid
3 Surplus on revaluation of properties
4 Proceeds of issuance of share capital

A All four items
B 1, 2 and 3 only
C 1, 3 and 4 only
D 2 and 4 only **(2 marks)**

---

3 Which of the following statements about company financial statements are true?

1 The statement of recognised income and expense must not include unrealised gains.

2 The number of employees at the end of the period or the average number of employees for the period must be disclosed by note.

3 Investments may appear in the balance sheet as either non-current assets or current assets.

4 When a revalued asset is sold, the revaluation surplus may be transferred from revaluation reserve to retained earnings in the balance sheet.

A 2, 3 and 4
B 3 and 4
C 1 and 2
D 1 and 4 **(2 marks)**

---

4 Which of the following items are required by IAS 1 *Presentation of financial statements* to be disclosed in the financial statements of a limited liability company?

1 Authorised share capital
2 Finance costs
3 Staff costs
4 Depreciation

A 1 and 4 only
B 1 , 2 and 3 only
C 2, 3 and 4 only
D All four items **(2 marks)**

---

5 Which of the following constitute a change of accounting policy according to IAS 8 *Accounting policies, changes in accounting estimates and errors?*

1 A change in the basis of valuing inventory

2 A change in depreciation method

3 A decision to capitalise borrowing costs relating to the construction of non-current assets, rather than writing them off as incurred

4 Adopting an accounting policy for a new type of transaction not previously dealt with

A 1 and 2
B 2 and 3
C 1 and 3
D 2 and 4 **(2 marks)**

---

6 Which of the following items would qualify for treatment as a change in accounting estimate, according to IAS 8 (revised) *Accounting policies, changes in accounting estimates and errors?*

1 Provision for obsolescence of inventory
2 Correction necessitated by a material error
3 A change as a result of the adoption of a new International Accounting Standard
4 A change in the useful life of a non-current asset

A All four items
B 2 and 3 only
C 1 and 3 only
D 1 and 4 only **(2 marks)**

---

7 A change in accounting policy is accounted for by:

A Changing the current year figures but not previous year's figures
B Retrospective application
C No alteration of any figures but disclosure in the notes
D No alteration of any figures nor disclosure in the notes **(2 marks)**

---

8 Shah changes the depreciation method for its motor vehicles from the straight line method to the reducing balance method. How would this be treated in the financial statements?

A Changing the current year figures but not previous year's figures
B Retrospective application
C No alteration of any figures but disclosure in the notes
D No alteration of any figures nor disclosure in the notes **(2 marks)**

---

9 IAS 8 –*Accounting Policies, Changes in Accounting Estimates and Errors* specifies the definition and treatment of a number of different items. Which of the following is NOT specified by IAS 8?

A The effect of a change in an accounting estimate
B Prior period adjustments
C Provisions
D Errors **(2 marks)**

Pilot paper

---

10 Which one of the following would be regarded as a change of accounting policy under IAS 8 *Accounting policies, changes in accounting estimates and errors*?

A An entity changes its method of depreciation of machinery from straight line to reducing balance.

B An entity has started capitalising borrowing costs for assets under the revised IAS 23 *Borrowing costs*. The borrowing costs previously had been charged to the income statement.

C An entity changes its method of calculating the provision for warranty claims on its products sold.

D An entity disclosed a contingent liability for a legal claim in the previous year's accounts. In the current year, a provision has been made for the same legal claim. **(2 marks)**

11/05

---

11 IAS 1 *Presentation of financial statements* requires some of the items to be disclosed on the face of the financial statements and others to be disclosed in the notes.

1 Depreciation
2 Revenue
3 Closing inventory
4 Finance cost
5 Dividends

Which two of the above have to be shown on the face of the income statement, rather than in the notes:

A 1 and 4
B 3 and 5
C 2 and 3
D 2 and 4 **(2 marks)**

11/05

---

12 IAS 1 *Presentation of Financial Statements* encourages an analysis of expenses to be presented on the face of the income statement. The analysis of expenses must use a classification based on either the nature of expense, or its function, within the entity such as:

1 Raw materials and consumables used;
2 Distribution costs;
3 Employee benefit costs;
4 Cost of sales;
5 Depreciation and amortisation expense.

Which of the above would be disclosed on the face of the income statement if a manufacturing entity uses analysis based on function?

A 1, 3 and 4
B 2 and 4
C 1 and 5
D 2, 3 and 5 **(2 marks)**

5/06

(Total = 24 marks)

---

6 Section B questions: Presentation **18 mins**

(a) Suggest reasons why companies should be expected to publish accounts using standard formats saying why and to whom the specific information shown in the formats would be useful. **(5 marks)**

(b) The following is an extract from the trial balance of CE at 31 March 20X6:

	$'000	$'000
Administration expenses	260	
Cost of sales	480	
Interest paid	190	
Interest bearing borrowings		2,200
Inventory at 31 March 20X6	220	
Property, plant and equipment at cost	1,500	
Property, plant and equipment, depreciation to 31 March 20X5		540
Distribution costs	200	
Revenue		2,000

Notes:

(i) Included in the closing inventory at the balance sheet date was inventory at a cost of $35,000, which was sold during April 20X6 for $19,000.

(ii) Depreciation is provided for on property, plant and equipment at 20% per year using the reducing balance method. Depreciation is regarded as cost of sales.

(iii) A member of the public was seriously injured while using one of CE's products on 4 October 20X5. Professional legal advice is that CE will probably have to pay $500,000 compensation.

Required

Prepare CE's Income Statement for the year ended 31 March 20X6 down to the line 'profit before tax'.

(5 marks)

5/06

(Total = 10 marks)

---

7 Objective test questions: Cash flow statements **47 mins**

1 The following is an extract from a cash flow statement prepared by a trainee accountant.

	$'000
Cash flows from operating activities	
Profit before taxation	3,840
Adjustments for	
Depreciation	(1,060)
Loss on sale of building	210
	2,990
Increase in inventories	(490)
Decrease in trade payables	290
Net cash from operating activities	2,790

Which of the following criticisms of this extract are correct?

1 Depreciation should have been added, not deducted.
2 Loss on sale of building should have been deducted, not added.
3 Increase in inventories should have been added, not deducted.
4 Decrease in trade payables should have been deducted, not added.

A	1 and 4
B	2 and 3
C	1 and 3
D	2 and 4

(2 marks)

---

2 In the year ended 31 December 20X4 a company sold some plant which had cost $100,000 for $20,000. At the time of sale the net book value of the plant was $18,000.

Which of the following correctly states the treatment of the transaction in the company's cash flow statement?

	Proceeds of sale	*Profit on sale*
A	Cash inflow under financing activities	Deducted from profit in calculating cash flow from operating activities.
B	Cash inflow under investing activities	Added to profit in calculating cash flow from operating activities.
C	Cash inflow under financing activities	Added to profit in calculating cash flow from operating activities.
D	Cash inflow under investing activities	Deducted from profit in calculating cash flow from operating activities.

(2 marks)

---

3 Which of the following items should not appear in a company's cash flow statement?

1 Proposed dividends
2 Dividends received
3 Bonus issue of shares
4 Surplus on revaluation of a non-current asset
5 Proceeds of sale of an investment not connected with the company's trading activities

A 1, 2, 3 and 5
B 3 and 4 only
C 1, 3 and 4
D 2 and 5

(2 marks)

---

4 Which, if any, of the following statements about cash flow statements are correct according to IAS 7 Cash flow statements?

1 The direct and indirect methods produce different figures for operating cash flow.

2 In calculating operating cash flow using the indirect method, an increase in inventory is added to operating profit.

3 Figures shown in the cash flow statement should include sales taxes.

4 The final figure in the cash flow statement is the increase or decrease in cash at bank.

A 1 and 4
B 2 and 3
C 2 only
D None of the statements is correct.

(2 marks)

---

5 A company's balance sheets at 31 December 20X4 and 20X5 included the following items.

	Balance sheets at	
	31.12.X5	*31.12.X4*
	$'000	$'000
Taxation payable	840	760
Retained earnings	1,660	1,470

The company paid no interest or interim dividends during these years, and the tax provision of $760,000 in the 20X4 balance sheet was the amount paid in 20X5. Using this information, what is the company's operating profit for 20X5 for inclusion in its cash flow statement?

A $190,000
B $1,030,000
C $ 950,000
D $1,660,000 **(2 marks)**

---

6 The balance sheets of R, a limited liability company, at 31 December 20X3 and 20X4 included these figures.

	31 December	
	20X3	*20X4*
	$m	$m
Property, plant and equipment: cost	40	50
Accumulated depreciation	(10)	(14)
	30	36

The income statement for the year ended 31 December 20X4 showed the following figures.

Depreciation charge for year	$6m
Loss on sales of property, plant and equipment	$1m

The company purchased new property, plant and equipment costing $16m during the year.

What figure should appear in the company's cash flow statement for 20X4 for receipts from the sale of property, plant and equipment?

A $3m
B $5m
C $4m
D The figure cannot be calculated from the information provided. **(2 marks)**

---

7 A cash flow statement shows the increase or decrease in cash and cash equivalents in the period.

Which of the following items are included in this movement?

1 Cash at bank

2 Overdraft at bank

3 Current asset investments readily convertible into known amounts of cash and which can be sold without disrupting the company's business.

4 Equity investments.

A All four items
B 1, 2 and 3 only
C 1 and 2 only
D 1 and 3 only **(2 marks)**

---

8 Which of the following should appear in a cash flow statement according to IAS 7 *Cash flow statements*?

1 Dividends paid on preference shares
2 Interest capitalised as part of the cost of a non-current asset
3 Cash flows resulting from share issues

A All three items
B 1 and 2 only
C 1 and 3 only
D 2 and 3 only **(2 marks)**

---

9 The IAS 7 format for a cash flow statement using the indirect method opens with adjustments to net profit before taxation to arrive at cash flow from operating activities.

Which of the following lists consists only of items that would be deducted in that calculation?

A Loss on sale of non-current assets, increase in inventories, decrease in trade payables
B Depreciation, increase in trade receivables, decrease in trade payables
C Increase in trade receivables, profit on sale of non-current assets, decrease in trade payables
D Profit on sale of non-current assets, increase in trade payables, decrease in trade receivables

(2 marks)

---

10 A company's accounting records contain the following figures.

	$'000
Sales for year	3,600
Purchases for year	2,400
Receivables: 31 December 20X2	600
31 December 20X3	700
Payables: 31 December 20X2	300
31 December 20X3	450
Salaries and other expenses paid during 20X3, excluding interest	760

What figure should appear in the company's cash flow statement for 20X3 for cash generated from operations, based on these figures?

A $490,000
B $390,000
C $1,250,000
D None of these figures

(2 marks)

---

11 At 30 September 20X5, BY had the following balances, with comparatives:

Balance Sheet extracts:

As at 30 September	20X5 $'000	20X4 $'000
Non-current tangible assets		
Property, plant and equipment	260	180
Equity and reserves		
Property, plant and equipment revaluation reserve	30	10

The income statement for the year ended 30 September 20X5 included:

Gain on disposal of an item of equipment	$10,000
Depreciation charge for the year	$40,000

Notes to the accounts:

Equipment disposed of had cost $90,000. The proceeds received on disposal were $15,000.

Calculate the property, plant and equipment purchases that BY would show in its cash flow statement for the year ended 30 September 20X5, as required by IAS 7 *Cash flow statements*. **(4 marks)**

11/05

---

12 At 1 October 20X4, BK had the following balance:

Accrued interest payable $12,000 credit

During the year ended 30 September 20X5, BK charged interest payable of $41,000 to its income statement. The closing balance on accrued interest payable account at 30 September 20X5 was $15,000 credit.

How much interest paid should BK show on its cash flow statement for the year ended 30 September 20X5?

A	$38,000
B	$41,000
C	$44,000
D	$53,000

(2 marks)

11/05

(Total = 26 marks)

8 Section B questions: Cash flow statements **9 mins**

The following financial information relates to FC for the year ended 31 March 20X8.

FC
INCOME STATEMENT FOR THE YEAR ENDED 31 MARCH 20X8

	$'000
Revenue	445
Cost of sales	(220)
Gross profit	225
Other income	105
	330
Administrative expense	(177)
	153
Finance costs	(20)
Profit before tax	133
Income tax expense	(43)
Profit	90

The following administrative expenses were incurred in the year.

	$'000
Wages	70
Other general expenses	15
Depreciation	92
	177
Other income:	
Rentals received	45
Gain on disposal of non-current assets	60
	105

Balance sheet extracts at:

	31 March 20X8	*31 March 20X7*
	$'000	$'000
Inventories	40	25
Trade receivables	50	45
Trade payables	(30)	(20)

Required

Prepare FC's cash flow statement for the year ended 31 March 20X8, down to the line 'Cash generated from operations', using the direct method. **(5 marks)**

5/08

9 Tex cash flow (Pilot paper amended) 54 mins

The following information has been extracted from the draft financial statements of Tex, a manufacturing company.

TEX
INCOME STATEMENT FOR THE YEAR ENDED 30 SEPTEMBER 20X1

	$'000
Revenue	15,000
Cost of sales	(9,000)
Gross profit	6,000
Other operating expenses	(2,300)
	3,700
Finance cost	(124)
Profit before taxation	3,576
Income tax expense	(1,040)
Profit for the period	2,536

TEX
BALANCE SHEET AS AT 30 SEPTEMBER 20X1

	20X1		*20X0*	
	$'000	$'000	$'000	$'000
Assets				
Property, plant and equipment		18,160		14,500
Current assets				
Inventories	1,600		1,100	
Trade receivables	1,500		800	
Bank	150		1,200	
		3,250		3,100
Total assets		21,410		17,600
Equity and liabilities				
Equity:				
Share capital		10,834		7,815
Retained earnings		6,536		5,000
		17,370		12,815
Non-current liabilities				
Interest-bearing borrowing	1,700		2,900	
Deferred tax	600		400	
		2,300		3,300
Current liabilities				
Trade payables	700		800	
Taxation	1,040		685	
		1,740		1,485
Tax equity and liabilities		21,410		17,600

Property, plant and equipment

	Property $'000	Plant $'000	Total $'000
Cost			
30 September 20X0	8,400	10,800	19,200
Additions	2,800	5,200	8,000
Disposals	–	(2,600)	(2,600)
30 September 20X1	11,200	13,400	24,600
Depreciation			
30 September 20X0	1,300	3,400	4,700
Disposals	–	(900)	(900)
Charge for year	240	2,400	2,640
30 September 20X1	1,540	4,900	6,440
Net book value			
30 September 20X1	9,660	8,500	18,160
30 September 20X0	7,100	7,400	14,500

The plant that was disposed of during the year was sold for $730,000.

All additions to property, plant and equipment were purchased for cash.

Dividends paid during the year were $1,000,000.

Required

(a) Prepare Tex's cash flow statement for the year ended 30 September 20X1. **(13 marks)**

(b) During the year to 30 September 20X2 Tex had the following results:

	$'000
Sales revenue	18,000
Purchases	9,000
Depreciation	3,000
Other operating expenses (all paid by the year end)	2,000
Finance charge (paid)	120
Cash received from customers	16,700
Cash paid to suppliers	8,300
Closing inventory	1,700
Tax charge	1,300
Dividend paid	1,000

The current tax charge for 20X1 has been paid in full.

There are no additions or disposals of property, plant or equipment.

There is no movement on share capital or non-current liabilities.

Required

Prepare the income statement of Tex for the year to 30 September 20X2 and a balance sheet at that date. **(17 marks)**

(Total = 30 marks)

10 AG (5/05 amended) — 54 mins

The financial statements of AG are given below:

BALANCE SHEETS AS AT	*31 March 20X5* $'000	$'000	*31 March 20X4* $'000	$'000
Non-current assets				
Property, plant and equipment	4,500		4,800	
Development expenditure	370	4,870	400	5,200
Current assets				
Inventories	685		575	
Trade receivables	515		420	
Cash and cash equivalents	552	1,752	232	1,227
Total assets		6,622		6,427
Equity and liabilities				
Equity				
Share capital	2,600		1,900	
Share premium account	750		400	
Revaluation surplus	425		300	
Retained earnings	1,430		1,415	
Total equity		5,205		4,015
Non-current liabilities				
10% loan notes	0		1,000	
5% loan notes	500		500	
Deferred tax	250		200	
Total non-current liabilities		750		1,700
Current liabilities				
Trade payables	480		350	
Income tax	80		190	
Accrued expenses	107		172	
Total current liabilities		667		712
Total equity and liabilities		6,622		6,427

INCOME STATEMENT FOR THE YEAR ENDED 31 MARCH 20X5

	$'000
Revenue	7,500
Cost of sales	(4,000)
Gross profit	3,500
Distribution costs	(900)
Administrative expenses	(2,300)
Finance costs	(45)
Profit before tax	255
Income tax expense	(140)
Profit for the period	115

Additional information

(a) On 1 April 20X4, AG issued 1,400,000 $0.50 ordinary shares at a premium of 50%.

(b) On 1 May 20X4, AG purchased and cancelled all its 10% loan notes at par.

(c) Non-current tangible assets include properties which were revalued upwards by $125,000 during the year.

(d) Non-current tangible assets disposed of in the year had a net book value of $75,000; cash received on disposal was $98,000. Any gain or loss on disposal has been included under cost of sales.

(e) Cost of sales includes $80,000 for development expenditure amortised during the year.

(f) Depreciation charged for the year was $720,000.

(g) The accrued expenses balance includes interest payable of $87,000 at 31 March 20X4 and $12,000 at 31 March 20X5.

(h) The income tax expense for the year to 31 March 20X5 is made up as follows:

	$'000
Corporate income tax	90
Deferred tax	50
	140

(i) Dividends paid during the year were $100,000.

Required

(a) Prepare a cash flow statement, using the indirect method, for AG for the year ended 31 March 20X5, in accordance with IAS 7 *Cash Flow Statements*. **(20 marks)**

(b) In auditing the accounts of AG the auditors discovered the following:

(i) The closing inventory at 31 March 20X4 had been overstated by $120,000.

(ii) The cash and cash equivalents figure at 31 March 20X5 was falsified. $250,000 of this amount had been misappropriated.

(iii) Tax allowances on one class of assets for the year exceeded depreciation by $60,000. The tax rate is 30%. This was not provided for.

(iv) An item of development expenditure costing $25,000 which should have been capitalised was written off to the income statement.

(v) The additional depreciation arising on the property revaluation (Note (c) above) was $5,000. This was included in the depreciation charged for the year but no further adjustment has been made in respect of it. It should be transferred to retained earnings as allowed under IAS 16.

Required

Redraft the balance sheet of AG at 31 March 20X5 to reflect these issues. Show your working for retained earnings.

Note. This does **not** affect your answer to (a). **(10 marks)**

(Total = 30 marks)

11 CJ (5/06 amended) 54 mins

The financial statements of CJ for the year to 31 March 20X6 were as follows:

BALANCE SHEETS AS AT	*31 March 20X6*		*31 March 20X5*	
	$'000	$'000	$'000	$'000
Assets				
Non-current assets				
Property	19,160		18,000	
Plant and equipment	8,500		10,000	
Available for sale investments	1,500		2,100	
		29,160		30,100
Current assets				
Inventory	2,714		2,500	
Trade receivables	2,106		1,800	
Cash at bank	6,553		0	
Cash in hand	409		320	
		11,782		4,620
Total assets		40,942		34,720

BALANCE SHEETS AS AT	*31 March 20X6*		*31 March 20X5*	
	$'000	$'000	$'000	$'000
Equity and liabilities				
Equity				
Ordinary shares $0.50 each	12,000			7,000
Share premium	10,000			5,000
Revaluation reserve	4,200			2,700
Retained earnings	3,009			1,510
		29,209		16,210
Non-current liabilities				
Interest bearing borrowings	7,000		13,000	
Provision for deferred tax	999	7,999	800	13,800
Current liabilities				
Bank overdraft	0		1,200	
Trade and other payables	1,820		1,700	
Corporate income tax payable	1,914		1,810	
		3,734		4,710
Total equity and liabilities		40,942		34,720

INCOME STATEMENT FOR THE YEAR TO 31 MARCH 20X6

	$'000
Revenue	31,000
Cost of sales	(19,000)
Gross profit	12,000
Other income	200
Administrative expenses	(3,900)
Distribution costs	(2,600)
	5,700
Finance cost	(1,302)
Profit before tax	4,398
Income tax expense	(2,099)
Profit for the period	2,299

Additional information

(a) On 1 April 20X5, CJ issued 10,000,000 $0.50 ordinary shares at a premium of 100%.

(b) No additional available for sale investments were acquired during the year.

(c) On 1 July 20X5, CJ repaid $6,000,000 of its interest bearing borrowings.

(d) Properties were revalued by $1,500,000 during the year.

(e) Plant disposed of in the year had a net book value of $95,000; cash received on disposal was $118,000.

(f) Depreciation charged for the year was properties $2,070,000 and plant and equipment $1,985,000.

(g) The trade and other payables balance includes interest payable of $650,000 at 31 March 20X5 and $350,000 at 31 March 20X6.

(h) Dividends paid during the year, $800,000 comprised last year's final dividend plus the current year's interim dividend. CJ's accounting policy is not to accrue proposed dividends.

(i) Other income comprises:

	$
Dividends received	180,000
Gain on disposal of available for sale investments	20,000
	200,000

Dividends receivable are not accrued.

(j) Income tax expense comprises:

	$
Corporate income tax	1,900,000
Deferred tax	199,000
	2,099,000

Required

(a) Prepare CJ's cash flow statement for the year ended 31 March 20X6, in accordance with IAS 7 *Cash flow statements.* **(20 marks)**

(b) CJ commenced a long-term contract in early 20X6. The details are as follows:

	$'000
Total contract price	5,000
Costs to date	700
Expected further costs to complete	2,500
Progress billings	500
Percentage completed	20%

CJ did not include any of these amounts in its financial statements. No payment has yet been received and it has not yet made any payments to its suppliers or subcontractors.

Required

Redraft CJ's balance sheet at 31 March 20X6 to include the results of the long-term contract. Ignore any tax implications. (This does not affect your answer to (a).) **(10 marks)**

(Total = 30 marks)

12 DN (11/06 amended) 54 mins

DN's draft financial statements for the year ended 31 October 20X6 are as follows:

DN

INCOME STATEMENT FOR THE YEAR TO 31 OCTOBER 20X6

	$'000	$'000
Revenue		2,600
Cost of sales		
Parts and sub-assemblies	(500)	
Labour	(400)	
Overheads	(400)	
		(1,300)
Gross profit		1,300
Administrative expenses	(300)	
Distribution costs	(100)	
		(400)
Profit from operations		900
Finance cost		(110)
Profit before tax		790
Income tax expense		(140)
Profit for the period		650

DN

BALANCE SHEET AS AT

	31 October 20X6		31 October 20X5	
	$'000	$'000	$'000	$'000
Assets				
Non-current assets				
Property, plant and equipment		4,942		4,205
Current assets				
Inventories	190		140	
Trade receivables	340		230	
Cash and cash equivalents	0		45	
		530		415
Total assets		5,472		4,620
Equity and liabilities				
Equity				
Equity shares of $0.50 each	1,300		1,000	
Share premium	300		0	
Revaluation reserve	400		0	
Retained earnings	1,660		1,410	
Total equity		3,660		2,410
Non-current liabilities				
Bank loans (various rates)		1,500		2,000
		5,160		4,410
Current liabilities		312		210
Total equity and liabilities		5,472		4,620

Additional information

(a) Property, plant and equipment comprises:

	2006	*2005*
	$'000	$'000
Property	3,100	2,800
Plant and equipment	1,842	1,405

(b) Plant and equipment sold during the year for $15,000 had originally cost $60,000 five years ago. The plant and equipment were depreciated on the straight line basis over six years. Any gain/loss on disposal has been included in overheads.

(c) Properties were revalued on 31 October 20X6.

(d) DN made an equity share issue on 31 October 20X6. The new shares do not rank for dividend until the following accounting period.

(e) DN's funding includes two bank loans:

- $1,500,000 6% loan commenced 30 June 20X6, due for repayment 29 June 20X9;
- $2,000,000 7% loan repaid early on 1 July 20X6.

(f) Current liabilities:

	20X6	*20X5*
	$'000	$'000
Trade payables	105	85
Interest payable	55	75
Tax payable	70	50
Bank overdraft	82	0
Total current liabilities	312	210

(g) A dividend of $0.20 per share was paid on 1 May 20X6.

(h) Overheads include the annual depreciation charge of $100,000 for property and $230,000 for plant and equipment.

Required

(a) Prepare DN's cash flow statement for the year ended 31 October 20X6, using the indirect method, in accordance with IAS 7 *Cash Flow Statements*. **(20 marks)**

(b) Over the next twelve months DN expects to make sales of $3,300,000, which will require purchases of $1,700,000. Inventory levels will remain constant.

It expects to collect $3,100,000 from customers and pay $1,600,000 to suppliers. Interest costs will be the same as 20X6 and the tax charge is estimated at $60,000. DN will use its improved cash position to clear both tax and interest payable by the year end.

No purchases or disposals of non-current assets are planned. Depreciation will be $330,000 and DN intends to hold other expenses to $500,000, which will be paid in cash.

Required

Draft DN's projected balance sheet at 31 October 20X7. **(10 marks)**

(Total = 30 marks)

13 Lemming Inc **54 mins**

The balance sheets of Lemming Inc at 31 August 20X8 and 20X9 are given below.

	Reference to notes	*Year ended 31 August* *20X8*		*20X9*	
		$'000	$'000	$'000	$'000
Property, plant and equipment	1		6,400		8,500
Current assets					
Inventory		1,200		1,400	
Receivables		1,500		1,400	
Cash at bank		200		300	
			2,900		3,100
			9,300		11,600
Equity					
Share capital			2,000		2,200
Share premium account			2,340		2,540
Revaluation reserve			-		1,000
Retained earnings			2,400		2,960
			6,740		8,700
Non current liabilities					
10% Loan notes 20Y5	3		1,000		1,500
			7,740		10,200
Current liabilities					
Trade payables		800		700	
Taxation		400		500	
Bank overdraft		360		200	
			1,560		1,400
			9,300		11,600

Notes

(a) *Movements in property, plant and equipment*

	Land	*Buildings*	*Plant and equipment*	*Total*
	$'000	$'000	$'000	$'000
Cost or valuation				
At 1 September 20X8	2,000	3,000	3,400	8,400
Additions			2,500	2,500
Disposals			(1,000)	(1,000)
Revaluation	1,000			1,000
At 31 August 20X9	3,000	3,000	4,900	10,900
Accumulated depreciation				
At 1 September 20X8		400	1,600	2,000
Charge for year		60	1,140	1,200
Disposals			(800)	(800)
At 31 August 20X9		460	1,940	2,400
Net book value				
At 31 August 20X9	3,000	2,540	2,960	8,500
At 1 September 20X8	2,000	2,600	1,800	6,400

(b) Dividends paid during the year amounted to $500,000.

(c) Issue of loan notes – A further $500,000 of 10% loan notes was issued at par on 1 September 20X8. Interest on all loan notes is paid on 28 February and 31 August each year.

(d) Plant sold during the year realised $250,000.

(e) The tax charge for the year in the income statement was $500,000.

(f) Sales revenue for the year to 31 August 20X9 was $14,050,000 and purchases were $10,690,000.

(g) Operating expenses of $700,000 were paid during the year.

Required

(a) Prepare the income statement of Lemming Inc for the year ended 31 August 20X9.

(b) Prepare the cash flow statement of Lemming Inc for the year ended 31 August 20X9, complying as far as possible with IAS 7 *Cash Flow Statements,* using the indirect method.

(30 marks)

14 Objective test questions: Non-current assets, inventories and construction contracts I — 52 mins

1 The components of the cost of a major item of equipment are given below.

	$
Purchase price	780,000
Import duties	117,000
Sales tax (refundable)	78,000
Site preparation	30,000
Installation	28,000
Initial operating losses before the asset reaches planned performance	50,000
Estimated cost of dismantling and removal of the asset, recognised as a provision under IAS 37 *Provisions, contingent liabilities and contingent assets*	100,000
	1,183,000

What amount may be recognised as the cost of the asset, according to IAS 16 *Property, plant and equipment?*

A $956,000
B $1,105,000
C $1,055,000
D $1,183,000 **(2 marks)**

---

2 Which of the following statements about IAS 36 *Impairment of assets* are correct?

1 Non-current assets must be checked annually for evidence of impairment.

2 An impairment loss must be recognised immediately in the income statement, except that all or part of a loss on a revalued asset should be charged against any related revaluation surplus.

3 If individual assets cannot be tested for impairment, it may be necessary to test a group of assets as a unit.

A 1 and 2 only
B 1 and 3 only
C 2 and 3 only
D 1, 2 and 3 **(2 marks)**

---

3 Which of the following statements is correct?

1 Negative goodwill should be shown on the balance sheet as a deduction from positive goodwill.

2 IAS 38 allows goodwill to be written off immediately against reserves as an alternative to capitalisation.

3 As a business grows, internally generated goodwill may be revalued upwards to reflect that growth.

4 Internally developed brands must not be capitalised.

A 1 and 4
B 2 and 3
C 3 only
D 4 only **(2 marks)**

---

4 Which of the following accounting policies would contravene International Accounting Standards if adopted by a company?

1 Goodwill on acquisitions is written off immediately against reserves.

2 Land on which the company's buildings stand is not depreciated.

3 Internally generated brands are capitalised at fair value as advised by independent consultants.

4 In calculating depreciation, the estimated useful life of an asset is taken as half the actual estimated useful life as a measure of prudence.

A 1, 3 and 4
B 2 and 4 only
C 1 and 3 only
D All four are unacceptable **(2 marks)**

---

5 Which of the following items should be included in arriving at the cost of the inventory of finished goods held by a manufacturing company, according to IAS 2 *Inventories?*

1 Carriage inwards on raw materials delivered to factory
2 Carriage outwards on goods delivered to customers
3 Factory supervisors' salaries
4 Factory heating and lighting
5 Cost of abnormally high idle time in the factory
6 Import duties on raw materials

A 1, 3, 4 and 6
B 1, 2, 4 ,5 and 6
C 3, 4 and 6
D 2, 3 and 5 **(2 marks)**

---

6 Which of the following statements about IAS 2 *Inventories* are correct?

1 Production overheads should be included in cost on the basis of a company's actual level of activity in the period.

2 In arriving at the net realisable value of inventories, trade discounts and settlement discounts must be deducted.

3 In arriving at the cost of inventories, FIFO, LIFO and weighted average cost formulas are acceptable.

4 It is permitted to value finished goods inventories at materials plus labour cost only, without adding production overheads.

A 1 only
B 2 only
C 3 only
D None of them **(2 marks)**

---

7 The position of a construction contract at 30 June 20X6 is as follows.

	$
Contract price	900,000
At 30 June 20X6	
Costs to date	720,000
Estimated costs to completion	480,000
Progress payments invoiced and received	400,000
Percentage complete	60%

What figures should appear for this contract in the accounts at 30 June 20X6, according to IAS 11 *Construction contracts*?

	Income statement		*Balance sheet*	
A	Sales revenue	$540,000	Receivables	$140,000
	Costs	$840,000		
B	Sales revenue	$540,000		
	Costs	$720,000		
C	Sales revenue	$540,000	Amount due from customer	$20,000
	Costs	$840,000		
D	Sales revenue	$540,000	Receivables	$140,000
	Costs	$720,000		

(2 marks)

---

8 According to IAS 16 *Property, plant and equipment*, which, if any, of the following statements about depreciation are correct?

1 The main purpose of depreciation is to reflect the fall in value of an asset in the balance sheet over its useful life.

2 When an asset is revalued, depreciation relating to the revaluation surplus should be debited to the revaluation reserve rather than the income statement.

3 Provision for depreciation ensures that there are funds available to replace an asset when this becomes necessary, though in times of inflation additional amounts may need to be set aside.

4 A change in depreciation method constitutes a change in accounting policy and must be accounted for as such.

A 1 and 4
B 2 and 3
C 4 only
D None of the statements is correct **(2 marks)**

---

9 The following measures relate to a non-current asset:

(i) Net book value $20,000
(ii) Net realisable value $18,000
(iii) Value in use $22,000
(iv) Replacement cost $50,000

The recoverable amount of the asset is

A $18,000
B $20,000
C $22,000
D $50,000 **(2 marks)**

11/05

---

10 BL started a contract on 1 November 20X4. The contract was scheduled to run for two years and has a sales value of $40 million.

At 31 October 20X5, the following details were obtained from BL's records:

	$m
Costs incurred to date	16
Estimated costs to completion	18
Percentage complete at 31 October 20X5	45%

Applying IAS 11 *Construction contracts*, how much revenue and profit should BL recognise in its income statement for the year ended 31 October 20X5? **(2 marks)**

11/05

11 CI purchased equipment on 1 April 20X2 for $100,000. The equipment was depreciated using the reducing balance method at 25% per year. CI's balance sheet date is 31 March.

Depreciation was charged up to and including 31 March 20X6. At that date, the recoverable amount was $28,000.

Calculate the impairment loss on the equipment according to IAS 36 Impairment of Assets. **(3 marks)**

5/06

The following data are given for sub-questions 12 and 13 below

CN started a three year contract to build a new university campus on 1 April 20X5. The contract had a fixed price of $90 million.

CN incurred costs to 31 March 20X6 of $77 million and estimated that a further $33 million would need to be spent to complete the contract.

CN uses the percentage of cost incurred to date to total cost method to calculate stage of completion of the contract.

---

12 Calculate revenue earned on the contract to 31 March 20X6, according to IAS 11 Construction Contracts. **(2 marks)**

5/06

---

13 State how much gross profit/loss CN should recognise in its income statement for the year ended 31 March 20X6, according to IAS 11 Construction Contracts. **(2 marks)**

5/06

---

14 IAS 16 *Property, Plant and Equipment* requires an asset to be measured at cost on its original recognition in the financial statements.

EW used its own staff, assisted by contractors when required, to construct a new warehouse for its own use.

Which ONE of the following costs would NOT be included in attributable costs of the non-current asset?

A Clearance of the site prior to work commencing.

B Professional surveyors' fees for managing the construction work.

C EW's own staff wages for time spent working on the construction.

D An allocation of EW's administration costs, based on EW staff time spent on the construction as a percentage of the total staff time. **(2 marks)**

11/07

(Total = 29 marks)

---

15 Objective test questions: Non-current assets, inventories and construction contracts II **63 mins**

1 A company purchased a machine for $50,000 on 1 January 20X1. It was judged to have a 5-year life with a residual value of $5,000. On 31 December 20X2 $15,000 was spent on an upgrade to the machine. This extended its remaining useful life to 5 years, with the same residual value. During 20X3, the market for the product declined and the machine was sold on 1 January 20X4 for $7,000.

What was the loss on disposal?

A $31,000
B $35,000
C $31,600
D $35,600 **(2 marks)**

2 A cash generating unit comprises the following:

	$m
Building	20
Plant and equipment	10
Goodwill	5
Current assets	10
	45

Following a downturn in the market, an impairment review has been undertaken and the recoverable amount of the cash generating unit is estimated to be $25m.

What is the carrying value of the building after adjusting for the impairment loss?

A $11m
B $10m
C $12.5m
D $20m **(2 marks)**

3 In less than 30 words, define 'impairment'. **(2 marks)**

4 Which of the following is *not* true regarding IAS 2 *Inventories*?

A Fixed production overheads must be allocated to items of inventory on the basis of the normal level of production.

B Plant lying idle will lead to a higher fixed overhead allocation to each unit.

C An abnormally high level of production will lead to a lower allocation of fixed production overhead to each unit

D Unallocated overheads must be recognised as an expense in the period in which they are incurred.

(2 marks)

5 In less than 20 words define *fair value.* **(2 marks)**

The following data is to be used to answer sub-questions 6 and 7 below

X acquired the business and assets from the owners of an unincorporated business: the purchase price was satisfied by the issue of 10,000 equity shares with a nominal market value of $10 each and $20,000 cash. The market value of X shares at the date of acquisition was $20 each.

The assets acquired were:

- Net tangible non-current assets with a book value of $20,000 and current value of $25,000.
- Patents for a specialised process valued by a specialist valuer at $15,000.
- Brand name, valued by a specialist brand valuer on the basis of a multiple of earnings at $50,000.
- Publishing rights of the first text from an author that the management of X expects to become a best seller. The publishing rights were a gift from the author to the previous owners at no cost. The management of X has estimated the future value of the potential best seller at $100,000. However, there is no reliable evidence available to support the estimate of the management.

6 In no more than **30 words**, explain the accounting treatment to be used for the publishing rights of the first text. **(2 marks)**

Pilot paper

---

7 Calculate the value of goodwill to be included in the accounts of X for this purchase. **(4 marks)**

Pilot paper

---

8 An item of plant and equipment was purchased on 1 April 20X1 and for $100,000. At the date of acquisition its expected useful economic life was 10 years. Depreciation was provided on a straight line basis, with no residual value.

On April 1 20X3, the asset was revalued to $95,000. On 1 April 20X4, the useful life of the asset was reviewed and the remaining useful life was reduced to 5 years, a total useful life of 8 years.

Calculate the amounts that would be included in the balance sheet for the asset cost/valuation and provision for accumulated depreciation at 31 March 20X5. **(4 marks)**

5/05

---

9 IAS 16 *Property, Plant and Equipment* provides definitions of terms relevant to non-current assets. Complete the following sentence, **in no more than 10 words.**

'Depreciable amount is ...' **(2 marks)**

5/05

---

10 Which ONE of the following items would CM recognise as subsequent expenditure on a non-current asset and capitalise it as required by IAS 16 *Property, Plant and Equipment*?

A CM purchased a furnace five years ago, when the furnace lining was separately identified in the accounting records. The furnace now requires relining at a cost of $200,000. When the furnace is relined it will be able to be used in CM's business for a further five years.

B CM's office building has been badly damaged by a fire. CM intends to restore the building to its original condition at a cost of $250,000.

C CM's delivery vehicle broke down. When it was inspected by the repairers it was discovered that it needed a new engine. The engine and associated labour costs are estimated to be $5,000.

D CM closes its factory for two weeks every year. During this time, all plant and equipment has its routine annual maintenance check and any necessary repairs are carried out. The cost of the current year's maintenance check and repairs was $75,000. **(2 marks)**

5/06

---

11 DS purchased a machine on 1 October 20X2 at a cost of $21,000 with an expected useful economic life of six years, with no expected residual value. DS depreciates its machines using the straight line basis.

The machine has been used and depreciated for three years to 30 September 20X5. New technology was invented in December 20X5, which enabled a cheaper, more efficient machine to be produced; this technology makes DS's type of machine obsolete. The obsolete machine will generate no further economic benefit or have any residual value once the new machines become available. However, because of production delays, the new machines will not be available on the market until 1 October 20X7.

Calculate how much depreciation DS should charge to its income statement for the year ended 30 September 20X6, as required by IAS 16 *Property, Plant and Equipment.* **(3 marks)**

11/06

---

12 IAS 38 *Intangible Assets* sets out six criteria that must be met before an internally generated intangible asset can be recognised.

List FOUR of IAS 38's criteria for recognition. **(4 marks)**

11/06

---

13 Details from DV's long-term contract, which commenced on 1 May 20X6, at 30 April 20X7:

	$'000
Invoiced to client for work done	2,000
Costs incurred to date:	
Attributable to work completed	1,500
Inventory purchased, but not yet used	250
Progress payment received from client	900
Expected further costs to complete project	400
Total contract value	3,000

DV uses the percentage of costs incurred to total costs to calculate attributable profit.

Calculate the amount that DV should recognise in its income statement for the year ended 30 April 20X7 for revenue, cost of sales and attributable profits on this contract according to IAS 11 *Construction Contracts.*

(4 marks)

5/07

(Total = 35 marks)

---

16 Section B questions: Non-current assets, inventories and construction contracts 45 mins

(a) (i) Discuss the criteria which IAS 38 *Intangible assets* states should be used when considering whether research and development expenditure should be written off in an accounting period or carried forward.

(ii) Discuss to what extent these criteria are consistent with the fundamental accounting assumptions within IAS 1. **(5 marks)**

(b) 'The cost of inventories should comprise all costs of purchase, costs of conversion and other costs incurred in bringing the inventories to their present location and condition' (IAS 2).

This statement results in problems of a practical nature in arriving at the amount at which inventories and short term work in progress are stated in the accounts.

Required

Comment on the above statement identifying and discussing both the accounting policy and the problems 'of a practical nature' that may arise when computing the amount at which inventories and short term work in progress are stated in financial accounts. **(5 marks)**

(c) A new type of delivery vehicle, when purchased on 1 April 20X0 for $20,000, was expected to have a useful life of four years. It now appears that the original estimate of the useful life was too short, and the vehicle is now expected to have a useful life of six years, from the date of purchase. All delivery vehicles are depreciated using the straight-line method and are assumed to have zero residual value.

Required

As the trainee management accountant, draft a memo to the transport manager explaining whether it is possible to change the useful life of the new delivery vehicle. Using appropriate International Accounting Standards, explain how the accounting transactions relating to the delivery vehicle should be recorded in the income statement for the year ended 31 March 20X3 and the balance sheet at that date **(5 marks)**

Pilot paper

(d) BI owns a building which it uses as its offices, warehouse and garage. The land is carried as a separate non-current tangible asset in the balance sheet.

BI has a policy of regularly revaluing its non-current tangible assets. The original cost of the building in October 20X2 was $1,000,000; it was assumed to have a remaining useful life of 20 years at that date, with no residual value. The building was revalued on 30 September 20X4 by a professional valuer at $1,800,000.

BI also owns a brand name which it acquired 1 October 20X0 for $500,000. The brand name is being amortised over 10 years.

The economic climate had deteriorated during 20X5, causing BI to carry out an impairment review of its assets at 30 September 20X5. BI's building was valued at a market value of $1,500,000 on 30 September 20X5 by an independent valuer. A brand specialist valued BI's brand name at market value of $200,000 on the same date.

BI's management accountant calculated that the brand name's value in use at 30 September 20X5 was $150,000.

Required

Explain how BI should report the events described above and quantify any amounts required to be included in its financial statements for the year ended 30 September 20X5. **(5 marks)**

11/05

(e) DV purchased two buildings on 1 September 1996. Building A cost $200,000 and had a useful economic life of 20 years. Building B cost $120,000 and had a useful economic life of 15 years. DV's accounting policies are to revalue buildings every five years and depreciate them over their useful economic lives on the straight line basis. DV does not make an annual transfer from revaluation reserve to retained profits for excess depreciation.

DV received the following valuations from its professionally qualified external valuer:

31 August 2001	Building A	$180,000
	Building B	$75,000
31 August 2006	Building A	$100,000
	Building B	$30,000

Required

Calculate the gains or impairments arising on the revaluation of Buildings A and B at 31 August 2006 and identify where they should be recognised in the financial statements of DV. **(5 marks)**

11/06

(Total = 25 marks)

17 Geneva **27 mins**

Geneva Co is a company involved in the building industry and often has a number of major construction contracts which fall into two or more accounting periods.

During the year ended 31 December 20X8, Geneva Co enters into three construction contracts as follows:

		Contract	
	Lausanne	*Bern*	*Zurich*
	$'000	$'000	$'000
Fixed contract price	2,000	2,000	2,000
Payments on account	1,080	950	800
Costs incurred to date	1,000	1,100	640
Estimated costs to complete the contract	600	1,100	1,160
Estimate percentage of work completed	60%	50%	35%

Required

Show how each contract would be reflected in the balance sheet and income statement of Geneva Co for the year ended 31 December 20X8. **(5 marks each)**

(Total = 15 marks)

18 Objective test questions: Capital transactions and financial instruments **47 mins**

1 A company made an issue of 100,000 ordinary shares of 50c at $1.10 each. The cash received was correctly recorded in the cash book but the whole amount was entered into ordinary share capital account.

Which of the following journal entries will correct the error made in recording the issue?

		Debit	*Credit*
		$	$
A	Share capital account	10,000	
	Share premium account		10,000
B	Cash	60,000	
	Share premium account		60,000
C	Share capital account	60,000	
	Share premium account		60,000
D	Share premium account	60,000	
	Share capital account		60,000

(2 marks)

---

2 A company issued 1,000,000 $1 shares at $1.50 each payable as follows.

On application (including premium)	70c
On allotment	30c
First and final call	50c

All monies were received except for the call due from a holder of 10,000 shares. These shares were subsequently forfeited and reissued at $1.60 per share.

What *total* will be credited to share premium account as a result of this issue?

A $501,000
B $506,000
C $511,000
D None of the above **(2 marks)**

---

3 At 1 January 20X4, a company's share capital consisted of 1,000,000 ordinary shares of 50c each, and there was a balance of $800,000 on its share premium account.

During 20X4, the following events took place.

1 March	The company made a bonus issue of 1 share for every 2 held, using the share premium account.
1 July	The company issued 600,000 shares at $2 per share.
1 October	The company made a rights issue of 1 share for every 3 held at $1.80 per share.

What are the balances on the company's share capital and share premium accounts at 31 December 20X4?

	Share capital	*Share premium*	
	$	$	
A	1,400,000	2,860,000	
B	2,800,000	1,460,000	
C	1,800,000	2,320,000	
D	1,400,000	2,360,000	**(2 marks)**

4 A company has forfeited shares for non-payment of calls, but has not yet reissued them.

How, if at all, will the forfeited shares be shown in the company's balance sheet?

A As a deduction from called up share capital
B As an asset under investments
C As a current asset under receivables
D No item appears in the balance sheet for the shares **(2 marks)**

5 Which of the following are normally permitted uses for a company's share premium account?

1 Issuing fully paid bonus shares
2 Being repaid to members as part of an authorised reduction of share capital
3 Writing off preliminary expenses of company formation
4 Writing off subsequent share issue expenses

A 1, 2 and 4 only
B 1, 3 and 4 only
C 2, 3 and 4 only
D All four are permitted **(2 marks)**

6 The balance sheet of X, a limited liability company, at 31 December 20X5 is shown below.

	$m
Issued share capital: ordinary shares of 50c each, fully paid	10
Retained earnings	3
	13
Sundry net assets	13

At this date X purchased 1,000,000 of its own ordinary shares at par. 300,000 $1 preference shares were issued at $1.20 each to help finance the purchase.

What balance should appear on the company's capital redemption reserve account when these transactions have been correctly recorded?

A $140,000
B $200,000
C $500,000
D None of these figures **(2 marks)**

7 Which of the following statements regarding share issues is incorrect?

A **Application** is where potential shareholders apply for shares in the company and send cash to cover their application

B **Allotment** is when the company allocates shares to the successful applicants and returns cash to unsuccessful applicants

C A **call** is where the purchase value is payable in instalments. The company will 'call' for instalments.

D If a shareholder fails to pay a call his allotment is cancelled and his money returned to him. His shares may then be reissued. **(2 marks)**

8 IAS 32 *Financial Instruments – Disclosure and Presentation* classifies issues shares as either equity instruments or financial liabilities. An entity has the following categories of funding on its balance sheet:

1 A preference share that is redeemable for cash at a 10% premium on 30 May 2015.
2 An ordinary share which is not redeemable and has no restrictions on receiving dividends.
3 A loan note that is redeemable at par in 2020.
4 A cumulative preference share that is entitled to receive a dividend of 7% a year.

Applying IAS 32, how would **each** of the above be categorised on the balance sheet?

	As an equity instrument	*As a financial liability*
A	1 and 2	3 and 4
B	2 and 3	1 and 4
C	2	1, 3 and 4
D	1, 2 and 3	4

(2 marks)

5/05

9 BN is a listed entity and has the following balances included on its opening balance sheet:

	$000
Equity and reserves	
Equity shares, $1 shares, fully paid	750
Share premium	250
Retained earnings	500
	1,500

BN reacquired 100,000 of its shares and classified them as 'treasury shares'. BN still held the treasury shares at the year end.

How should BN classify the treasury shares on its closing balance sheet in accordance with IAS 32 *Financial instruments – presentation*?

A As a non-current asset investment.
B As a deduction from equity.
C As a current asset investment.
D As a non-current liability. **(2 marks)**

11/05

10 R issued 500,000 new $1 equity shares on 1 April 20X2. The issue price of the share was $1.50 per share. Applicants paid $0.20 per share with their applications and a further $0.80 per share on allotment. All money was received on time.

A final call of $0.50 per share was made on 31 January 20X3. One holder of 5,000 shares failed to pay the call by the due date and the shares were forfeited. The forfeited shares were reissued for $1 per share on 31 March 20X3.

Which of the following is the correct set of accounting entries to record the reissue of the forfeited shares?

	Investment in own shares account	*Bank account*	*Investment in own shares account*	*Share premium account*
A	$5,000 credit	$5,000 debit	$2,500 debit	$2,500 credit
B	$5,000 credit	$5,000 debit	0	0
C	$5,000 credit	$5,000 debit	$2,500 credit	$2,500 debit
D	$5,000 debit	$5,000 credit	$2,500 credit	$2,500 debit

(2 marks)

The following data applies to questions 11 and 12.

On 1 January 20X8 PX issued 10m 7% $1 preference shares, redeemable after 4 years at a 5% premium. Issue charges amount to $500,000 and the effective interest rate is 10%.

11 What is the total finance charge on the issue? **(3 marks)**

---

12 At what amount will the preference shares be shown in the balance sheet at 31 December 20X9? **(3 marks)**

(Total = 26 marks)

---

19 Objective test questions: Accounting standards I — 61 mins

1 A company leases some plant on 1 January 20X4. The cash price of the plant is $9,000, and the company leases it for four years, paying four annual instalments of $3,000 beginning on 31 December 20X4.

The company uses the sum of the digits method to allocate interest.

What is the interest charge for the year ended 31 December 20X5?

A $900
B $600
C $1,000
D $750 **(2 marks)**

---

2 A company leases some plant on 1 January 20X4. The cash price is $9,000, and the company is to pay four annual instalments of $3,000, beginning on 1 January 20X4.

The company uses the sum of the digits method to allocate interest.

What is the interest charge for the year ended 31 December 20X5?

A $750
B $500
C $900
D $1,000 **(2 marks)**

---

3 Which of the following statements about IAS 10 *Events after the balance sheet date* are correct?

1 Notes to the financial statements must give details of all material adjusting events reflected in those financial statements.

2 Notes to the financial statements must give details of non-adjusting events affecting users' ability to understand the company's financial position.

3 Financial statements should not be prepared on a going concern basis if after the balance sheet date the directors have decided to liquidate the company.

A All three statements are correct.
B 1 and 2 only
C 1 and 3 only
D 2 and 3 only **(2 marks)**

---

4 A company's income statement showed a profit before tax of $1,800,000

After the balance sheet date and before the financial statements were authorised for issue, the following events took place.

1 The value of an investment held at the balance sheet date fell by $85,000.

2 A customer who owed $116,000 at the balance sheet date went bankrupt owing a total of $138,000.

3 Inventory valued at cost $161,000 in the balance sheet was sold for $141,000.

4 Assets with a carrying value at the balance sheet date of $240,000 were unexpectedly expropriated by government.

What is the company's profit after making the necessary adjustments for these events?

A $1,399,000
B $1,579,000
C $1,664,000
D None of these figures **(2 marks)**

---

5 Which of the following events after the balance sheet date would normally be classified as *adjusting*, according to IAS 10 *Events after the balance sheet date*?

1 Destruction of a major non-current asset
2 Issue of shares and debentures
3 Discovery of error or fraud
4 Evidence of impairment in value of a property as at the balance sheet date
5 Purchases and sales of non-current assets

A 1, 2 and 5 only
B 3 and 4 only
C 3, 4 and 5 only
D 1, 3 and 4 only **(2 marks)**

---

6 Which of the following events after the balance sheet date would normally be classified as *non-adjusting*, according to IAS 10 *Events after the balance sheet date*?

1 Opening new trading operations
2 Sale of goods held at the balance sheet date for less than cost
3 A customer is discovered to be insolvent
4 Announcement of plan to discontinue an operation
5 Expropriation of major assets by government

A 2 and 3 only
B 1, 2 and 3 only
C 2, 3, 4 and 5 only
D 1, 4 and 5 only **(2 marks)**

---

7 In compiling its financial statements, the directors of a company have to decide on the correct treatment of the following items.

1 An employee has commenced an action against the company for wrongful dismissal. The company's solicitors estimate that the ex-employee has a 40 per cent chance of success in the action.

2 The company has guaranteed the overdraft of another company, not at present in any financial difficulties. The possibility of a liability arising is thought to be remote.

3 Shortly after the balance sheet date, a major installation owned by the company was destroyed in a flood. The company's going concern status is not affected.

What are the correct treatments for these items, assuming all are of material amount?

A All three should be disclosed by note.
B A provision should be made for item 1 and items 2 and 3 disclosed by note.
C Items 1 and 3 should be disclosed by note, with no disclosure for item 2.
D Item 1 should be disclosed by note. No disclosure is required for items 2 and 3. **(2 marks)**

---

8 Which of the following statements about IAS 37 *Provisions, contingents liabilities and contingent assets* are correct?

1 Provisions should be made for constructive obligations (those arising from a company's pattern of past practice) as well as for obligations enforceable by law.

2 Discounting may be used when estimating the amount of a provision if the effect is material.

3 A restructuring provision must include the estimated costs of retraining or relocating continuing staff.

4 A restructuring provision may only be made when a company has a detailed plan for the reconstruction and a firm intention to carry it out.

A All four statements are correct
B 1, 2 and 4 only
C 1, 3 and 4 only
D 2, 3 and 4 only **(2 marks)**

---

9 Which of the following criteria must be present in order for a company to recognise a provision?

1 There is a present obligation as a result of past events.
2 It is probable that a transfer of economic benefits will be required to settle the obligation.
3 A reliable estimate of the obligation can be made.

A All three criteria must be present.
B 1 and 2 only
C 1 and 3 only
D 2 and 3 only **(2 marks)**

---

10 Which **one** of the following would be treated as a non-adjusting event after the balance sheet date, as required by IAS 10 *Events after the Balance Sheet Date*, in the financial statements of AN for the period ended 31 January 20X5? The financial statements were approved for publication on 15 May 20X5.

A Notice was received on 31 March 20X5 that a major customer of AN had ceased trading and was unlikely to make any further payments.

B Inventory items at 31 January 20X5, original cost $30,000, were sold in April 20X5 for $20,000.

C During 2004, a customer commenced legal action against AN. At 31 January 20X5, legal advisers were of the opinion that AN would lose the case, so AN created a provision of $200,000 for the damages claimed by the customer. On 27 April 20X5, the court awarded damages of $250,000 to the customer.

D There was a fire on 2 May 20X5 in AN's main warehouse which destroyed 50% of AN's total inventory. **(2 marks)**

5/05

---

11 DT's final dividend for the year ended 31 October 20X5 of $150,000 was declared on 1 February 20X6 and paid in cash on 1 April 20X6. The financial statements were approved on 31 March 20X6.

The following statements refer to the treatment of the dividend in the accounts of DT:

1 The payment clears an accrued liability set up in the balance sheet as at 31 October 20X5;

2 The dividend is shown as a deduction in the income statement for the year ended 31 October 20X6;

3 The dividend is shown as an accrued liability in the balance sheet as at 31 October 20X6;

4 The $150,000 dividend was shown in the notes to the financial statements at 31 October 20X5;

5 The dividend is shown as a deduction in the statement of changes in equity for the year ended 31 October 20X6.

Which of the above statements reflect the correct treatment of the dividend?

A 1 and 2
B 1 and 4
C 3 and 5
D 4 and 5 **(2 marks)**

11/06

---

12 List the THREE criteria specified in IAS 37 *Provisions, Contingent Liabilities and Contingent Assets* that must be satisfied before a provision is recognised in the financial statements. **(3 marks)**

11/06

---

13 DH has the following two legal claims outstanding:

- A legal action against DH claiming compensation of $700,000, filed in February 20X7. DH has been advised that it is probable that the liability will materialise.
- A legal action taken by DH against another entity, claiming damages of $300,000, started in March 20X4. DH has been advised that it is probable that it will win the case.

How should DH report these legal actions in its financial statements for the year ended 30 April 20X7?

	Legal action against DH	Legal action taken by DH
A	Disclose by a note to the accounts	No disclosure
B	Make a provision	No disclosure
C	Make a provision	Disclose as a note
D	Make a provision	Accrue the income

(2 marks)

5/07

---

14 During its 20X6 accounting year, DL made the following changes.

Which ONE of these changes would be classified as 'a change in accounting policy' as determined by IAS 8 *Accounting Policies, Changes in Accounting Estimates and Errors?*

A Increased the bad debt provision for 20X6 from 5% to 10% of outstanding debts.

B Changed the treatment of borrowing costs from capitalising borrowing costs incurred on capital projects to treating all borrowing costs as an expense in the year incurred.

C Changed the depreciation of plant and equipment from straight line depreciation to reducing balance depreciation.

D Changed the useful economic life of its motor vehicles from six years to four years. **(2 marks)**

5/07

---

15 Define an operating segment as per IFRS 8 *Operating segments.* **(3 marks)**

---

16 Which ONE of the following is a criteria for determining a reportable segment under IFRS 8 *Operating segments*?

A Its revenue is 15% or more of the total revenue of all segments
B Its revenue is 10% or more of the total revenue of all operating segments
C Its assets are 10% or more of the combined assets of all operating segments
D Its assets are 15% or more of the combined assets of all operating segments **(2 marks)**

(Total = 34 marks)

20 Objective test questions: Accounting standards II   74 mins

1 IAS 37 *Provisions, contingent liabilities and contingent assets* governs the recognition of contingent items. Which of the following statements about contingencies, if any, are correct according to IAS 37?

1 A contingent liability should be disclosed by note if it is probable that an obligation will arise and its amount can be estimated reliably.

2 A contingent asset should be disclosed by note if it is probable that it will arise.

3 An entity should not recognise a contingent asset.

A None of the statements is correct.
B 1 and 2
C 2 and 3
D All of the statements are correct. **(2 marks)**

---

2 IAS 24 *Related party disclosures* governs disclosures required for transactions between a company and parties deemed to be related to it.

Which of the following parties will normally be held to be related parties of a company?

1 Its subsidiary companies
2 Its directors
3 Close family of the company's directors
4 Providers of finance to the company
5 A customer or supplier with whom the company has a significant volume of business

A All of the parties listed
B 1, 2, 3 and 4 only
C 1, 2 and 3 only
D 3, 4 and 5 only **(2 marks)**

---

3 Which of the following statements defines a finance lease?

A A short term hire agreement
B A long term hire agreement where the legal title in the asset passes on the final payment
C A long term hire agreement where substantially all the risks and rewards of ownership are transferred
D A long term hire agreement where the hirer is responsible for maintenance of the asset **(2 marks)**

---

4 An asset is hired under a finance lease with a deposit of $30,000 on 1 January 20X1 plus 8 six monthly payments in arrears of $20,000 each. The fair value of the asset is $154,000. The finance charge is to be allocated using the sum of the digits method.

What is the finance charge for the year ending 31 December 20X3?

A $7,000
B $8,000
C $10,000
D $11,000 **(2 marks)**

---

5 The directors of Robin (year end 31 December 20X6) were informed on 27 February 20X7 that a serious fire at one of the company's factories had stopped production there for at least six months to come. On 3 March 20X7 the directors of Robin were informed that a major customer had gone into liquidation owing a substantial amount to Robin as at the year end. The liquidator was pessimistic about the prospect of recovering anything for unsecured creditors. The financial statements for the year ended 31 December 20X6 were approved on 20 March 20X7.

In accordance with IAS 10 *Events after the balance sheet date*, how should the two events be treated in the financial statements?

	Fire	*Liquidation*
A	Accrued in accounts	Disclosed in notes
B	Disclosed in notes	Disclosed in notes
C	Accrued in accounts	Accrued in accounts
D	Disclosed in notes	Accrued in accounts

(2 marks)

6 In which of the following circumstances would a provision be recognised under IAS 37 *Provisions, contingent liabilities and contingent assets* in the financial statements for the year ending 31 March 20X6?

1 A board decision was made on 15 March to close down a division with potential costs of $100,000. At 31 March the decision had not been communicated to managers, employees or customers.

2 There are anticipated costs from returns of a defective product in the next few months of $60,000. In the past all returns of defective products have always been refunded to customers.

3 It is anticipated that a major refurbishment of the company Head Office will take place from June onwards costing $85,000.

A 1 and 2 only
B 2 and 3 only
C 2 only
D 3 only **(2 marks)**

7 According to IAS 24 *Related party disclosures*, which of the following would be presumed to be a related party of Fredo unless it can be demonstrated otherwise?

A The bank which has given a loan to Fredo
B The husband of the managing director of Fredo
C Fredo's major supplier
D The assistant accountant of Fredo **(2 marks)**

8 List the three criteria set out in IAS 37 *Provisions, Contingent Liabilities and Contingent Assets* for the recognition of a provision. **(3 marks)**

5/05

9 AP has the following two legal claims outstanding:

- A legal action claiming compensation of $500,000 filed against AP in March 20X4.
- A legal action taken by AP against a third party, claiming damages of $200,000 was started in January 20X3 and is nearing completion.

In both cases, it is more likely than not that the amount claimed will have to be paid.

How should AP report these legal actions in its financial statements for the year ended 31 March 20X5?

	Legal action against AP	*Legal action by AP*
A	Disclose by a note	No disclosure
B	Make a provision	No disclosure
C	Make a provision	Disclose as a note
D	Make a provision	Accrue the income

(2 marks)

5/05

10 Which one of the following would be regarded as a related party of BS?

A BX, a customer of BS.

B The president of the BS Board, who is also the chief executive officer of another entity, BU, that supplies goods to BS.

C BQ, a supplier of BS.

D BY, BS's main banker. **(2 marks)**

11/05

11 An item of machinery leased under a five year finance lease on 1 October 20X3 had a fair value of $51,900 at date of purchase.

The lease payments were $12,000 per year, payable in arrears.

If the sum of digits method is used to apportion interest to accounting periods, calculate the finance cost for the year ended 30 September 20X5. **(3 marks)**

11/05

---

12 Which one of the following would require a provision to be created by BW at its balance sheet date of 31 October 20X5?

A The government introduced new laws on data protection which come into force on 1 January 20X6. BW's directors have agreed that this will require a large number of staff to be retrained. At 31 October 20X5, the directors were waiting on a report they had commissioned that would identify the actual training requirements.

B At the balance sheet date, BW is negotiating with its insurance provider about the amount of an insurance claim that it had filed. On 20 November 20X5, the insurance provider agreed to pay $200,000.

C BW makes refunds to customers for any goods returned within 30 days of sale, and has done so for many years.

D A customer is suing BW for damages alleged to have been caused by BW's product. BW is contesting the claim and, at 31 October 20X5, the directors have been advised by BW's legal advisers it is very unlikely to lose the case. **(2 marks)**

11/05

---

13 IAS 18 *Revenue recognition* defines when revenue may be recognised on the sale of goods.

List four of the five conditions that IAS 18 requires to be met for income to be recognised. **(4 marks)**

11/05

The following data are given for sub-questions 14 and 15 below

CS acquired a machine, using a finance lease, on 1 January 20X4. The machine had an expected useful life of 12,000 operating hours, after which it would have no residual value.

The finance lease was for a five-year term with rentals of $20,000 per year payable in arrears. The cost price of the machine was $80,000 and the implied interest rate is 7.93% per year. CS used the machine for 2,600 hours in 20X4 and 2,350 hours in 20X5.

---

14 Using the actuarial method, calculate the non-current liability and current liability figures required by IAS 17 *Leases* to be shown in CS's balance sheet at 31 December 20X5. **(3 marks)**

5/06

---

15 Calculate the non-current asset – property, plant and equipment net book value that would be shown in CS's balance sheet at 31 December 20X5. Calculate the depreciation charge using the machine hours method. **(2 marks)**

5/06

---

16 On 31 March 20X7, DT received an order from a new customer, XX, for products with a sales value of $900,000. XX enclosed a deposit with the order of $90,000.

On 31 March 20X7, DT had not completed credit referencing of XX and had not despatched any goods. DT is considering the following possible entries for this transaction in its financial statements for the year ended 31 March 20X7.

1 Include $900,000 in income statement revenue for the year
2 Include $90,000 in income statement revenue for the year
3 Do not include anything in income statement revenue for the year
4 Create a trade receivable for $810,000
5 Create a trade payable for $90,000

According to IAS 18 *Revenue Recognition*, how should DT record this transaction in its financial statements for the year ended 31 March 20X7?

A 1 and 4
B 2 and 5
C 3 and 4
D 3 and 5 **(2 marks)**

5/07

The following data are given for sub questions 17 and 18 below

Company X closed one of its divisions 12 months ago. It has yet to dispose of one remaining machine. The carrying value of the machine at the date when business ceased was $750,000. It was being depreciated at 25% on a reducing balance basis. Company X has been advised that the fair value of the machine is $740,000 and expects to incur costs of $10,000 in making the sale. It has located a probable buyer but the sale will not be completed before the year end.

17 At what amount should the machine be shown in the year end financial statements of Company X?

A $750,000
B $562,500
C $740,000
D $730,000 **(2 marks)**

18 Where should the carrying value of the machine be shown in Company X's balance sheet?

A Under non-current assets
B Under current assets
C Included within inventory
D Included within receivables **(2 marks)**

(Total = 41 marks)

21 Section B questions: Accounting standards I 72 mins

(a) The following definitions have been taken from the International Accounting Standards Committee's *Framework for the Preparation and Presentation of Financial Statements.*

- 'An asset is a resource controlled by the entity as a result of past events and from which future economic benefits are expected to flow to the entity.'
- 'A liability is a present obligation of the entity arising from past events, the settlement of which is expected to result in an outflow from the entity of resources embodying economic benefits.'

IAS 17 *Leases* requires lessees to capitalise finance leases in their financial statements.

Required

Explain how IAS 17's treatment of finance leases applies the definitions of assets and liabilities. **(5 marks)**

(b) NDL drilled a new oil well, which started production on 1 March 20X3. The licence granting permission to drill the new oil well included a clause that requires NDL to 'return the land to the state it was in before drilling commenced'.

NDL estimates that the oil well will have a 20-year production life. At the end of that time, the oil well will be de-commissioned and work carried out to reinstate the land. The cost of this de-commissioning work is estimated to be $20 million.

Required

As the trainee management accountant, draft a memo to the production manager explaining how NDL must treat the de-commissioning costs in its financial statements for the year to 31 March 20X3. Your memo should refer to appropriate International Accounting Standards. **(5 marks)**

Pilot paper

(c) BJ is an entity that provides a range of facilities for holidaymakers and travellers.

At 1 October 20X4 these included:

- a short haul airline operating within Europe; and
- a travel agency specialising in arranging holidays to more exotic destinations, such as Hawaii and Fiji.

BJ's airline operation has made significant losses for the last two years. On 31 January 20X5, the directors of BJ decided that, due to a significant increase in competition on short haul flights within Europe, BJ would close all of its airline operations and dispose of its fleet of aircraft. All flights for holiday makers and travellers who had already booked seats would be provided by third party airlines. All operations ceased on 31 May 20X5.

On 31 July 20X5, BJ sold its fleet of aircraft and associated non-current assets for $500 million, the carrying value at that date was $750 million.

At the balance sheet date, BJ were still in negotiation with some employees regarding severance payments. BJ has estimated that in the financial period October 20X5 to September 20X6, they will agree a settlement of $20 million compensation.

The closure of the airline operation caused BJ to carry out a major restructuring of the entire entity. The restructuring has been agreed by the directors and active steps have been taken to implement it. The cost of restructuring to be incurred in year 20X5/20X6 is estimated at $10 million.

Required

Explain how BJ should report the events described above and quantify any amounts required to be included in its financial statements for the year ended 30 September 20X5. (Detailed disclosure notes are not required.) **(5 marks)**

11/05

(d) CB is an entity specialising in importing a wide range of non-food items and selling them to retailers. George is CB's president and founder and owns 40% of CB's equity shares:

- CB's largest customer, XC, accounts for 35% of CB's revenue. XC has just completed negotiations with CB for a special 5% discount on all sales.
- During the accounting period, George purchased a property from CB for $500,000. CB had previously declared the property surplus to its requirements and had valued it at $750,000.
- George's son, Arnold, is a director in a financial institution, FC. During the accounting period, FC advanced $2 million to CB as an unsecured loan at a favourable rate of interest.

Required

Explain, with reasons, the extent to which each of the above transactions should be classified and disclosed in accordance with IAS 24 *Related Party Disclosures* in CB's financial statements for the period. **(5 marks)**

5/06

(e) CR issued 200,000 $10 redeemable 5% preference shares at par on 1 April 20X5. The shares were redeemable on 31 March 20Y0 at a premium of 15%. Issue costs amounted to $192,800.

Required

(a) Calculate the total finance cost over the life of the preference shares. **(2 marks)**

(b) Calculate the annual charge to the income statement for finance expense, as required by IAS 39 Financial Instruments: Recognition and Measurement, for each of the five years 20X6 to 20Y0. Assume the constant annual rate of interest as 10%. **(3 marks)**

(Total = 5 marks)

5/06

(f) You are in charge of the preparation of the financial statements for DF. You are nearing completion of the preparation of the accounts for the year ended 30 September 20X6 and two items have come to your attention.

(i) Shortly after A senior employee left in April 20X6, a number of accounting discrepancies were discovered. With further investigation, it became clear that fraudulent activity had been going on. DF has calculated that, because of the fraud, the profit for the year ended 30 September 20X5 had been overstated by $45,000.

(ii) On 1 September 20X6, DF received an order from a new customer enclosing full payment for the goods ordered; the order value was $90,000. DF scheduled the manufacture of the goods to commence on 28 November 20X6. The cost of manufacture was expected to be $70,000. DF's management want to recognise the $20,000 profit in the income statement for the year ended 30 September 20X6. It has been suggested that the $90,000 should be recognised as revenue and a provision of $70,000 created for the cost of manufacture.

DF's income statement for the year ended 30 September 20X5 showed a profit of $600,000. The draft income statement for the year ended 30 September 20X6 showed a profit of $700,000. The 30 September 20X5 accounts were approved by the directors on 1 March 20X6.

Required

Explain how the events described above should be reported in the financial statements of DF for the years ended 30 September 20X5 and 20X6. **(5 marks)**

11/06

(g) On 1 June 20X6 the directors of DP commissioned a report to determine possible actions they could take to reduce DP's losses. The report, which was presented to the directors on 1 December 20X6, proposed that DP cease all of its manufacturing activities and concentrate on its retail activities. The directors formally approved the plan to close DP's factory. The factory was gradually shut down, commencing on 5 December 20X6, with production finally ceasing on 15 March 20X7. All employees had ceased working or had been transferred to other facilities in the company, by 29 March 20X7. The plant and equipment was removed and sold for $25,000 (net book value $95,000) on 30 March 20X7.

The factory and building as being advertised for sale but had not been sold by 31 March 20X7. The net book value of the land and building at 31 March 20X7, based on original cost, was $750,000. The estimated net realisable value of the land and building at 31 March 20X7 was $1,125,000.

Closure costs incurred (and paid) up to 31 March 20X7 were $620,000.

The cash flows, revenues and expenses relating to the factory were clearly distinguishable from DP's other operations. The output of the factory was sold directly to third parties and to DP's retail outlets. The manufacturing facility was shown as a separate segment in DP's segmental information.

Required

With reference to relevant International Accounting Standards, explain how DP should treat the factory closure in its financial statements for the year ended 31 March 20X7. **(5 marks)**

5/07

(h) On 1 September 20X7, the Directors of EK decided to sell EK's retailing division and concentrate activities entirely on its manufacturing division.

The retailing division was available for immediate sale, but EK had not succeeded in disposing of the operation by 31 October 20X7. EK identified a potential buyer for the retailing division, but negotiations were at an early stage. The Directors of EK are certain that the sale will be completed by 31 August 20X8.

The retailing division's carrying value at 31 August 20X7 was:

	$'000
Non-current tangible assets – property, plant and equipment	300
Non-current tangible assets – goodwill	100
Net current assets	43
Total carrying value	443

The retailing division has been valued at $423,000, comprising:

	$'000
Non-current tangible assets – property, plant and equipment	320
Non-current tangible assets – goodwill	60
Net current assets	43
Total carrying value	423

EK's directors have estimated that EK will incur consultancy and legal fees for the disposal of $25,000.

Required

(i) Explain whether EK can treat the sale of its retailing division as a 'discontinued operation', as defined by IFRS 5 *Non-current Assets held for Sale and Discontinued Operations*, in its financial statements for the year ended 31 October 20X7. **(3 marks)**

(ii) Explain how EK should treat the retailing division in its financial statements for the year ended 31 October 20X7, assuming the sale of its retailing division meets the classification requirements for a disposal group (IFRS 5). **(2 marks)**

(Total = 5 marks)

11/07

(Total = 40 marks)

22 Section B questions: Accounting standards II — 72 mins

(a) IAS 37 defines the meaning of a provision and sets out when a provision should be recognised.

Required

Using the IAS 37 definition of a provision, explain how a provision meets the International Accounting Standards Board's *Framework for the Preparation and Presentation of Financial Statements*' definition of a liability. **(5 marks)**

Pilot paper

(b) A lessee leases a non-current asset on a non-cancellable lease contract of five years, the details of which are:

- The asset has a useful life of five years.
- The rental is $21,000 per annum payable at the end of each year.
- The lessee also has to pay all insurance and maintenance costs.
- The fair value of the asset was $88,300.

The lessee uses the sum of digits method to calculate finance charges on the lease.

Required

Prepare income statement and balance sheet extracts for years one and two of the lease. **(5 marks)**

Pilot paper

(c) AE has a three year contract which commenced on 1 April 20X4. At 31 March 20X5, AE had the following balances in its ledger relating to the contract:

	$'000	$'000
Total contract value		60,000
Cost incurred up to 31 March 20X5:		
Attributable to work completed	21,000	
Inventory purchased for use in 20X5/6	3,000	24,000
Progress payments received		25,000
Other information:		
Expected further costs to completion		19,000

At 31 March 20X5, the contract was certified as 50% complete.

Required

Prepare the income statement and balance sheet extracts showing the balances relating to this contract, as required by IAS 11 *Long term contracts*. **(5 marks)**

5/05

(d) A five year finance lease commenced on 1 April 20X3. The annual payments are $30,000 in arrears. The fair value of the asset at 1 April 20X3 was $116,000. Use the sum of digits method for interest allocations and assume that the asset has no residual value at the end of the lease term.

Required

In accordance with IAS 17 *Leases*:

(i) Calculate the amount of finance cost that would be charged to the income statement for the year ended 31 March 20X5

(ii) Prepare balance sheet extracts for the lease at 31 March 20X5. **(5 marks)**

5/05

(e) CD is a manufacturing entity that runs a number of operations including a bottling plant that bottles carbonated soft drinks. CD has been developing a new bottling process that will allow the bottles to be filled and sealed more efficiently.

The new process took a year to develop. At the start of development, CD estimated that the new process would increase output by 15% with no additional cost (other than the extra bottles and their contents). Development work commenced on 1 May 20X5 and was completed on 20 April 20X6. Testing at the end of the development confirmed CD's original estimates.

CD incurred expenditure of $180,000 on the above development in 20X5/X6.

CD plans to install the new process in its bottling plant and start operating the new process from 1 May 20X6.

CD's balance sheet date is 30 April.

Required

(i) Explain the requirements of IAS 38 *Intangible Assets* for the treatment of development costs. **(3 marks)**

(ii) Explain how CD should treat its development costs in its financial statements for the year ended 30 April 20X6. **(2 marks)**

(Total = 5 marks)

5/06

(f) On 1 April 20X5, DX acquired plant and machinery with a fair value of $900,000 on a finance lease. The lease is for five years with the annual lease payments of $228,000 being paid in advance on 1 April each year. The interest rate implicit in the lease is 13.44%. The first payment was made on 1 April 20X5.

Required

(i) Calculate the finance charge in respect of the lease that will be shown in DX's income statement for the year ended 31 March 20X7.

(ii) Calculate the amount to be shown as a current liability and a non-current liability in DX's balance sheet at 31 March 20X7.

(All workings should be to the nearest $'000.) **(5 marks)**

5/07

(g) EJ publishes trade magazines and sells them to retailers. EJ has just concluded negotiations with a large supermarket chain for the supply of a large quantity of several of its trade magazines on a regular basis.

EJ has agreed a substantial discount on the following terms:

- The same quantity of each trade magazine will be supplied each month;
- Quantities can only be changed at the end of each six month period;
- Payment must be made six monthly in advance.

The supermarket paid $150,000 on 1 September 20X7 for six months supply of trade magazines to 29 February 20X8. At 31 October 20X7, EJ had supplied two months of trade magazines.

EJ estimates that the cost of supplying the supermarket each month is $20,000.

Required

(i) State the criteria in IAS 18 *Revenue Recognition* for income recognition. **(2 marks)**

(ii) Explain, with reasons, how EJ should treat the above in its financial statements for the year ended 31 October 20X7. **(3 marks)**

(Total = 5 marks)

11/07

(h) The objective of IAS 24 *Related Party Disclosures* is to ensure that financial statements disclose the effect of the existence of related parties.

Required

With reference to IAS 24, explain the meaning of the terms 'related party' and 'related party transaction'. **(5 marks)**

11/07

(Total = 40 marks)

23 AZ (Pilot paper/amended) **54 mins**

AZ is a quoted manufacturing entity. Its finished products are stored in a nearby warehouse until ordered by customers. AZ has been re-organising the business to improve performance.

The trial balance for AZ at 31 March 20X3 was as follows:

	$'000	$'000
7% Loan Notes (redeemable 20X7)		18,250
Retained earnings at 31 March 20X2		14,677
Administrative expenses	16,020	
Bank and Cash	26,250	
Cost of goods manufactured in the year to 31 March 20X3 (excluding depreciation)	94,000	
Distribution costs	9,060	
Dividends paid	1,000	
Dividends received		1,200
Equity shares $1 each, fully paid		20,000
Interest paid	639	
Inventory at 31 March 20X2	4,852	
Plant and Equipment	30,315	
Allowance for depreciation at 31 March 20X2:		
Plant and Equipment		6,060
Vehicles		1,670
Allowance for doubtful trade receivables		600
Restructuring costs	121	
Sales revenue		124,900
Share issue expenses	70	
Share premium		500
Trade payables		8,120
Trade receivables	9,930	
Vehicles	3,720	
	195,977	195,977

Additional information provided

(a) Non-current assets are being depreciated as follows:

Plant & Equipment	20% per annum straight line
Vehicles	25% per annum reducing balance

Depreciation of plant and equipment is considered to be part of cost of sales, while depreciation of vehicles should be included under distribution costs.

(b) Tax due for the year to 31 March 20X3 is estimated at $15,000.

(c) The closing inventory at 31 March 20X3 was $5,180,000.

(d) A dividend of 5 cents per ordinary share was paid in February 20X3.

(e) The 7% loan notes are 10-year loans due for repayment by 31 March 20X7. AZ incurred no other interest charges in the year to 31 March 20X3.

(f) The restructuring costs in the trial balance represent the cost of the final phase of a major fundamental restructuring of the entity to improve competitiveness and future profitability.

(g) At 31 March 20X3, AZ was engaged in defending a legal action against the entity. Legal advisers have indicated that it is reasonably certain that the outcome of the case will be against the entity. The amount of compensation is currently estimated at $25,000 and has not been included in the trial balance.

(h) On 1 October 20X2, AZ issued 1,000,000 equity shares at $1·50 each. All money had been received and correctly accounted for by the year end.

(i) The auditors have drawn attention to the following issues not reflected in the trial balance:

(i) Inventory brought forward at the beginning of the year had been understated by $500,000.

(ii) Items included in closing inventory at cost of $1.2m were damaged in transit. They will require remedial work costing $250,000 and can then be sold for $1.35m.

(iii) Administrative expenses include $600,000 paid on leasing a machine from 1 April 20X2. This should not have been treated as an operating lease. It is actually a finance lease. The original cost of the machine was $2m and the agreement provides for four annual payments in arrears of $600,000. The interest rate implicit in the lease is 7.7%.

Required

Prepare AZ's income statement for the year to 31 March 20X3, a balance sheet at that date, and a statement of changes in equity for the year. These should be in a form suitable for presentation to the shareholders, in accordance with the requirements of International Accounting Standards.

Notes to the financial statements are NOT required, but all workings must be clearly shown. DO NOT prepare a statement of accounting policies or a statement of recognised income and expense. **(30 marks)**

24 AF (5/05 amended) — 54 mins

AF is a furniture manufacturing entity. The trial balance for AF at 31 March 20X5 was as follows:

	$'000	$'000
6% loan notes (redeemable 20Y0)		1,500
Retained earnings at 31 March 20X4		388
Administrative expenses	1,540	
Available for sale investments at market value 31 March 20X4	1,640	
Bank and cash	822	
Cost of sales	3,463	
Distribution costs	1,590	
Dividend paid 1 December 20X4	275	
Interest paid on loan notes – half year to 30 September 20X4	45	
Inventory at 31 March 20X5	1,320	
Investment income received		68
Land and buildings at cost	5,190	
Ordinary shares of $1 each, fully paid		4,500
Plant and equipment at cost	3,400	
Provision for deferred tax		710
Accumulated depreciation at 31 March 20X4: Buildings		1,500
Accumulated depreciation at 31 March 20X4: Plant and equipment		1,659
Revaluation reserve		330
Sales revenue		8,210
Share premium		1,380
Trade payables		520
Trade receivables	1,480	
	20,765	20,765

Additional information provided

(a) Available for sale investments are carried in the financial statements at market value. The market value of the available for sale investments at 31 March 20X5 was $1,750,000.

(b) There were no sales or purchases of non-current assets or available for sale investments during the year ended 31 March 20X5.

(c) Income tax due for the year ended 31 March 20X5 is estimated at $250,000. The tax rate is 30%. There is no balance outstanding in relation to previous years' corporate income tax. At 31 March 20X5 capital allowances exceed depreciation by $2,700,000.

(d) Depreciation is charged on buildings using the straight-line basis at 3% each year. The cost of land included in land and buildings is $2,000,000. Plant and equipment is depreciated using the reducing balance method at 20%. Depreciation is regarded as a cost of sales.

(e) The company's head office building which was bought 10 years ago for $500,000 has been revalued to $600,000. There is no change required to the depreciation rate which should continue at 3% pa. No entries have yet been made for the revaluation. The excess depreciation should be transferred back to retained earnings, as allowed under IAS 16.

(f) AF entered into a non-cancellable five year operating lease on 1 April 20X4 to acquire machinery to manufacture a new range of kitchen units. Under the terms of the lease, AF will receive the first year rent free, then $62,500 is payable for four years commencing in year two of the lease. The machine is estimated to have a useful economic life of 20 years.

(g) The 6% loan notes are 10 year loans due for repayment in March 20Y0. AF incurred no other finance costs in the year to 31 March 20X5.

Required

Prepare the income statement of AF for the year to 31 March 20X5, a statement of changes in equity and a balance sheet at that date, in a form suitable for presentation to the shareholders and in accordance with the requirements of International Financial Reporting Standards.

Notes to the financial statements are **not** required, but all workings must be clearly shown. **(30 marks)**

25 Murdoch Co **54 mins**

Murdoch Co compiles its financial statements to 30 June annually. At 30 June 20X9, the company's trial balance was as follows.

	$'000	$'000
Sales revenue		14,800
Purchases	8,280	
Inventory at 1 July 20X8	1,390	
Distribution costs	1,080	
Administration expenses	1,460	
Land at valuation	10,500	
Building: cost	8,000	
accumulated depreciation at 1 July 20X8		2,130
Plant and equipment: cost	12,800	
accumulated depreciation at 1 July 20X8		2,480
Trade receivables and payables	4,120	2,240
Cash at bank	160	
Ordinary shares of 50c each: as at 1 July 20X8		10,000
issued during year		4,000
Share premium account: as at 1 July 20X8		2,000
arising on shares issued during year		2,000
Revaluation reserve as at 1 July 20X8		3,000
Retained earnings		3,140
10% loan notes (redeemable 20Y8) (issued 1 April 20X9 with interest payable 31 March and 30 September each year)		2,000
	47,790	47,790

The following matters remain to be adjusted for in preparing the financial statements for the year ended 30 June 20X9:

(a) Inventory at 30 June 20X9 amounted to $1,560,000 at cost. A review of inventory items revealed the need for some adjustments for two inventory lines:

(i) Items which had cost $80,000 and which would normally sell for $120,000 were found to have deteriorated. Remedial work costing $20,000 would be needed to enable the items to be sold for $90,000.

(ii) Some items sent to customers on sale or return terms had been omitted from inventory and included as sales in June 20X9. The cost of these items was $16,000 and they were included in sales at $24,000. In July 20X9 the items were returned in good condition by the customers.

(b) During May 20X9 the company announced the closure of one of its factories. The factory is a single cash-generating unit. Its carrying value before the announcement was $1.8m. After the announcement its fair value less costs to sell was $1.5m. This value relates entirely to the building as all the plant was fully depreciated, and has already been scrapped. The factory building is included in the trial balance at its original carrying value of $1.8m ($2m less depreciation). A buyer has been found and the factory building will be sold in 3 months time. It should now be re-classified under current assets as a 'non-current asset classified as held for sale'.

The factory has now ceased operation and during the year to 30 June 20X9 it made a loss of $0.5m and ran up a corresponding overdraft of $0.5m. This will be paid off when the building is sold. The trading loss, the overdraft and the impairment loss on the building are **not** included in the trial balance, but should be included in the financial statements in accordance with IFRS 5 *Non-current Assets Held for Sale and Discontinued Operations.*

(c) Depreciation is to be provided as follows.

Buildings	2% per year on cost
Plant and equipment	20% per year on cost

80% of the depreciation is to be charged in cost of sales, and 10% each in distribution costs and administrative expenses.

(d) The land is to be revalued to $12,000,000. No change was required to the value of the buildings apart from the factory as noted above.

(e) Accruals and prepayments were:

	Accruals	*Prepayments*
	$'000	$'000
Distribution costs	190	120
Administrative expenses	70	60

Required

Prepare the company's income statement for the year ended 30 June 20X9 and balance sheet as at that date for publication, complying as far as possible with the provisions of accounting standards. Ignore taxation. **(30 marks)**

26 BG (11/05 amended)

54 mins

BG provides office cleaning services to a range of organisations in its local area. BG operates through a small network of depots that are rented spaces situated in out-of-town industrial developments. BG has a policy to lease all vehicles on operating leases.

The trial balance for BG at 30 September 20X5 was as follows:

	$'000	$'000
10% bonds (redeemable 20Y0)		150
Administrative expenses	239	
Available for sale investments at market value 30 September 20X4	205	
Bank and cash	147	
Bond interest paid – half year to 31 March 20X5	8	
Cost of cleaning materials consumed	101	
Direct operating expenses (including cleaning staff)	548	
Dividend paid	60	
Equipment and fixtures, cost at 30 September 20X5	752	
Equity shares $1 each, fully paid		200
Income tax	9	
Inventory of cleaning materials at 30 September 20X5	37	
Investment income received		11
Provision for deferred tax		50
Accumulated depreciation at 30 September 20X4:		
Equipment and fixtures		370
Provision for legal claim balance at 30 September 20X4		190
Retained earnings at 30 September 20X4		226
Revaluation reserve at 30 September 20X4		30
Revenue		1,017
Share premium		40
Trade payables		24
Trade receivables	141	
Vehicle operating lease rentals paid	61	
	2,308	2,308

Additional information

(a) Available for sale investments are carried in the financial statements at market value. The market value of the available for sale investments at 30 September 20X5 was $225,000. There were no purchases or sales of available for sale investments held during the year.

(b) The income tax balance in the trial balance is a result of the underprovision of tax for the year ended 30 September 20X4.

(c) The taxation due for the year ended 30 September 20X5 is estimated at $64,000 and the deferred tax provision needs to be increased by $15,000.

(d) Equipment and fixtures are depreciated at 20% per annum straight line. Depreciation of equipment and fixtures is considered to be part of direct cost of sales. BG's policy is to charge a full year's depreciation in the year of acquisition and no depreciation in the year of disposal.

(e) The 10% bonds were issued in 20X0.

(f) BG paid an interim dividend during the year, but does not propose to pay a final dividend as profit for the year is well below expectations.

(g) At 30 September 20X4, BG had an outstanding legal claim from a customer alleging that BG had caused a major fire in the customer's premises. BG was advised that it would very probably lose the case, so a provision of $190,000 was set up at 30 September 20X4. During 20X5, new evidence was discovered and the case against BG was dropped. As there is no further liability, the directors have decided that the provision is no longer required.

Required

(a) Prepare the income statement and a statement of changes in equity for BG for the year to 30 September 20X5 and a balance sheet at that date, in a form suitable for presentation to the shareholders and in accordance with the requirements of International Financial Reporting Standards. **(20 marks)**

BG currently has 9 vans leased on operating leases. All of the leases were taken out on 1 October 20X3 when the vans were new and priced at $20,000 each. At that time BG could have acquired them under finance leases, paying 3 annual instalments of $8,000 for each van on 1 October 20X3, 20X4 and 20X5. The directors are wondering whether this would have been a better option.

Required

(b) Redraft the retained earnings balance at 30 September 20X5 of BG as it would be if the vans had been acquired as above under finance leases and depreciated at 20% per annum. Assume an interest rate of 21.53% pa. **(10 marks)**

(Total = 30 marks)

27 DM (11/06 amended) 54 mins

The trial balance for DM, a trading entity, at 30 September 20X6 was as follows:

	$'000	$'000
6% Loan (repayable 20Z5)		140
Administrative expenses	91	
Cash and cash equivalents	43	
Distribution costs	46	
Dividend paid 1 June 20X6	25	
Inventory at 30 September 20X5	84	
Inventory purchases	285	
Land and buildings at cost	500	
Equity shares $1 each, fully paid		300
Plant and equipment at cost	211	
Provision for deferred tax at 30 September 20X5		40
Provision for depreciation at 30 September 20X5 – Buildings		45
Provision for depreciation at 30 September 20X5 – Plant and equipment		80
Retained earnings at 30 September 20X5		32
Sales revenue		602
Share premium		50
Trade payables		29
Trade receivables	6	
Vehicle lease rental paid	27	
	1,318	1,318

Additional information

(a) Inventory at 30 September 20X6 was $93,000.

(b) There were no sales of non-current assets during the year ended 30 September 20X6.

(c) The income tax due for the year ended 30 September 20X6 is estimated at $24,000. The deferred tax provision needs to be increased by $15,000.

(d) Depreciation is charged on buildings using the straight line method at 3% per annum. The cost of land included in land and buildings is $200,000. Buildings depreciation is treated as an administration expense.

(e) Plant and equipment is depreciated using the reducing balance method at 20%. Plant and equipment depreciation is regarded as a cost of sales.

(f) Vehicles are depreciated using the straight line method at 20% per year. Vehicles depreciation is regarded as a distribution cost.

(g) During the year DM issued 100,000 new $1 equity shares at a premium of 50%. The proceeds were all received before 30 September 20X6 and are included in the trial balance figures.

(h) DM entered into a non-cancellable five-year finance lease on 1 October 20X5 to acquire a number of vehicles for use in the entity. The vehicles had a fair value of $100,000 and the annual lease payment is $27,000 per year in arrears. The finance charge is to be allocated using the actuarial method. The interest rate implicit in the lease is 10.92%. All the vehicles have economic useful lives of five years. The only entry in the accounting system is the lease payments made to date of $27,000.

(i) The 6% loan was taken out on 1 December 20X5.

(j) DM is diversifying into construction and has a contract in progress to build a warehouse. At 30 September 20X6 the following figures were available.

	$'000
Contract value	240
Costs to date	105
Estimated further costs to completion	35
Progress billings	25

DM estimates percentage completion on the basis of costs incurred. No invoices have yet been paid by the customer.

DM has not included revenue from this contract in its financial statement as the contract is incomplete. However, costs to date for this contract have been charged to inventory purchases.

Required

Prepare the income statement and a statement of changes in equity for the year ended 30 September 20X6 and a balance sheet at that date, in a form suitable for presentation to the shareholders and in accordance with the requirements of International Financial Reporting Standards.

(Notes to the financial statements are NOT required, but all workings must be clearly shown and should be to the nearest $'000. Do not prepare a statement of accounting policies.) **(30 marks)**

28 DZ (5/07) 54 mins

DZ is a manufacturing entity and produces one group of products, known as product Y.

DZ' trial balance at 31 March 20X7 is shown below.

	$'000	$'000
8% loan 20Z0 (see note (n))		2,000
Administration expenses	891	
Bank and cash	103	
Cash received on disposal of land		1,500
Cash received on disposal of plant		5
Cost of raw materials purchased in year	2,020	
Direct production labour costs	912	
Distribution costs	462	
Equity shares $1 each, fully paid		1,000
Income tax (see note (k))	25	
Inventory of finished goods at 31 March 20X6	240	
Inventory of raw materials at 31 March 20X6	132	
Land at valuation at 31 March 20X6	1,250	
Loan interest paid – half year	80	
Plant and equipment at cost at 31 March 20X6	4,180	
Production overheads (excluding depreciation)	633	
Property at cost at 31 March 20X6	11,200	
Provision for deferred tax at 31 March 20X6 (see note (l))		773
Provision for depreciation at 31 March 20X6 (see notes (d) and (e))		
Property		1,900
Plant and equipment		2,840
Research and development (see note (f))	500	
Retained earnings at 31 March 20X6		2,024
Revaluation reserve at 31 March 20X6		2,100
Revenue		8,772
Trade payables		773
Trade receivables	1,059	
	23,687	23,687

Further information

(a) The property cost of $11,200,000 consisted of land $3,500,000 and buildings $7,700,000.

(b) During the year, DZ disposed of non-current assets as follows.

- A piece of surplus land was sold on 1 March 20X7 for $1,500,000
- Obsolete plant was sold for $5,000 scrap value on the same date
- All the cash received is included in the trial balance

Details of the assets sold were:

Asset type	*Cost*	*Revalued amount*	*Accumulated dep'n*
Land	$500,000	$1,250,000	$0
Plant and equipment	$620,000		$600,000

(c) On 31 March 20X7, DZ revalued its properties to $9,800,000 (land $4,100,000 and buildings $5,700,000).

(d) Buildings are depreciated at 5% per annum on the straight line basis. Buildings depreciation is treated as 80% production overhead and 20% administration.

(e) Plant and equipment is depreciated at 25% per annum using the reducing balance method, the depreciation being treated as a production overhead

(f) Product Y was developed in-house. Research and development is carried out on a continuous basis to ensure that the product range continues to meet customer demands. The research and development figure in the trial balance is made up as follows.

	$'000
Development costs capitalised in previous years	867
Less amortisation to 31 March 20X6	534
	333
Research costs incurred in the year to 31 March 20X7	119
Development costs (all meet IAS 38 *Intangible Assets* criteria) incurred in the year to 31 March 20X7	48
Total	500

(g) Development costs are amortised on a straight line basis at 20% per annum.

(h) Research and development costs are treated as cost of sales when charged to the income statement.

(i) DZ charges a full year's amortisation and depreciation in the year of acquisition and none in the year of disposal.

(j) Inventory of raw materials at 31 March 20X7 was $165,000. Inventory of finished goods at 31 March 20X7 was $270,000.

(k) The director estimate the income tax charge on the year's profits at $811,000. The balance on the income tax account represents the underprovision for the previous year's tax charge.

(l) The deferred tax provision is to be reduced to $665,000.

(m) No interim dividend was paid during the year.

(n) The 8% loan is a 20-year loan issued in 20X0.

Required

(a) Prepare DZ's property, plant and equipment note to the accounts for the year ended 31 March 20X7.

(6 marks)

(b) Prepare the income statement and a statement of changes in equity for the year to 31 March 20X7 and a balance sheet at that date, in a form suitable for presentation to the shareholders and in accordance with the requirements of International Financial Reporting Standards.

(All workings should be to the nearest $'000). **(24 marks)**

Notes to the financial statements are NOT required (except as specified in part (a) of the question) but ALL workings must be clearly shown. Do NOT prepare a statement of accounting policies.

(Total = 30 marks)

29 EY (11/07) 54 mins

EY is an office and industrial furniture manufacturing entity that specialises in developing and using new materials and manufacturing processes in the production of its furniture.

The balance sheet below relates to the previous year, 31 October 20X6, which is followed by a summary of EY's cash book for the year to 31 October 20X7.

EY

BALANCE SHEET AT 31 OCTOBER 20X6

	$'000	$'000	$'000
Assets			
Non-current assets			
Development costs – cost	1,000		
– amortisation	200	800	
Property, plant and equipment – cost	7,300		
– depreciation	1,110	6,190	6,990
Current assets			
Inventory	1,200		
Trade receivables	753		
Cash and cash equivalents	82		
			2,035
			9,025
Equity and liabilities			
Equity			
Share capital		3,000	
Revaluation reserve		600	
Retained earnings		1,625	
			5,225
Non-current liabilities			
Loan notes	2,260		
Deferred tax	180		
		2,440	
Current liabilities			
Trade and other payables	573		
Tax payable	670		
Interest payable	117		
		1,360	
Total equity and liabilities			3,800
			9,025

EY

SUMMARISED CASH BOOK FOR THE YEAR ENDED 31 OCTOBER 20X7

	Receipts/(Payments)	
	Note	$'000
Cash book balance at 1 November 20X6		82
Expenditure incurred on government contract	(i)	(600)
Interest paid during the year	(ii)	(160)
Administration expenses paid		(500)
Research and development costs	(iii)	(1,600)
Income tax	(iv)	(690)
Purchase cost of property, plant and equipment	(v)	(3,460)
Final dividend of 25c per share for year ended 31 October 20X6		(750)
Receipt for disposal of land	(vi)	1,200
Cash received from customers		7,500
Payments to suppliers of production materials, wages and other production costs		(3,000)
Distribution and selling costs		(730)
Cash received from increase in loan notes		2,500
Cash book balance at 31 October 20X7		(208)

Notes

(a) The government contract is a long-term project for the supply of a new type of seating for government offices involving the development of new materials. The total contract value is $1,400,000. The expenditure includes all costs incurred during the first year of the contract. The project leader is confident that the remainder of the work will cost no more than $400,000. The contract provides that EY can charge for the proportion of work completed by 31 October each year. The percentage of cost incurred to total cost should be used to apportion profit/losses on the contract.

(b) Interest outstanding at 31 October 20X7 was $130,000.

(c) During the year EY spent $1,600,000 on research and development. This comprised three projects:

- Cost in the year $300,000 – Funded research projects carried out at the local university;
- Cost in the year $500,000 – Development of a new type of laminate expected to be a very profitable product line. The final development phase has just finished, and production of the laminate is expected from January 20X8.
- Cost in the year $800,000 – Development of a new type of artificial wood, to replace real wood in some furniture and help reduce EY's use of wood. The development produced a good substitute for wood, but was five times more expensive and hence not viable.

Capitalised development expenditure is amortised on the straight line basis over five years and treated as a cost of sale.

(d) Income tax due for the year was estimated by EY at $420,000.

(e) The property, plant and equipment balance at 31 October 20X6 was made up as follows.

	Land	*Premises*	*Plant & equipment*	*Total*
	$'000	$'000	$'000	$'000
Cost/valuation	2,000	1,500	3,800	7,300
Depreciation	0	350	760	1,110
Net book value	2,000	1,150	3,040	6,190

During the year EY purchased new premises at a cost of $1,600,000, and new plant and equipment for $1,860,000. Premises are depreciated on the straight line basis at 6% per year, and plant and machinery are depreciated on the reducing balance at 15% per year and are treated as a cost of sale. EY charges a full year's depreciation in the year of acquisition. No assets were fully depreciated at 31 October 20X6.

(f) Land originally costing $600,000, which had previously been revalued to $1,000,000 was sold during the year for $1,200,000.

(g) A bonus issue of shares was made on the basis of one new share for every six shares held.

(h) Deferred tax is to be increased by $42,000.

(i) Balances at 31 October 20X7 included.

Trade receivables	$620,000
Outstanding trade payables	$670,000
Inventory	$985,000

Required

Prepare the income statement and a statement of changes in equity for the year to 31 October 20X7 and a balance sheet at that date, in a form suitable for presentation to the shareholders and in accordance with the requirements of International Financial Reporting Standards. (All workings should be to the nearest $000)

Notes to the financial statements are NOT required, but all workings must be clearly shown. Do NOT prepare a statement of accounting policies. **(Total = 30 marks)**

30 FZ (5/08) **54 mins**

FZ is an entity which owns a number of factories that specialise in packaging and selling fresh dairy products in bulk to wholesale entities and large supermarkets. FZ also own a chain of small newsagents' shops.

At its meeting on 1 January 20X8, the Board of FZ decided that, to maximise its strategic opportunities, it would sell the newsagents' shops and concentrate on its dairy product business.

FZ's trial balance at 31 March 20X8 is shown below.

	Notes	$'000	$'000
5% Loan notes (redeemable 20Z0)			1,000
Administrative expenses		440	
Cash and cash equivalents		853	
Cash received on disposal of vehicles			15
Cost of goods sold		4,120	
Distribution costs		432	
Equity dividend paid		500	
Factory buildings at valuation		12,000	
Goodwill		300	
Inventory at 31 March 20X8		900	
Newsagents shops at cost		6,200	
Ordinary shares $1 each, fully paid at 31 March 20X8			5,000
Plant and equipment		2,313	
Provision for deferred tax at 31 March 20X7			197
Provision for property, plant and equipment depreciation at 31 March 20X7	(c)		3,337
Retained earnings at 31 March 20X7			5,808
Revaluation reserve			190
Sales revenue			10,170
Share premium at 31 March 20X8			3,000
Trade payables			417
Trade receivables		929	
Vehicles at cost		147	
		29,134	29,134

Additional information

(a) The newsagents' shops were valued at $5,000,000 by an external valuer on 1 January 20X8. On the same date, a prospective buyer expressed an interest at that price. At 31 March 20X8, detailed negotiations were continuing, with the sale expected to be concluded by 31 July 20X8, for the full valuation of $5,000,000.

The net book values (all included in the relevant figures in the trial balance) of the assets relating to the newsagents' shops at 1 January 20X8, before revaluation, were:

	$'000
Goodwill	300
Newsagents' shops	4,960
	5,260

The newsagents' shops are regarded as a cash generating unit. The cost of selling the shops is estimated at $200,000.

The revenue and expenses of the newsagents' shops for the year ended 31 March 20X8, all included in the trial balance figures, were as follows.

	$'000
Revenue	772
Cost of sales	580
Administrative expenses	96
Distribution costs	57

The sales agreement provides for all employee contracts to be transferred to the new owners of the shops.

Loan note interest does not relate to newsagents shops.

(b) At their meeting on 1 February 20X8, the directors of FZ agreed a $2,000,000 reorganisation package for all of FZ, excluding the newsagents' shops. The restructuring was announced to the staff on 16 February 20X8. it was scheduled to begin implementation on 1 July 20X8 and to be completed by 31 December 20X8. The reorganisation package covered staff retraining, staff relocation and development of new computer systems.

(c) Property, plant and equipment depreciation at 31 March 20X7 comprised:

	$'000
Factory buildings	720
Plant and equipment	1,310
Vehicles	67
Newsagents' shops	1,240

(d) On 1 May 20X8, FZ was informed that one of its customers, X, had ceased trading. The liquidators advised FZ that it was very unlikely to receive payment of any of the $62,000 due from X at 31 March 20X8.

(e) The taxation due for the year ended 31 March 20X8 is estimated at $920,000 (net of tax credit for newsagents' shops of $120,000) and the deferred tax provision needs to be increased to $237,000 (all relating to continuing activities).

(f) Depreciation is to be charged on non-current assets as follows.

- Factory buildings, straight line basis at 3%
- Plant and equipment, straight line basis at 20%
- Newsagents' shops, straight line basis at 10%

These items of depreciation are regarded as a cost of sales.

- Vehicles, reducing balance at 25%

This depreciation is regarded as a distribution cost.

FZ provides a full year's depreciation in the year of purchase and no depreciation in the year of sale.

(g) During the year, FZ disposed of old vehicles for $15,000. The original cost of these vehicles was $57,000 and accumulated depreciation at 31 March 20X7 was $52,000.

(h) The revaluation reserve arose when the factory buildings were revalued in 20X5.

(i) During the year, FZ raised new capital by making a rights issue of 1,000,000 $1 equity shares at $1.50 each. All rights were taken up and all amounts are included in the trial balance.

(j) The 5% loan notes were issued in 20X0.

(k) FZ want to disclose the minimum information allowed by IFRS in its primary financial statements.

Required

(a) Explain, with reasons, how items (a) and (b) above should be treated in FZ's financial statements for the year ended 31 March 20X8. **(5 marks)**

(b) Prepare FZ's income statement and a statement of changes in equity for the year to 31 March 20X8 and a balance sheet at that date, in a form suitable for presentation to the shareholders and in accordance with the requirements of International Financial Reporting Standards. **(25 marks)**

Notes to the financial statements are not required, but all workings must be clearly shown. Do not prepare a statement of accounting policies. **(Total = 30 marks)**

Part C: Principles of Business Taxation

Questions 31 to 38 cover Principles of Business Taxation, the subject of Part C of the BPP Study Text for Paper P7.

31 Objective test questions: General principles of taxation

76 mins

1 Country X uses a Pay-As-You-Earn (PAYE) system for collecting taxes from employees. Each employer is provided with information about each employee's tax position and tables showing the amount of tax to deduct each period. Employers are required to deduct tax from employees and pay it to the revenue authorities on a monthly basis

From the perspective of the government, list THREE advantages of the PAYE system. **(3 marks)**

5/07

---

2 Where is employee tax recorded in a set of financial accounts?

A Charged to employee costs in the income statement
B Charged to cost of sales in the income statement
C Included as a payable in the balance sheet
D Included as a receivable in the balance sheet **(2 marks)**

---

3 Which of the following powers is *not* available to tax authorities.

A Power to review and query filed returns
B Power to detain company officials
C Power to request special returns
D Power to enter and search premises **(2 marks)**

---

4 Complete the blanks:

Direct taxation is charged directly on the .... or .... that is intended to pay the tax. **(2 marks)**

---

5 Complete the following equation.

Accounting profit + ? – non-taxable income – tax allowable expenditure = ? **(2 marks)**

---

6 In 1776, Adam Smith proposed that an acceptable tax should meet four characteristics. Three of these characteristics were certainty, convenience and efficiency.

Identify the FOURTH characteristic.

A Neutrality
B Transparency
C Equity
D Simplicity **(2 marks)**

11/06

---

7 Define tax evasion. **(2 marks)**

---

8 DR makes a taxable profit of $400,000 and pays an equity dividend of $250,000. Income tax on DR's profit is at a rate of 25%.

Equity shareholders pay tax on their dividend income at a rate of 30%.

If DR and its equity shareholders pay a total of $175,000 tax between them, what method of corporate income tax is being used in that country?

A The classical system
B The imputation system
C The partial imputation system
D The split rate system **(2 marks)**

11/06

---

9 List (using no more than five words per item) the four main sources of tax rules in a country. **(4 marks)**

Pilot paper

---

10 A withholding tax is

A tax withheld from payment to the tax authorities.
B tax paid less an amount withheld from payment.
C tax deducted at source before payment of interest or dividends.
D tax paid on increases in value of investment holdings. **(2 marks)**

Pilot paper

---

11 The effective incidence of a tax is

A the date the tax is actually paid.
B the person or entity that finally bears the cost of the tax.
C the date the tax assessment is issued.
D the person or entity receiving the tax assessment. **(2 marks)**

5/05

---

12 In no more than 15 words, define the meaning of 'competent jurisdiction'. **(2 marks)**

5/05

---

13 Which **one** of the following powers is a tax authority least likely to have granted to them?

A Power of arrest.
B Power to examine records.
C Power of entry and search.
D Power to give information to other country's tax authorities. **(2 marks)**

5/05

---

14 An entity sells furniture and adds a sales tax to the selling price of all products sold. A customer purchasing furniture from the entity has to pay the cost of the furniture plus the sales tax. The customer therefore bears the cost of the sales tax.

This is referred to as

A formal incidence.
B indirect incidence.
C effective incidence.
D direct incidence. **(2 marks)**

11/05

---

15 BM has a taxable profit of $30,000 and receives a tax assessment of $3,000.

BV has a taxable profit of $60,000 and receives a tax assessment of $7,500.

BM and BV are resident in the same tax jurisdiction.

This tax could be said to be

A A progressive tax.
B A regressive tax.
C A direct tax.
D A proportional tax. **(2 marks)**

11/05

---

16 List three possible reasons why governments set deadlines for filing returns and/or paying taxes. **(3 marks)**

5/06

---

17 The 'tax gap' is the difference between:

A When a tax payment is due and the date it is actually paid

B The tax due calculated by the entity and the tax demanded by the tax authority

C The amount of tax due to be paid and the amount actually collected

D The date when the entity was notified by the tax authority of the tax due and the date the tax should be paid **(2 marks)**

5/08

---

18 What is 'hypothecation'?

A Process of earmarking tax revenues for specific types of expenditure
B Estimation of tax revenue made by the tax authorities for budget purposes
C Refund made by tax authorities for tax paid in other countries
D Payment of taxes due to tax authorities, net of tax refunds due from tax authorities **(2 marks)**

5/08

---

19 State two reasons why a group of entities might want to claim group loss relief rather than use the loss in the entity to which it relates. (Group loss relief is where, for tax purposes the loss for the year of one entity in the group is offset against the profit of the year of one or more other entities in the group.) **(2 marks)**

5/08

(Total = 42 marks)

---

32 Objective test questions: International tax 49 mins

1 Company Z has a factory in Malaysia with retail outlets in Hong Kong. The company's registered office is in London but the head office is located in the Cayman Islands. All board meetings take place in the Cayman Islands. Where is Company Z's country of residence?

A Malaysia
B Hong Kong
C England
D Cayman Islands **(2 marks)**

---

2 Which of the following is a source of tax rules?

A International accounting standards
B Local company legislation
C International tax treaties
D Domestic accounting practice **(2 marks)**

---

3 The European Union (EU) is an example of a supranational body. In not more than 20 words, describe the effect the EU has on its member states' tax rules. **(2 marks)**

---

4 In countries such as the UK, different types of income are taxed according to different rules. What is the name of this system? **(2 marks)**

---

5 Name four payments that are usually affected by withholding tax. **(2 marks)**

---

6 Name three methods of giving double taxation relief. **(2 marks)**

---

7 Double tax relief is used to:

A Ensure that you do not pay tax twice on any of your income.
B Mitigate taxing overseas income twice.
C Avoid taxing dividends received from subsidiaries in the same country twice.
D Provide relief where a company pays tax at double the normal rate. **(2 marks)**

Pilot paper

---

8 The OECD model tax convention defines a permanent establishment to include a number of different types of establishments:

1 A place of management
2 A warehouse
3 A workshop
4 A quarry
5 A building site that was used for 9 months

Which of the above are included in the OECD's list of permanent establishments?

A 1, 2 and 3 only
B 1, 3 and 4 only
C 2, 3 and 4 only
D 3, 4 and 5 only **(2 marks)**

5/05

---

9 Corporate residence for tax purposes can be determined in a number of ways, depending on the country concerned.

Which ONE of the following is NOT normally used to determine corporate residence for tax purposes?

A The country from which control of the entity is exercised.
B The country of incorporation of the entity.
C The country where management of the entity hold their meetings.
D The country where most of the entity's products are sold **(2 marks)**

11/06

---

10 An entity, DP, in Country A receives a dividend from an entity in Country B. The gross dividend of $50,000 is subject to a withholding tax of $5,000 and $45,000 is paid to DP.

Country A levies a tax of 12% on overseas dividends.

Country A and Country B have both signed a double taxation treaty based on the OECD model convention and both apply the credit method when relieving double taxation.

How much tax would DP be expected to pay in Country A on the dividend received from the entity in Country B?

A $400
B $1,000
C $5,400
D $6,000

(2 marks)

11/06

---

11 Where a resident entity runs an overseas operation as a branch of the entity, certain tax implications arise.

Which one of the following does not usually apply in relation to an overseas branch?

A Assets can be transferred to the branch without triggering a capital gain
B Corporate income tax is paid on profits remitted by the branch
C Tax depreciation can be claimed on any qualifying assets used in the trade of the branch
D Losses sustained by the branch are immediately deductible against the resident entity's income.

(2 marks)

5/08

---

12 EB has an investment of 25% of the equity shares in XY, an entity resident in a foreign country.

EB receives a dividend of $90,000 from XY, the amount being after the deduction of withholding tax of 10%.

XY had profits before tax for the year of $1,200,000 and paid corporate income tax of $200,000.

How much underlying tax can EB claim for double taxation relief? **(3 marks)**

11/07

---

13 The following details relate to EA:

- Incorporated in Country A.
- Carries out its main business activities in Country B.
- Its senior management operate from Country C and effective control is exercised from Country C.

Assume countries A, B and C have all signed double tax treaties with each other, based on the OECD model tax convention.

Which country will EA be deemed to be resident in for tax purposes?

A Country A
B Country B
C Country C
D Both Countries B and C

(2 marks)

11/07

(Total = 27 marks)

---

33 Objective test questions: Indirect taxes **41 mins**

1 Excise duties are deemed to be most suitable for commodities that have certain specific characteristics.

List THREE characteristics of a commodity that, from a revenue authority's point of view, would make that commodity suitable for an excise duty to be imposed. **(3 marks)**

5/07

---

2 Which of the following is an indirect tax?

A Withholding tax
B Employee tax
C Sales tax
D Company income tax **(2 marks)**

---

3 The cost of a sales tax is borne by which person?

A The supplier of raw materials
B The end consumer
C The retailer
D The wholesaler **(2 marks)**

The following data are given for sub-questions 4 and 5 below

Country D uses a value added tax (VAT) system whereby VAT is charged on all goods and services at a rate of 15%. Registered VAT entities are allowed to recover input VAT paid on their purchases.

Country E uses a multi-stage sales tax system, where a cumulative tax is levied every time a sale is made. The tax rate is 7% and tax paid on purchases is not recoverable.

DA is a manufacturer and sells products to DB, a retailer, for $500 excluding tax. DB sells the products to customers for a total of $1,000 excluding tax.

DA paid $200 plus VAT/sales tax for the manufacturing cost of its products.

---

4 Assume DA operates in Country D and sells products to DB in the same country.

Calculate the net VAT due to be paid by DA and DB for the products. **(2 marks)**

11/06

---

5 Assume DA operates in Country E and sells products to DB in the same country.

Calculate the total sales tax due to be paid on all of the sales of the products. **(2 marks)**

11/06

---

6 Country Z has a VAT system which allows entities to reclaim input tax paid.

In Country Z, the VAT rates are:

Zero rated	0%
Standard rated	15%

FE owns and runs a small retail store. The store's sales include items that are zero rated, standard rated and exempt.

FE's electronic cash register provides an analysis of sales. The figures for the three months to 30 April 20X8 were:

	Sales value, including VAT where appropriate
	$
Zero rated	13,000
Standard rated	18,400
Exempt	11,000
Total	42,400

FE's analysis of expenditure for the same period provided the following:

	Expenditure, excluding VAT
	$
Zero rated purchases	6,000
Standard rated purchases relating to standard rate outputs	10,000
Standard rated purchases relating to zero rate outputs	4,000
Standard rated purchases relating to exempt outputs	5,000
	25,000

Calculate the VAT due to/from FE for the three months ended 30 April 20X8. **(3 marks)**

5/08

---

7 Which of the following types of taxes is regarded as an indirect tax?

A Taxes on income.

B Taxes on capital gains.

C Taxes on inherited wealth.

D Sales tax (Value added tax). **(2 marks)**

Pilot paper

---

8 AE purchases products from a foreign entity and imports them into a country A. On import, the products are subject to an excise duty of $5 per item and Value Added Tax (VAT) of 15% on cost plus excise duty.

AE purchased 200 items for $30 each and after importing them sold all of the items for $50 each plus VAT at 15%.

How much is due to be paid to the tax authorities for these transactions?

A $450

B $1,450

C $2,050

D $2,500 **(3 marks)**

5/05

---

9 Country OS has a value added tax (VAT) system where VAT is charged on all goods and services. Registered VAT entities are allowed to recover input VAT paid on their purchases.

VAT operates at different levels in OS:

- Standard rate 10%
- Luxury rate 20%
- Zero rate 0%

During the last VAT period, an entity, BZ, purchased materials and services costing $100,000, excluding VAT. All materials and services were at standard rate VAT.

BZ converted the materials into two products Z and L; product Z is zero rated and product L is luxury rated for VAT purposes.

During the VAT period, BZ made the following sales, excluding VAT:

	$
Z	60,000
L	120,000

At the end of the period, BZ paid the net VAT due to the tax authorities.

Assuming BZ had no other VAT-related transactions, how much VAT did BZ pay? **(2 marks)**

11/05

---

10 CU manufactures clothing and operates in a country that has a Value Added Tax system (VAT). The VAT system allows entities to reclaim input tax that they have paid on taxable supplies. VAT is at 15% of the selling price at all stages of the manufacturing and distribution chain.

CU manufactures a batch of clothing and pays expenses (taxable inputs) of $100 plus VAT. CU sells the batch of clothing to a retailer CZ for $250 plus VAT. CZ unpacks the clothing and sells the items separately to various customers for a total of $600 plus VAT.

How much VAT do CU and CZ each have to pay in respect of this one batch of clothing? **(2 marks)**

5/06

(Total = 23 marks)

---

34 Objective test questions: Company taxation **67 mins**

1 Company G makes an accounting profit of $350,000 during the year. This includes non-taxable income of $25,000 and depreciation of $30,000. In addition, $15,000 of the expenses are disallowable for tax purposes. If the tax allowable depreciation totals $32,000, what is the taxable profit?

A $323,000
B $338,000
C $352,000
D $362,000 **(2 marks)**

---

2 Company G makes a taxable profit of $350,000 during the year. This includes adjustments for non-taxable income of $25,000, depreciation of $30,000 and $15,000 disallowed expenses. If the tax allowable depreciation totals $32,000, what is the accounting profit?

A $323,000
B $338,000
C $352,000
D $362,000 **(2 marks)**

---

3 Company G makes an accounting loss of $350,000 during the year. This includes non-taxable income of $25,000 and depreciation of $30,000. In addition, $400,000 of the expenses are disallowable for tax purposes. If the tax allowable depreciation totals $32,000, what is the taxable amount?

A $23,000 profit
B $23,000 loss
C $123,000 profit
D $123,000 profit **(2 marks)**

---

4 Company W makes a taxable profit of $50m during the year. This is after adjustments for non-taxable income of $3m, depreciation of $15m and $1m disallowed expenses. If the tax allowable depreciation totals $4m, what is the accounting profit?

A $38m
B $41m
C $58m
D $59m **(2 marks)**

---

5 Company M makes an accounting profit of $250,000 during the year. This includes depreciation of $45,000 and disallowable expenses of $20,000. If the tax allowable depreciation totals $30,000 and the tax rate is 30%, what is the tax payable?

A $64,500
B $75,000
C $79,500
D $85,500 **(2 marks)**

---

6 Company B makes an accounting profit of $360,000 during the year. This includes non-taxable income of $35,000 and depreciation of $40,000. In addition, $10,000 of the expenses are disallowable for tax purposes. If the tax allowable depreciation totals $30,000 and the tax rate is 20%, what is the tax payable?

A $60,000
B $65,000
C $69,000
D $72,000 **(2 marks)**

---

7 Company X makes an accounting profit of $500,000 during the year. This includes non-taxable income of $25,000 and depreciation of $50,000.

The finance director finds that $5,000 of the expenses are disallowable for tax purposes. If the tax allowable depreciation totals $60,000 and the tax rate is 25%, what is the tax payable?

A $116,250
B $117,500
C $123,750
D $132,500 **(2 marks)**

---

8 Company G makes an accounting profit of $250,000 during the year. This is after charging depreciation of $40,000 and tax disallowable expenses of $2,000. If the tax allowable depreciation totals $30,000 and the tax rate is 30%, what is the tax payable?

A $71,400
B $72,000
C $77,400
D $78,600 **(2 marks)**

---

9 Tax on an entity's trading profits could be referred to as:

1 Income tax
2 Profits tax
3 Indirect tax
4 Direct tax
5 Earnings tax

Which TWO of the above would most accurately describe tax on an entity's trading profits:

A 1 and 3
B 1 and 4
C 2 and 3
D 4 and 5 **(2 marks)**

Pilot paper

---

10 E has an accounting profit before tax of $95,000. The tax rate on trading profits applicable to E for the year is 25%. The accounting profit included non-taxable income from government grants of $15,000 and non-tax allowable expenditure of $10,000 on entertaining expenses.

How much tax is E due to pay for the year? **(2 marks)**

Pilot paper

---

11 AC made the following payment during the year ended 30 April 20X5:

	$'000
Operating costs (excluding depreciation)	23
Finance costs	4
Capital repayment of loans	10
Payments for the purchase of new computer equipment for use in AC's business	20

AC's revenue for the period was $45,000 and the corporate income tax rate applicable to AC's profits was 25%. The computer equipment qualifies for tax allowances of 10% per year on a straight line basis.

Calculate AC's tax payable for the year ended 30 April 20X5. **(3 marks)**

5/05

---

12 Country B has a corporate income tax system that treats capital gains/losses separately from trading profits/losses. Capital gains/losses cannot be offset against trading profits/losses. All losses can be carried forward indefinitely, but cannot be carried back to previous years. Trading profits and capital gains are both taxed at 20%.

BD had no brought forward losses on 1 October 20X2. BD's results for 20X3 to 20X5 were as follows:

	Trading profit/(loss)	*Capital gains/(loss)*
	$'000	$'000
Year to September 20X3	200	(100)
Year to September 20X4	(120)	0
Year to September 20X5	150	130

Calculate BD's corporate income tax due for each of the years ended 30 September 20X3 to 20X5. **(3 marks)**

11/05

---

13 A full imputation system of corporate income tax is one where an entity is taxable on

A all of its income and gains whether they are distributed or not. The shareholder is liable for taxation on all dividends received.

B all of its income and gains whether they are distributed or not, but all the underlying corporation tax is passed to the shareholder as a tax credit.

C all of its income and gains whether they are distributed or not, but only part of the underlying corporation tax is passed to the shareholder as a tax credit.

D its retained profits at one rate and on its distributed profits at another (usually lower) rate of tax.

(2 marks)

5/06

---

14 DZ recognised a tax liability of $290,000 in its financial statements for the year ended 30 September 20X5. This was subsequently agreed with and paid to the tax authorities as $280,000 on 1 March 20X6. The directors of DZ estimate that the tax due on the profits for the year to 30 September 20X6 will be $320,000. DZ has no deferred tax liability.

What is DZ's income statement tax charge for the year ended 30 September 20X6?

A $310,000
B $320,000
C $330,000
D $600,000 **(2 marks)**

11/06

---

15 DD purchased an item of plant and machinery costing $500,000 on 1 April 20X4, which qualified for 50% capital allowances in the first year, and 20% each year thereafter on the reducing balance basis.

DD's policy in respect of plant and machinery is to charge depreciation on a straight line basis over five years, with no residual value. On 1 April 20X6, DD decides to revalue the item of plant and machinery upwards, from its net book value, by $120,000.

Assuming there are no other capital transactions in the three year period and a tax rate of 30% throughout, calculate the amount of deferred tax to be shown in DD's income statement for the year ended 31 March 20X7, and the deferred tax provision to be included in its balance sheet at 31 March 20X7. **(4 marks)**

5/07

---

16 EG purchased a property for $630,000 on 1 September 20X0. EG incurred additional costs for the purchase of $3,500 surveyors' fees and $6,500 legal fees. EG then spent $100,000 renovating the property prior to letting it. All of EG's expenditure was classified as capital expenditure according to the local tax regulations.

Indexation of the purchase and renovation costs is allowed on EE's property. The index increased by 50% between September 20X0 and October 20X7. Assume that acquisition and renovation costs were incurred in September 20X0. EG sold the property on 1 October 20X7 for $1,250,000, incurring tax allowable costs on disposal of $2,000.

Calculate EG's tax due on disposal assuming a tax rate of 30%. **(3 marks)**

11/07

(Total = 37 marks)

---

35 Objective test questions: Deferred tax **67 mins**

1 A company had a credit balance brought forward on current tax of $20,000. During the year it paid tax of $18,000 and it has a provision for the current year of $50,000. It has increased the deferred tax provision by $5,000. What is the total charge to tax for the year in the income statement?

A $53,000
B $55,000
C $57,000
D $68,000 **(2 marks)**

---

2 A company had a debit balance brought forward on current tax of $2,000. During the year it has paid no tax and received a tax refund of $1,800. It has a provision for the current year of $30,000. It has decreased the deferred tax provision by $5,000. What is the total charge to tax for the year in the income statement?

A $23,200
B $24,800
C $25,200
D $35,200 **(2 marks)**

---

3 In accounting for deferred tax, which of the following items can give rise to temporary differences?

1 Differences between accounting depreciation and tax allowances for capital expenditure
2 Expenses charged in the income statement but disallowed for tax
3 Revaluation of a non-current asset
4 Unrelieved tax losses

A 1, 3 and 4 only
B 1 and 2 only
C 3 and 4 only
D All four items **(2 marks)**

---

4 Which of the following are examples of assets or liabilities whose carrying amount is always equal to their tax base?

1 Accrued expenses that will never be deductible for tax purposes

2 Accrued expenses that have already been deducted in determining the current tax liability for current or earlier periods

3 Accrued income that will never be taxable

4 A loan payable in the balance sheet at the amount originally received, which is also the amount eventually repayable

A 1 and 3 only
B 1 and 2 only
C 2 and 4 only
D All four items **(2 marks)**

---

5 Which of the following statements about IAS 12 *Income taxes* are correct?

1 Companies may discount deferred tax assets and liabilities if the effect would be material.

2 The financial statements must disclose an explanation of the relationship between tax expense and accounting profit.

3 Deferred tax may not be recognised in respect of goodwill unless any impairment of that goodwill is deductible for tax purposes.

4 The tax base of an asset or liability is the amount attributed to that asset or liability for tax purposes.

A All the statements are correct
B 2, 3 and 4 only are correct
C 1 and 4 only are correct
D None of the statements is correct. **(2 marks)**

---

6 The following information relates to an entity.

- At 1 January 20X8, the net book value of non-current assets exceeded their tax written down value by $850,000.
- For the year ended 31 December 20X8, the entity claimed depreciation for tax purposes of $500,000 and charged depreciation of $450,000 in the financial statements.
- During the year ended 31 December 20X8, the entity revalued a freehold property. The revaluation surplus was $250,000. The entity has no plans to sell the property and realise the gain in the foreseeable future.
- The tax rate was 30% throughout the year.

What is the provision for deferred tax required by IAS 12 *Income taxes* at 31 December 20X8?

A $240,000
B $270,000
C $315,000
D $345,000 **(2 marks)**

---

7 A company had a credit balance brought forward on current tax of $25,000. During the year it has paid no tax and received a tax refund of $2,500. It has a provision for the current year of $30,000. It has decreased the deferred tax provision by $10,000. What is the total charge to tax for the year in the income statement?

A $5,000 debit
B $5,000 credit
C $7,500 debit
D $7,500 credit **(2 marks)**

---

8 A country had a current tax regime whereby relief is given for tax paid on dividends. What system of tax is this? **(2 marks)**

---

9 A company had a credit balance brought forward on current tax of $25,000. During the year it paid tax of $27,800. It has a provision for the current year of $28,000. It has increased the deferred tax provision by $5,000. What is the total charge to tax for the year in the income statement?

A $31,200
B $33,000
C $33,800
D $35,800 **(2 marks)**

---

10 BC, a small entity, purchased its only non-current tangible asset on 1 October 20X3. The asset cost $900,000, all of which qualified for tax depreciation.

BC's asset qualified for an accelerated first year tax allowance of 50%. The second and subsequent years qualified for tax depreciation at 25% per year on the reducing balance method.

BC's accounting depreciation policy is to depreciate the asset over its useful economic life of five years, assuming a residual value of $50,000.

Assume that BC pays tax on its income at the rate of 30%.

Calculate BC's deferred tax balance required in the balance sheet as at 30 September 20X5 according to IAS 12 *Income taxes.* **(4 marks)**

11/05

---

11 CY had the following amounts for 20X3 to 20X5:

Year ended 31 December:	*20X3*	*20X4*	*20X5*
	$	$	$
Accounting depreciation for the year	1,630	1,590	1,530
Tax depreciation allowance for the year	2,120	1,860	1,320

At 31 December 20X2, CY had the following balances brought forward:

	$
Cost of property, plant and equipment qualifying for tax depreciation	20,000
Accounting depreciation	5,000
Tax depreciation	12,500

CY had no non-current asset acquisitions or disposals during the period 20X3 to 20X5.
Assume the corporate income tax rate is 25% for all years.
Calculate the deferred tax provision required by IAS 12 *Income taxes* at 31 December 20X5. **(3 marks)**

5/06

---

12 On 31 March 20X6, CH had a credit balance brought forward on its deferred tax account of $642,000. There was also a credit balance on its corporate income tax account of $31,000, representing an over-estimate of the tax charge for the year ended 31 March 20X5.

CH's taxable profit for the year ended 31 March 20X6 was $946,000. CH's directors estimated the deferred tax provision required at 31 March 20X6 to be $759,000 and the applicable income tax rate for the year to 31 March 20X6 as 22%.

Calculate the income tax expense that CH will charge in its income statement for the year ended 31 March 20X6, as required by IAS 12 *Income taxes.* **(3 marks)**

5/06

---

13 FD purchased an item of plant and machinery costing $600,000 on 1 April 20X5, which qualified for 50% capital allowances in the first year and 25% per year thereafter, on the reducing balance basis.

FD's policy in respect of plant and machinery is to charge depreciation on a straight line basis over five years, with no residual value.

On 1 April 20X7, FD carried out an impairment review of all its non-current assets. This item of plant and machinery was found to have a value in use of $240,000. FD adjusted its financial records and wrote the plant and machinery down to its value in use on 1 April 20X7.

Assuming there are no other temporary differences in the period and a tax rate of 25% per annum over the five years, calculate the amount of any deferred tax balances outstanding at 31 March 20X7 and 31 March 20X8. (Work to the nearest $1,000.) **(4 marks)**

5/08

---

14 EE reported accounting profits of $822,000 for the period ended 30 November 20X7. This was after deducting entertaining expenses of $32,000 and a donation to a political party of $50,000, both of which are disallowable for tax purposes.

EE's reported profit also included $103,000 government grant income that was exempt from taxation. EE paid dividends of $240,000 in the period.

Assume EE had no temporary differences between accounting profits and taxable profits.

Assume that a classical tax system applies to EE's profits and that the tax rate is 25%.

What would EE's tax payable be on its profits for the year to 30 November 20X7? **(2 marks)**

11/07

---

15 A government wanted to encourage investment in new non-current assets by entities and decided to change tax allowances for non-current assets to give a 100% first year allowance on all new non-current assets purchased after 1 January 20X5.

ED purchased new machinery for $400,000 on 1 October 20X5 and claimed the 100% first year allowance. For accounting purposes ED depreciated the machinery on the reducing balance basis at 25% per year. The rate of corporate income tax to be applied to ED's taxable profits was 22%.

Assume ED had no other temporary differences.

Calculate the amount of deferred tax that ED would show in its balance sheet at 30 September 20X7. **(3 marks)**

11/07

(Total = 37 marks)

---

36 Section B questions: Taxation I — 63 mins

(a) Define a taxable person and give three examples. What is a competent jurisdiction for tax purposes? **(5 marks)**

(b) (i) Give a definition of an indirect tax and explain how it works. **(3 marks)**

(ii) There are two types of indirect taxes. State what these are and give two examples of each. **(2 marks)**

(Total = 5 marks)

(c) F has sales of $587,500 including sales tax. Its purchases for the same period were $350,000 excluding sales tax. The sales tax rate is 17.5%. Calculate the tax payable to the tax authorities if 20% of the total amount of B's sales represents exempt outputs and its deductible input tax is to be apportioned accordingly. **(5 marks)**

(d) On 1 January 20X3, SPJ had an opening credit balance of $5,000 on its tax account, which represented the balance on the account after settling its tax liability for the previous year. SPJ had a credit balance on its deferred tax account of $1·6 million at the same date.

SPJ has been advised that it should expect to pay $1 million tax on its trading profits for the year ended 31 December 20X3 and increase its deferred tax account balance by $150,000.

Required

Prepare extracts from the income statement for the year ended 31 December 20X3, balance sheet at that date and notes to the accounts showing the tax entries required. **(5 marks)**

Pilot paper

(e) *Required*

(i) Explain the difference between tax avoidance and tax evasion. **(2 marks)**

(ii) Briefly explain the methods that governments can use to reduce tax avoidance and tax evasion. **(3 marks)**

(Total = 5 marks)

11/05

(f) CW owns 40% of the equity shares in Z, an entity resident in a foreign country. CW receives a dividend of $45,000 from Z; the amount received is after deduction of withholding tax of 10%. Z had before tax profits for the year of $500,000 and paid corporate income tax of $100,000.

Required

(i) Explain the meaning of 'withholding tax' and 'underlying tax.' **(2 marks)**

(ii) Calculate the amount of withholding tax paid by CW. **(1 mark)**

(iii) Calculate the amount of underlying tax that relates to CW's dividend. **(2 marks)**

(Total = 5 marks)

5/06

(g) EF is an importer and imports perfumes and similar products in bulk. EF repackages the products and sells them to retailers. EF is registered for Value Added Tax (VAT).

EF imports a consignment of perfume priced at $10,000 (excluding excise duty and VAT) and pays excise duty of 20% and VAT on the total (including duty) at 15%.

EF pays $6,900 repackaging costs, including VAT at 15% and then sells all the perfume for $40,250 including VAT at 15%.

EF has not paid or received any VAT payments to/from the VAT authorities for this consignment.

Required

(i) Calculate EF's net profit on the perfume consignment.

(ii) Calculate the net VAT due to be paid by EF on the perfume consignment. **(Total = 5 marks)**

11/07

(Total = 35 marks)

37 Section B questions: Taxation II **27 mins**

(a) Tax authorities have various powers to enforce compliance with the tax rules.

State what these powers are and give examples of each. **(5 marks)**

(b) What is withholding tax and why do tax authorities use it? Give two examples of payments affected by withholding tax. **(5 marks)**

(c) Why do countries need to enter into double taxation agreements? What are the three main methods of giving double taxation relief? **(5 marks)**

(Total = 15 marks)

38 Section B questions: Taxation III **54 mins**

(a) H is a major manufacturing entity. According to the entity's records, temporary differences of $2.00 million had arisen at 30 April 20X4 because of differences between the carrying amount of non-current assets and their tax base, due to H claiming accelerated tax relief in the earlier years of the asset lives.

At 30 April 20X3, the temporary differences attributable to non-current assets were $2.30 million.

H's tax rate has been 30% in the past. On 30 April 20X4, the directors of H were advised that the rate of taxation would decrease to 28% by the time that the temporary differences on the non-current assets reversed.

Required

Prepare the note in respect of deferred tax as it would appear in the financial statements of H for the year ended 30 April 20X4. (Your answer should be expressed in $ million and you should work to two decimal places.) **(5 marks)**

(b) B is a retail entity. Its tax rate is 30%. It has a current tax payable brought forward from the year ended 30 April 20X3 of $750,000 and a deferred tax payable of $250,000.

On 30 April 20X4, the estimated tax charge for the year ended 30 April 20X4 was $1,400,000. The actual tax charge for the year ended 30 April 20X3 was agreed with the tax authority and settled with a payment of $720,000. The deferred tax payable needs to be increased to $300,000 as at 30 April 20X4.

Required

Prepare the notes in respect of current and deferred tax as they would appear in the financial statements of B for the year ended 30 April 20X4. (Your answer should be expressed in $ million and you should work to two decimal places.) **(5 marks)**

(c) DG purchased its only non-current tangible asset on 1 October 20X2. The asset cost $200,000, all of which qualified for tax depreciation. DG's accounting depreciation policy is to depreciate the asset over its useful economic life of five years, assuming no residual value, charging a full year's depreciation in the year of acquisition and no depreciation in the year of disposal.

The asset qualified for tax depreciation at a rate of 30% per year on the reducing balance method. DG sold the asset on 30 September 20X6 for $60,000.

The rate of income tax to apply to DG's profit is 20%. DG's accounting period is 1 October to 30 September.

Required

(i) Calculate DG's deferred tax balance at 30 September 20X5.

(ii) Calculate DG's accounting profit/loss that will be recognised in its income statement on the disposal of the asset, in accordance with IAS 16 *Property, Plant and Equipment.*

(iii) Calculate DG's tax balancing allowance/charge arising on the disposal of the asset. **(5 marks)**

11/06

(d) Country Z has the following tax regulations in force for the years 20X5 and 20X6 (each year January to December).

- Corporate income is taxed at the following rates.
  - $1 to $10,000 at 0%
  - $10,001 to $25,000 at 15%
  - $25,001 and over at 25%
- When calculating corporate income tax, Country Z does **not** allow the following types of expense to be charged against taxable income:
  - Entertaining expenses
  - Taxes paid to other public bodies
  - Accounting depreciation of non-current asset
- Tax relief on capital expenditure is available at the following rates:
  - Buildings at 4% per annum on straight line basis
  - All other non-current tangible assets are allowed tax depreciation at 27% per annum on reducing balance basis.

DB commenced business on 1 January 20X5 when all assets were purchased. No first year allowances were available for 20X5.

NON-CURRENT ASSETS COST AS AT 1 JANUARY 20X5

	$
Land	27,000
Buildings	70,000
Plant and equipment	80,000

On 1 January 20X6, DB purchased another machine for $20,000. This machine qualified for a first year tax allowance of 50%.

DB
INCOME STATEMENT FOR THE YEAR TO 31 DECEMBER 20X6

	$
Gross profit	160,000
Administrative expenses	81,000
Entertaining	600
Tax paid to local government	950
Depreciation on buildings	1,600
Depreciation on plant and equipment	20,000
Distribution costs	20,000
	35,850
Finance cost	1,900
Profit before tax	33,950

Required

Calculate DB's corporate income tax due for the year 20X6. **(5 marks)**

5/07

(e) AB acquired non-current assets on 1 April 20X3 costing $250,000. The assets qualified for accelerated first year tax allowance at the rate of 50% for the first year. The second and subsequent years were at a tax depreciation rate of 25% per year on the reducing balance method.

AB depreciates all non-current assets at 20% a year on the straight line basis.

The rate of corporate tax applying to AB for 20X3/X4 and 20X4/X5 was 30%. Assume AB has no other qualifying non-current assets.

Required

Apply IAS 12 *Income taxes* and calculate:

(i) the deferred tax balance required at 31 March 20X4
(ii) the deferred tax balance required at 31 March 20X5
(iii) the charge to the income statement for the year ended 31 March 20X5 **(5 marks)**

5/05

(f) Country X has the following tax regulations in force.

- The tax year is 1 May to 30 April
- All corporate profits are taxed at 20%
- When calculating corporate taxable income, depreciation of non-current assets cannot be charged against taxable income.
- Tax depreciation is allowed at the following rates.
  - Buildings at 5% per annum on a straight line basis
  - All other non-current tangible assets are allowed tax depreciation at 25% per annum on a reducing balance basis
- No tax allowances are allowed on land or furniture and fittings.

FB commenced trading on 1 May 20X5 when it purchased all its non-current assets.

FB's non-current asset balances were:

	Cost	*Net book value*	*Tax written down value*
	1 May 20X5	*1 May 20X7*	*1 May 20X7*
	$	$	$
Land	20,000	20,000	–
Buildings	80,000	73,600	72,000
Plant and equipment	21,000	1,000	11,812
Furniture and fittings	15,000	5,000	–

FB did not purchase any non-current assets between 1 May 20X5 and 30 April 20X7. On 2 May 20X7, FB disposed of all its plant and equipment for $5,000 and purchased new plant and equipment for $30,000. The new plant and equipment qualified for a first year tax allowance of 50%.

FB INCOME STATEMENT FOR THE YEAR ENDED 30 APRIL 20X8

	$
Gross profit	210,000
Administrative expenses	(114,000)
Gain on disposal of plant and equipment	4,000
Depreciation – furniture and fittings	(5,000)
Depreciation – buildings	(3,200)
Depreciation – plant and equipment	(6,000)
Distribution costs	(49,000)
	36,800
Finance cost	(7,000)
Profit before tax	29,800

Required

Calculate FB's corporate income tax due for the year ended 30 April 20X8. **(Total = 5 marks)**

05/08

(Total = 30 marks)

Part D: Managing short term finance

Questions 39 to 46 cover Managing Short-term Finance, the subject of Part D of the BPP Study Text for Paper P7.

39 Objective test questions: Short-term finance I — 72 mins

1 DK is considering investing in government bonds. The current price of a $100 bond with 10 years to maturity is $88. The bonds have a coupon rate of 6% and repay face value of $100 at the end of the 10 years.

Calculate the yield to maturity. **(4 marks)**

11/06

---

2 Which of the following could a company NOT use as a source of short-term credit?

A Trade credit from suppliers
B Bank overdraft
C Factoring of trade debts
D Mortgage on property **(2 marks)**

---

3 Which one of the following statements about an overdraft facility is correct?

A An overdraft is a permanent loan
B Assets are always required as security
C Interest is paid on the full facility
D Compared with other types of loan it is quick and easy to set up **(2 marks)**

5/08

---

4 Of what is the following statement a definition?

'A document issued by a bank on behalf of a customer authorising a person to draw money to a specified amount from its branches or correspondents, usually in another country, when the conditions set out in the document have been met.'

A Bill of exchange
B Export guarantee
C Banker's draft
D Letter of credit **(2 marks)**

---

5 Which of the following is the LEAST IMPORTANT consideration when assessing how to invest a short-term cash surplus?

A Length of time for which the funds are available
B Maximising the return generated by the funds
C Ease of realisation
D Risk associated with calling in the investment early **(2 marks)**

---

6 Which of the following services is LEAST LIKELY to be offered by a factoring company?

A Provision of finance by advancing, say 80% of invoice value immediately, and the remainder on settlement of the debt by the customer
B Taking over responsibility for administration of the client's sales ledger
C Deciding what credit limits customers should be given
D Non-recourse finance, ie taking over responsibility for bad debts **(2 marks)**

---

7 KEN is awaiting the go-ahead to start its new building programme. This is likely to take place within the next 90 days, but the precise start date and timing of the cash flows are still uncertain. The company has $150,000 available in cash in anticipation of the investment. Which of the following is the LEAST APPROPRIATE use of the funds in the interim period?

A Investment in equities
B Treasury bills
C Bank deposits
D Local authority deposits **(2 marks)**

---

8 A bond has a coupon rate of 6% and a current price of $85. It is redeemable in 5 years time at its face value of $100.

What is its yield to maturity? **(4 marks)**

---

9 An entity's working capital financing policy is to finance working capital using short-term financing to fund all the fluctuating current assets as well as some of the permanent part of the current assets.

The above policy is an example of

A an aggressive policy.
B a conservative policy.
C a short-term policy.
D a moderate policy. **(2 marks)**

11/05

---

10 BE has been offering 60 day payment terms to its customers, but now wants to improve its cash flow. BE is proposing to offer a 1.5% discount for payment within 20 days.

Assume a 365 day year and an invoice value of $1,000.

What is the effective annual interest rate that BE will incur for this action? **(4 marks)**

11/05

---

11 A bond has a current market price of $83. It will repay it face value of $100 in seven years' time and has a coupon rate of 4%.

If the bond is purchased at $83 and held, what is its yield to maturity? **(4 marks)**

5/07

---

12 Which one of the following is correct?

A cash budget prepared on a monthly basis is done to calculate:

A The amount of inventory to purchase in the following month
B When to pay workers' wages
C Next month's sales volumes
D Whether there will be sufficient cash in the bank to meet requirements **(2 marks)**

5/08

---

13 A $1,000 bond has a coupon rate of 12% and will repay its face value on redemption in four year's time.

If the bond is purchased for $1,090 ex interest and held, what is its yield to maturity? **(4 marks)**

5/08

---

14 A bond has a coupon rate of 7%. It will repay its face value of $1,000 at the end of six years. The market expects this type of bond to have a yield to maturity of 10%.

What is the current market value of the bond? **(4 marks)**

11/07

(Total = 40 marks)

40 Objective test questions: Short-term finance II — 65 mins

1 A company with large amounts of surplus cash may decide to invest it in short-term money market instruments. Which of the following money market investments would carry the LOWEST interest rate?

A Sterling certificates of deposit (CDs)
B Treasury bills
C Finance house deposits
D Local authority deposits **(2 marks)**

2 A company uses the Baumol cash management model. Cash disbursements are constant at $20,000 each month. Money on deposit earns 5% a year, while money in the current account earns a zero return. Switching costs (that is, for each purchase or sale of securities) are $30 for each transaction.

What is the optimal amount (to the nearest $100) to be transferred in each transaction? **(2 marks)**

Pilot paper

3 A manufacturer of china commemorating the Olympic Games is facing a short-term liquidity shortage. Which of the following assets could it sell in order to make good the cash shortfall while doing the minimum damage to its core activities?

A 10% of its fleet of delivery vehicles
B The pigment blending plant
C The patent on a new design of china pouring device intended to commemorate the Olympic Games
D Its 60% equity stake in the company that supplies its gold leaf **(2 marks)**

4 List **four** forms of short-term finance generally available to small entities. **(2 marks)**

5/05

5 A bond with a coupon rate of 7% is redeemable in 8 year's time for $100. Its current purchase price is $82. What is the percentage yield to maturity? **(2 marks)**

5/05

6 An investor buys $11,000 (nominal value) of a bond with a coupon rate of 10%, for the current market value of $10,000. Average market returns are 12%. What is the interest yield to the nearest one percent?

A 9%
B 10%
C 11%
D 12% **(2 marks)**

7 In less than 30 words, define 'float'. **(2 marks)**

8 CT uses the Miller-Orr cash management model to help manage cash flows. The management accountant has agreed with the directors that the lower limit for cash will be $2,500.

The current rate of interest that CT pays is 0.025% per day. Each transaction costs CT $30. CT's daily cash flows have been measured and the variance calculated as $300,000.

Calculate, for CT, the Miller-Orr return point and upper limit. **(3 marks)**

5/06

---

9 Which one of the following MOST APPROPRIATELY describes forfaiting?

A It is a method of providing medium-term export finance.
B It provides long-term finance to importers.
C It provides equity finance for the redemption of shares.
D It is the surrender of a share because of the failure to make a payment on a partly-paid share.

(2 marks)

---

10 Which of the following statements about certificates of deposit is FALSE?

A Certificates of deposit are negotiable instruments issued by banks.
B Certificates of deposit will typically have maturity periods of between three and five years.
C Certificates of deposit are non-negotiable.
D Certificates of deposit are issued in bearer form. **(2 marks)**

---

11 Which of the following investments carries the highest level of risk?

A Local authority stocks
B Company loan stocks
C Convertible loan stocks
D Preference shares **(2 marks)**

---

12 In less than 30 words define 'redemption yield' (yield to maturity). **(2 marks)**

---

13 After a bill of exchange has been accepted, there are a number of possible actions that the drawer could take.

Which ONE of the following is NOT a possible course of action?

A Ask the customer for immediate payment.
B Discount the bill with a bank.
C Hold the bill until the due date and then present it for payment.
D Use the bill to settle a trade payable. **(2 marks)**

5/06

---

14 FW holds a 91 day treasury bill, with a face value of $10,000. FW wants to sell the treasury bill, which has 40 days remaining to maturity.

The market yield for treasury bills is 6%.

Calculate the expected selling price of the treasury bill. (Assume 365 days in a year for interest calculation purposes.) **(3 marks)**

5/08

---

15 Treasury shares are defined as

A Equity shares sold by an entity in the period.
B Equity shares repurchased by the issuing entity, not cancelled before the period end.
C Non-equity shares sold by an entity in the period.
D Equity shares repurchased by the issuing entity and cancelled before the period end. **(2 marks)**

11/07

---

16 List FOUR advantages of forfaiting for an exporter. **(4 marks)**

11/07

(Total = 36 marks)

---

41 Section B questions: Short-term finance 81 mins

(a) HRD owns a number of small hotels. The room occupancy rate varies significantly from month to month. There are also high fixed costs. As a result, the cash generated each month has been very difficult to estimate.

Christmas is normally a busy period and large cash surpluses are expected in December. There is, however, a possibility that a rival group of hotels will offer large discounts in December and this could damage December trade for HRD to a significant extent.

January is a poor period for the industry and therefore all the company's hotels will close for the month, resulting in a negative cash flow. The Finance Director has identified the following possible outcomes and their associated probabilities:

	$'000	*Probability*
Expected cash balance at 30 November 20X3	+175	1.0
Net operating cash flow in December 20X3	+700	0.7
	–300	0.3
Net operating cash flow in January 20X4	–900	1.0

Assume cash flows arise at month ends.

After January 20X4, trade is expected to improve, but there is still a high degree of uncertainty in relation to the cash surpluses or deficits that will be generated in each month.

Required

Calculate the expected cash balance or overdraft of HRD at 31 January 20X4.

Explain why your answer may not be useful for short-term cash planning and outline alternative approaches that could be used. **(5 marks)**

Pilot paper

(b) Official statistics show that over the past four to five years, overdraft usage has been falling by around 5% per annum and is being replaced by other forms of asset-based lending.

Required

Explain the main uses of overdraft facilities as part of a company's working capital management policy **(5 marks)**

(c) Discuss the alternative sources of finance which are available to companies which do not want to run an overdraft. **(5 marks)**

(d) AM is a trading entity operating in a country where there is no sales tax. Purchases are on credit, with 70% paid in the month following the date of purchase and 30% paid in the month after that.

Sales are partly on credit and partly for cash. Customers who receive credit are given 30 days to pay. On average 60% pay within 30 days, 30% pay between 30 and 60 days and 5% pay between 60 and 90 days. The balance is written off as irrecoverable. Other overheads, including salaries, are paid within the month incurred.

AM plans to purchase new equipment at the end of June 20X5, the expected cost of which is $250,000. The equipment will be purchased on 30 days credit, payable at the end of July.

The cash balance on 1 May 20X5 is $96,000.

The actual/budgeted figures for the six month to July 20X5 were:

		Actual			*Budgeted*	
	Feb	*Mar*	*Apr*	*May*	*Jun*	*Jul*
	$'000	$'000	$'000	$'000	$'000	$'000
Credit sales	100	100	110	110	120	120
Cash sales	30	30	35	35	40	40
Credit purchases	45	50	50	55	55	60
Other overhead expense	40	40	40	50	50	50

Required

Prepare a monthly cash budget for the period May to July 20X5 and assess the likelihood of AM being able to pay for the equipment when it falls due. (Round all figures to the nearest $'000) **(5 marks)**

5/05

(e) BH purchased a bond with a face value of $1,000 on 1 June 20X3 for $850. The bond has a coupon rate of 7%. BH intends holding the bond to its maturity on 31 May 20X8 when it will repay its face value.

Required

(i) Explain the difference between the coupon rate of a security and its yield to maturity. **(2 marks)**

(ii) Calculate the bond's yield to maturity. **(3 marks)**

11/05

(f) DH raised cash through an equity share issue to pay for a new factory it planned to construct. However, the factory contract has been delayed and payments are not expected to be required for three or four months. DH is going to invest its surplus funds until they are required.

One of the directors of DH has identified three possible investment opportunities:

(i) Treasury bills issued by the central bank of DH's country. They could be purchased on 1 December 20X6 for a period of 91 days. The likely purchase price is $990 per $1,000.

(ii) Equities quoted on DH's local stock exchange. The stock exchange has had a good record in recent months with the equity index increasing in value for 14 consecutive months. The director recommends that DH invests in three large multinational entities each paying an annual dividend that provides an annual yield of 10% on the current share price.

(iii) DH's bank would pay 3.5% per year on money placed in a deposit account with 30 day's notice.

Required

As Assistant Management Accountant, you have been asked to prepare notes on the risk and effective yield of each of the above investment opportunities for use by the Management Accountant at the next board meeting. **(5 marks)**

11/06

(g) DF, a sports training equipment wholesaler has prepared its forecast cash flow for the next six months and has calculated that it will need $2 million additional short-term finance in three months' time.

DF has an annual gross revenue of $240 million and achieves a gross margin of 50%. It currently has the flowing outstanding working capital balances:

- $16 million trade payables
- $20 million trade receivables
- $5 million bank overdraft

DF forecasts that it will be able to repay half the $2 million within three months and the balance within a further three months.

Required

Advise DF of possible sources of funding available to it. **(5 marks)**

5/07

(h) FG issued 10,000,000 $1, 5% preferred shares at par on 1 May 20X6. The shares are redeemable at a 10% premium four years after issue on 30 April 20Y0. Issue costs were $601,500.

Required

(i) Calculate the finance charge for each of the four years 1 May 20X6 to 30 April 20Y0 using the sum of digits method. **(3 marks)**

(ii) Prepare extracts from FG's income statement for the year ended 30 April 20X8 and its balance sheet at that date, to show the accounting entries required for the preferred shares. **(2 marks)**

5/08

(i) ES estimates from its cash flow forecast that it will have $120,000 to invest for 12 months.

ES is considering the following investments:

(i) Purchase of fixed term bonds issued by a "blue chip" entity quoted on the local stock exchange. The bonds have a maturity date in 12 months' time and pay 12·5% interest on face value. The bonds will be redeemed at face value in 12 months' time. ES will incur commission costs on purchasing the bonds of 1% of cost. The bonds are currently trading at $102 per $100.

(ii) An internet bank is offering a deposit account that pays interest on a monthly basis at 0·8% per month.

Required:

Identify which is the most appropriate investment for the year, giving your reasons. **(5 marks)**

11/07

(Total = 45 marks)

42 Objective test questions: Working capital management I

63 mins

1 HMP has decided to adopt a moderate working capital policy. It has fluctuating current assets of $1m, permanent current assets of $5m, and non-current assets of $9m. Which of the following mixes of finance is the company MOST LIKELY to choose?

A Short-term financing of $1m; permanent financing of $14m
B Short-term financing of $0.5m; permanent financing of $14.5m
C Short-term financing of $2m; permanent financing of $13m
D Short-term financing of $4m; permanent financing of $11m **(2 marks)**

2 The following figures are taken from the accounts of GRE:

	$
Inventories	400,000
Receivables	600,000
Cash	200,000
Payables	800,000
Loan stock redeemable in three years time	800,000

What is the quick ratio?

A 0.75
B 1.50
C 0.50
D 1.00 **(2 marks)**

3 Which ONE of the following is NOT a stage in the credit cycle?

A Negotiation of the price of the goods
B Receipt of the customer order
C Checking the credit limit
D Goods despatched with delivery note **(2 marks)**

4 The following figures have been extracted from the accounts of WI:

	$
Total sales	200,000
Cash sales	20,000
Credit sales	180,000
Year end receivables	25,000
Bad debts	5,000

What is the average debt collection period in days (based on 365 days per year)?

A 50.7
B 60.8
C 54.8
D 45.6 **(2 marks)**

5 DEN is considering whether to factor its sales ledger. It has been offered a 'without recourse' package by the factor at a cost of 2% sales, plus an administration fee of $5,000 per year. Annual sales are currently $1m, with bad debts of 1%. What is the annual cost of the package to DEN likely to be?

A $5,000
B $20,000
C $24,800
D $25,000 **(2 marks)**

6 GOR is considering changing its credit policy. It currently allows customers 90 days credit, but suffers bad debts amounting to 3% of its annual sales of $2m. It is proposing to reduce the credit period to 30 days, which should cause the bad debts to fall to 1% of turnover. However, it expects that this will result in a reduction in sales of 20%. This reduction will also be reflected in the level of purchases and inventory holding. What will be the effect of this on the annual financing cost? Current figures are:

Inventories (raw materials and finished goods)	$500,000
Annual purchases	$360,000
Payables	$30,000
Cost of capital	10%

A Saving of $46,000
B Increase of $46,000
C Saving of $36,000
D Increase of $36,000 **(2 marks)**

7 Z requires a rate of return of 13% each year.

Two of Z's suppliers, Y and X are offering the following terms for immediate cash settlement.

Company	*Discount*	*Normal settlement period*
X	3%	3 months
Y	4%	4 months

Which of the following discounts should be accepted to achieve the required rate of return?

A X's
B Y's
C Both X's and Y's
D Neither X's nor Y's **(2 marks)**

---

8 WM's major supplier, INT, supplies electrical tools and is one of the largest companies in the industry, with international operations. Deliveries from INT are currently made monthly, and are constant throughout the year. Delivery and invoicing both occur in the last week of each month.

Details of the credit terms offered by INT are as follows:

Normal credit period	*Cash discount*	*Average monthly purchases*
40 days	2% for settlement in 10 days	$100,000

WM always takes advantage of the cash discount from INT.

Calculate the annual rate of interest (to two decimal places) implied in the cash discount offered by INT. Assume a 365-day year. **(3 marks)**

Pilot paper

---

9 A company has a current ratio of 2 :1. Due to having significant surplus cash balances, it has decided to pay its trade payable accounts after 30 days in future, rather than after 50 days, as it has in the past.

What will be the effect of this change on the company's current ratio and its cash operating cycle?

	Current ratio	*Cash operating cycle*
A	Increase	Increase
B	Increase	Decrease
C	Decrease	Increase
D	Decrease	Decrease

(2 marks)

Pilot paper

---

10 The economic order quantity formula includes the cost of placing an order. However, the Management Accountant is unsure which of the following items should be included in 'cost of placing an order'.

1 Administrative costs
2 Postage
3 Quality control cost
4 Unit cost of products
5 Storekeeper's salary

Which **three** of the above would usually be regarded as part of the cost of placing an order?

A 1, 2 and 3 only
B 1, 4 and 5 only
C 2, 3 and 4 only
D 1, 2 and 5 only **(2 marks)**

5/05

11 SK sells bathroom fittings throughout the country in which it operates. In order to obtain the best price, it has decided to purchase all its annual demand of 10,000 shower units from a single supplier. RR has offered to provide the required number of showers each year under an exclusive long-term contract.

Demand for shower units is at a constant rate all year. The cost to SK of holding one shower unit in inventory for one year is $4 plus 3% of the purchase price.

RR is located only a few miles from the SK main showroom. It has offered to supply each shower unit at $400 with a transport charge of $200 per delivery. It has guaranteed such a regular and prompt delivery service that SK believes it will not be necessary to hold any safety inventory (that is buffer inventory) if it uses RR as its supplier.

Using the economic order quantity model (EOQ model), calculate the optimal order size, assuming that RR is chosen as the sole supplier of shower units for SK. **(3 marks)**

---

12 DS uses the Economic Order Quantity (EOQ) model. Demand for DS's product is 95,000 units per annum. Demand is evenly distributed throughout the year. The cost of placing an order is $15 and the cost of holding a unit of inventory for a year is $3.

How many orders should DS make in a year? **(3 marks)**

5/07

---

13 DY's trade receivables balance at 1 April 20X6 was $22,000. DY's income statement showed revenue from credit sales of $290,510 during the year ended 31 March 20X7.

DY's trade receivables at 31 March 20X7 were 49 days.

Assume DY's sales occur evenly throughout the year and that all balances outstanding at 1 April 20X6 have been received.

Also, it should be assumed all sales are on credit there were no bad debts and no trade discount was given.

How much cash did DY receive from its customers during the year to 31 March 20X7?

A $268,510
B $273,510
C $312,510
D $351,510 **(2 marks)**

5/07

---

14 DR has the following balances under current assets and current liabilities.

Current assets

	$
Inventory	50,000
Trade receivables	70,000
Bank	10,000

Current liabilities

	$
Trade payables	88,000
Interest payable	7,000

DR's quick ratio is

A 0.80:1
B 0.84:1
C 0.91:1
D 1.37:1 **(2 marks)**

5/07

15 Which ONE of the following is most likely to increase an entity's working capital?

A Delaying payment to trade payables
B Reducing the credit period given to customers
C Purchasing inventory on credit
D Paying a supplier and taking an early settlement discount **(2 marks)**

5/07

16 The trial balance of EH at 31 October 20X7 showed trade receivables of $82,000 before adjustments.

On 1 November 20X7 EH discovered that one of its customers had ceased trading and was very unlikely to pay any of its outstanding balance of $12,250.

On the same date EH carried out an assessment of the collectability of its other trade receivable balances. Using its knowledge of its customers and past experience EH determined that the remaining trade receivables had suffered a 3% impairment at 31 October 20X7.

What is EH's balance of trade receivables, as at 31 October 20X7?

A $66,202
B $67,290
C $67,657
D $79,540 **(2 marks)**

11/07

(Total = 35 marks)

43 Objective test questions: Working capital management II

77 mins

1 The trade receivables ledger account for customer C shows the following entries:

		Debits	*Credits*
		$	$
Balance brought forward		0	
10 June X6	Invoice 201	345	
19 June X6	Invoice 225	520	
27 June X6	Invoice 241	150	
3 July X6	Receipt 1009 – Invoice 201		200
10 July X6	Invoice 311	233	
4 August X6	Receipt 1122 – Invoice 225		520
6 August X6	Invoice 392	197	
18 August X6	Invoice 420	231	
30 August X6	Receipt 1310 – Invoice 311		233
7 September X6	Invoice 556	319	
21 September X6	Receipt 1501 – Invoice 392		197
30 September X6	Balance	845	

Prepare an age analysis showing the outstanding balance on a monthly basis for customer C at 30 September 20X6. **(4 marks)**

11/06

2 DX had the following balances in its trial balance at 30 September 20X6:

Trial balance extract at 30 September 20X6

	$'000	$'000
Revenue		2,400
Cost of sales	1,400	
Inventories	360	
Trade receivables	290	
Trade payables		190
Cash and cash equivalents	95	

Calculate the length of DX's working capital cycle at 30 September 20X6. **(4 marks)**

11/06

3 DY had a balance outstanding on trade receivables at 30 September 20X6 of $68,000. Forecast credit sales for the next six months are $250,000 and customers are expected to return goods with a sales value of $2,500.

Based on past experience, within the next six months DY expects to collect $252,100 cash and to write off as bad debts 5% of the balance outstanding at 30 September 20X6.

Calculate DY's forecast trade receivables days outstanding at 31 March 20X7. **(4 marks)**

11/06

4 (a) A company's sales are made up of 75% on credit and 25% for cash.

(b) Bad debts are 2% of credit sales on average.

(c) Half the company's credit customers pay in the month following the sale and the remainder who pay, pay in the month after that.

(d) Sales have grown at a constant rate of 10% per month for every month since October 20X0 and are expected to grow at this rate throughout 20X1.

(e) Sales for January 20X1 were $220,000.

The cash received during February 20X1 was:

A $214,850
B $215,000
C $216,700
D $218,000 **(2 marks)**

5 KEN manufactures shopping trolleys. It produces 2,500 trolleys per year, each of which has four wheels. The wheels are purchased from a single supplier, and it costs $25 to place an order. The cost of holding a single wheel in inventory for a year is 50c. How many wheels should be ordered each time to minimise inventory costs (answer to the nearest 10)?

A 350
B 500
C 710
D 1,000 **(2 marks)**

6 FIN manufactures shopping trolleys. It produces 10,000 trolleys per year, each of which has four wheels. The wheels are purchased from a single supplier, and it costs $100 to place an order. The cost of holding a single wheel in inventory for a year is $2. How many orders should be placed each year to minimise inventory costs?

A 3
B 10
C 14
D 20 **(2 marks)**

---

7 STAN manufactures shopping trolleys. It produces 40,000 trolleys per year, each of which has four wheels. The wheels are purchased from a single supplier, and it costs $400 to place an order. The cost of holding a single wheel in inventory for a year is $8. How long is it between each order?

A 1.3 weeks
B 2.6 weeks
C 3.9 weeks
D 5.2 weeks **(2 marks)**

---

8 Which of the following would NOT NORMALLY form part of the purchasing manager's responsibilities?

A Liaising with the R & D department to find suppliers for materials which are to the specifications required by the designers

B Locating and selecting suppliers

C Agreeing prices, discounts and lead times with suppliers

D Issuing payments to suppliers **(2 marks)**

---

9 FRA is a small restaurant business. It has just acquired a new van under a lease agreement, and it must make a monthly payment to the finance company of $276.53. Which of the following payment methods is the MOST APPROPRIATE for FRA to use?

A Cheque
B Standing order
C Direct debit
D Banker's draft **(2 marks)**

---

10 AYS is a small domestic cleaning business. It has just acquired a new van for $12,750, which is needed urgently since the old one has been written off in an accident. The garage will not accept a company cheque on collection of the vehicle. Which of the following payment methods is the MOST APPROPRIATE for AYS to use?

A Cash
B Standing order
C Direct debit
D Banker's draft **(2 marks)**

---

11 FR INCOME STATEMENT FOR THE YEAR ENDED 31 MARCH 20X8

	$'000
Revenue	270
Cost of goods sold	139
Gross profit	131

Assume all sales and all purchases are on credit and that there are no returns or discounts. All trade payables relate to cost of sales.

FR BALANCE SHEET AS AT 31 MARCH 20X8 (EXTRACT)

	$'000
Current assets	
Inventory	79
Trade receivables	52
Cash	25
	156
Current liabilities	
Trade payables	40
Accrued interest	21
Income tax	88
	149

Inventory balance at 31 March 20X7 was $79,000.

Calculate the number of days in FR's working capital cycle. **(4 marks)**

5/08

---

12 FJ commences business on 1 April 20X8. Sales in April 20X8 were $60,000. This is forecast to increase by 2% per month.

Credit sales accounted for 50% of sales. Credit sales customers are allowed one month to pay; 75% of April credit customers paid on time. A further 20% are expected to pay after more than one month, but before two months. The remaining 5% are not expected to pay. All these percentages are expected to continue in the near future.

Calculate the total amount of cash FJ should forecast to be received in June 20X8. **(4 marks)**

5/08

---

13 If an entity regularly fails to pay its suppliers by the normal due dates, it may lead to a number of problems:

1 Having insufficient cash to settle trade payables;
2 Difficulty in obtaining credit from new suppliers;
3 Reduction in credit rating;
4 Settlement of trade receivables may be delayed.

Which TWO of the above could arise as a result of exceeding suppliers' trade credit terms?

A 1 and 2
B 1 and 3
C 2 and 3
D 3 and 4 **(2 marks)**

5/06

---

14 A conservative policy for financing working capital is one where short-term finance is used to fund

A All of the fluctuating current assets, but no part of the permanent current assets.
B All of the fluctuating current assets and part of the permanent current assets.
C Part of the fluctuating current assets and part of the permanent current assets.
D Part of the fluctuating current assets, but no part of the permanent current assets. **(2 marks)**

5/06

---

15 When receivables are sold to a debt factoring company, which of the following is LEAST likely?

A Cash will be received sooner than if debts were not sold.
B The receivables will be sold at a profit to the selling company.
C The debt factoring company will make a profit on the service provided.
D Working capital will decrease. **(2 marks)**

---

16 EP sells refrigerators and freezers and provides a one year warranty against faults occurring after sale.

EP estimates that if all goods with an outstanding warranty at the balance sheet date need minor repairs the total cost would be $3 million. If all the products under warranty needed major repairs the total cost would be $12 million.

Based on previous years' experience, EP estimates that 85% of the products will require no repairs; 14% will require minor repairs and 1% will require major repairs.

Calculate the expected value of the cost of the repair of goods with an outstanding warranty at the balance sheet date. **(3 marks)**

11/07

(Total = 43 marks)

---

44 Objective test questions: Working capital management III

65 mins

1 A company has a current ratio of 1.5:1. It decides to use surplus cash balances to settle 30% of its total current liabilities.

The current ratio will

A Decrease by more than 30%
B Decrease by less than 30%
C Increase by more than 30%
D Increase by less than 30% **(2 marks)**

---

2 A company buys goods on credit and then, before payment is made, it is forced to sell all of these goods on credit for less than the purchase price. What is the consequence of these two transactions immediately after the sale has taken place?

A Inventory decreases and cash decreases.
B Cash decreases and payables increase.
C Inventory decreases and receivables increase.
D Receivables increase and payables increase. **(2 marks)**

---

3 Which one of the following would NOT NORMALLY be considered a cost of holding inventory?

A Inventory obsolescence
B Insurance cost of inventories
C Lost interest on cash invested in inventories
D Loss of sales from running out of inventory **(2 marks)**

---

4 The following items were extracted from a company's budget for next month:

	$
Purchases on credit	360,000
Expected decrease in inventories over the month	12,000
Expected increase in trade payables over the month	15,000

What is the budgeted payment to trade payables for the month?

A $333,000
B $345,000
C $357,000
D $375,000 **(2 marks)**

---

5 Y Co has funding requirements of $10,000 per month. Money on deposit earns 2% per annum, while the interest cost of new funds is 5% per annum. Transaction costs are $50.

Using the Baumol model what is the optimum amount of securities to transfer into cash in each transaction? **(2 marks)**

---

6 A retailing company has an annual turnover of $36 million. The company earns a constant margin of 20% on sales. All sales and purchases are on credit and are evenly distributed over the year. The following amounts are maintained at a constant level throughout the year.

	$m
Inventories	6
Receivables	8
Payables	3

What is the company's cash cycle to the nearest day (that is, the average time from the payment of a supplier to the receipt from a customer)?

A 81 days
B 111 days
C 119 days
D 195 days **(2 marks)**

---

7 A company uses the economic order quantity model (EOQ model). Demand for the company's product is 36,000 units each year and is evenly distributed each day. The cost of placing an order is $10 and the cost of holding a unit of stock for a year is $2.

How many orders should the company make in a year?

A 60
B 120
C 300
D 600 **(2 marks)**

---

8 Working capital is MOST LIKELY to increase when

A Payments to suppliers are delayed.
B The period of credit extended to customers is reduced.
C Non-current assets are sold.
D Inventory levels are increased. **(2 marks)**

---

9 Which ONE of the following transactions is most likely to affect the overall amount of working capital?

A Receipt of full amount of cash from a customer to settle their trade receivable account.
B Payment of a trade payable account in full.
C Sale of a non-current asset on credit at its net book value.
D Purchase of inventory on credit. **(2 marks)**

Pilot paper

---

10 A company maintains a minimum cash holding of $1,000. The variance of its daily cash flows has been measured as $250,000. The transaction cost for each sale or purchase of treasury bills is $20. The daily interest rate is 0.025% per day and is not expected to change in the foreseeable future. Using the Miller-Orr cash management model, the maximum cash holding level would be:

A $1,594
B $2,594
C $7,400
D $8,400 **(2 marks)**

---

11 Which of the following would be LEAST LIKELY to arise from the introduction of a Just-in-Time inventory ordering system?

A Lower inventory holding costs.
B Less risk of inventory shortages.
C More frequent deliveries.
D Increased dependence on suppliers. **(2 marks)**

Pilot paper

---

12 AL's customers all pay their accounts at the end of 30 days. To try and improve its cash flow, AL is considering offering all customers a 1.5% discount for payment within 14 days.

Calculate the implied annual (interest) cost to AL of offering the discount, using compound interest methodology and assuming a 365 day year. **(3 marks)**

5/05

---

13 Calculate the economic order quantity (EOQ) for the following item of inventory:

- Quantity required per year 32,000 items;
- Order costs are $15 per order;
- Inventory holding costs are estimated at 3% of inventory value per year;
- Each unit currently costs $40. **(2 marks)**

5/06

---

14 CX purchased $10,000 of unquoted bonds when they were issued by Z. CX now wishes to sell the bonds to B. The bonds have a coupon rate of 7% and will repay their face value at the end of five years. Similar bonds have a yield to maturity of 10%.

Calculate the current market price for the bonds. **(3 marks)**

5/06

---

15 EX is preparing its cash forecast for the next three months.

Which ONE of the following items should be left out of its calculations?

A Expected gain on the disposal of a piece of land.
B Tax payment due, that relates to last year's profits.
C Rental payment on a leased vehicle.
D Receipt of a new bank loan raised for the purpose of purchasing new machinery. **(2 marks)**

11/07

---

16 EV had inventory days outstanding of 60 days and trade payables outstanding of 50 days at 31 October 20X7.

EV's inventory balance at 1 November 20X6 was $56,000 and trade payables were $42,000 at that date.

EV's cost of goods sold comprises purchased goods cost only. During the year to 31 October 20X7, EV's cost of goods sold was $350,000.

Assume purchases and sales accrue evenly throughout the year and use a 365 day year. Further assume that there were no goods returned to suppliers and EV claimed no discounts.

Calculate how much EV paid to its credit suppliers during the year to 31 October 20X7. **(4 marks)**

11/07

(Total = 36 marks)

45 Section B questions: Working capital management I

81 mins

(a) Extracts from the financial statements of PRT for the years ended 31 March are as follows.

	20X6	*20X7*
	$'000	$'000
Raw material inventories	55	80
Finished goods inventories	185	185
Purchases of raw materials	600	850
Cost of sales	1,570	1,830
Administrative expenses	45	65
Sales	1,684	1,996
Trade receivables	114	200
Trade payables	50	70
Overdraft	400	950
Additions to non-current assets	700	900

Cost of sales includes all relevant production costs including manufacturing overheads and labour.

Required

Calculate the length in days of the company's operating cycle for the year ended 31 March 20X7. **(5 marks)**

(b) AAD is a newly-created subsidiary of a large listed company. It commenced business on 1 October 20X2, to provide specialist contract cleaning services to industrial customers. All sales are on credit.

More favourable credit terms are offered to larger customers (class A) than to smaller customers (class B). All sales are invoiced at the end of the month in which the sale occurs. Class A customers will be given credit terms requiring payment within 60 days of invoicing, while class B customers will be required to pay within 30 days of invoicing.

Since it is recognised, however, that not all customers comply with the credit terms they are allowed, receipts from customers have prudently been estimated as follows:

Customer type	*Within 30 days*	*31 to 60 days*	*61 to 90 days*	*91 to 120 days*	*Bad debts*
Class A		50%	30%	15%	5%
Class B	60%	25%	10%		5%

The above table shows that customers are expected either to pay within 60 days of the end of the credit period, or not at all. Bad debts will therefore be written off 60 days after the end of the credit period.

Budgeted credit sales for each class of customer in the first 4 months of trading are as follows:

Customer type	*October*	*November*	*December*	*January*
	$'000	$'000	$'000	$'000
Class A	100	150	200	300
Class B	60	80	40	50

Assume all months are of 30 days.

Required

Prepare a statement showing the budgeted cash to be received by AAD from customers in each of the three months of November 20X2, December 20X2 and January 20X3, based upon the prudently estimated receipts from customers. **(5 marks)**

(c) Discuss:

(i) The significance of trade payables in a firm's working capital cycle
(ii) The dangers of over-reliance on trade credit as a source of finance **(5 marks)**

(d) AD, a manufacturing entity, has the following balances at 30 April 20X5:

Extract from financial statements:	$'000
Trade receivables	216
Trade payables	97
Revenue (all credit sales)	992
Cost of sales	898
Purchases in year	641
Inventories at 30 April 20X5	
Raw materials	111
Work in progress	63
Finished goods	102

Required

Calculate AD's working capital cycle. **(5 marks)**

5/05

(e) BF manufactures a range of domestic appliances. Due to past delays in suppliers providing goods, BF has had to hold an inventory of raw materials, in order that the production could continue to operate smoothly. Due to recent improvements in supplier reliability, BF is re-examining its inventory holding policies and recalculating economic order quantities (EOQ).

- Item 'Z' costs BF — $10.00 per unit
- Expected annual production usage is — 65,000 units
- Procurement costs (cost of placing and processing one order) are — $25.00
- The cost of holding one unit for one year has been calculated as — $3.00

The supplier of item 'Z' has informed BF that if the order was 2,000 units or more at one time, a 2% discount would be given on the price of the goods.

Required

(i) Calculate the EOQ for item 'Z' before the quantity discount. **(2 marks)**

(ii) Advise BF if it should increase the order size of item 'Z' so as to qualify for the 2% discount. **(3 marks)**

11/05

(f) DJ maintains a minimum cash holding of $1,000. The standard deviation of its daily cash flows has been measured at $300 (variance is $90,000). DJ's annual cash outgoings are $420,000 spread evenly over the year. The transaction cost of each sale or purchase of treasury bills is $25. The daily interest rate is 0.02% (7.3% per year).

Required

(i) Using the Baumol cash management model, calculate the optimum amount of treasury bills to be sold each time cash is required.

(ii) Using the Miller-Orr cash management model, calculate the optimum amount of securities to sell when cash holding reaches the lower limit. **(5 marks)**

11/06

(g) DN currently has an overdraft on which it pays interest at 10% per year. DN has been offered credit terms from one of its suppliers, whereby it can either claim a cash discount of 2% if payment is made within 10 days of the date of the invoice or pay on normal credit terms, within 40 days of the date of the invoice.

Assume a 365 day year and an invoice value of $100.

Required

Explain to DN, with reasons and supporting calculations, whether it should pay the supplier early and take advantage of the discount offered. **(5 marks)**

5/07

(h) *Required*

Explain the possible benefits and limitations of a Just-In-Time (JIT) purchasing system. **(5 marks)**

5/08

(i) The trade receivables ledger account for customer X is as follows:

		Debits	*Credits*	*Balance*
01-Jul-X7	Balance b/fwd			162
12-Jul-X7	Invoice AC34	172		334
14-Jul-X7	Invoice AC112	213		547
28-Jul-X7	Invoice AC215	196		743
08-Aug-X7	Receipt RK 116 (Balance + AC34)		334	409
21-Aug-X7	Invoice AC420	330		739
03-Sep-X7	Receipt RL162 (AC215)		196	543
12-Sep-X7	Credit note CN92 (AC112)		53	490
23-Sep-X7	Invoice AC615	116		606
25-Sep-X7	Invoice AC690	204		810
05-Oct-X7	Receipt RM223 (AC420)		330	480
16-Oct-X7	Invoice AC913	233		713
25-Oct-X7	Receipt RM360 (AC615)		116	597

Required:

(i) Prepare an age analysis showing the outstanding balance on a monthly basis for customer X. **(3 marks)**

(ii) Explain how an age analysis of receivables can be useful to an entity. **(2 marks)**

(Total = 45 marks)

46 Section B questions: Working capital management II

72 mins

This information covers questions (a) to (c).

BB is a private sector training entity, which provides short courses and various in-house courses for large employers.

BB's forecast financial statements for the year ended 31 December includes the following:

Forecast Balance Sheet at 31 December 20X5 (extract)

Current assets	
Trade receivables: In-house training courses	\$34,100
Bank	\$12,460

Forecast Income Statement for the year ended 31 December 20X5 (extract)

Revenue: In-house training courses	\$125,000

BB is preparing its budgets for the year 1 January 20X6 to 31 December 20X6, but the cash budget has not yet been completed. The Finance Director is concerned about the cash flow forecast for the first six months and has asked you, a trainee management accountant, to prepare a cash budget for the six months from January to June 20X6 from the budgeted information provided.

Budgeted revenue

Short training courses

Short training courses budgeted charge \$100 per person per course.

Short courses are generally one night a week for four weeks commencing on the first of each month, except December and January.

Budgeted short course information:	*Jan*	*Feb*	*Mar*	*Apr*	*May*	*Jun*	*Jul*
Number of courses	0	2	3	3	4	4	4
Forecast students per course	0	10	12	12	14	13	15

BB expects to receive payment in advance of each course. Experience shows that, on average, one third of students pay one month in advance and the rest pay on the first day of the course.

In-house training courses

The exact number and type of in-house training courses is unknown at present but, during 20X6, BB is expecting to earn \$130,000 spread evenly throughout the year. Based on previous experience, the following receipts are forecast:

	Jan	*Feb*	*Mar*	*Apr*	*May*	*Jun*
In-house training course fee receipts (including trade receivables at 31 December 20X5)	\$5,000	\$8,000	\$10,000	\$11,000	\$12,000	\$6,000

BB has previously experienced problems of slow payment from some large employers and is monitoring the trade receivables collection period.

Budgeted expenditure

BB employs permanent full-time members of staff to run the entity and provide key lecturing skills. Most of the trainers are part-time tutors at an hourly rate.

Budgeted wages 20X6	*Jan*	*Feb*	*Mar*	*Apr*	*May*	*Jun*
Part-time tutor wages	\$0	\$2,500	\$4,000	\$4,000	\$5,000	\$6,000

Permanent staff salaries are currently \$4,000 a month. All full-time staff will receive an increase of 5% from 1 March 20X6.

BB rents the premises for $2,500 a year, payable in quarterly installments in January, April, July and October.

Teaching materials, printing and photocopying average $150 per short course (paid in the month of the course). The in-house courses cost, on average, $100 per month.

Budgeted payments in respect of overheads (electricity, telephone and so on) for January and April are $1,500 and for February, March, May and June are $600.

Capital expenditure in the first six months of 2006 is planned as follows:

(i) New furniture for the managing director's office $5,000 payable in April.

(ii) BB needs to replace all the IT equipment in one of its computer labs early in 20X6. This is currently planned to take place in April, with payment in May 20X6. The budgeted cost of the equipment is $40,000 for 20 top-of-the-range PCs and related equipment.

Other information

BB has negotiated an overdraft facility with the bank for an overdraft up to $5,000.

Required

(a) Calculate BB's in-house training course trade receivables days outstanding

(i) according to the forecast at 31 December 20X5;

(ii) according to the projected figures at 30 June 20X6, assuming the revenue and cash flow budgets are implemented. **(5 marks)**

11/05

(b) Prepare BB's cash budget for the first six months of 20X6 (January to June) (equivalent to two Section B questions). **(10 marks)**

11/05

(c) Advise BB of any actions it can take to make sufficient funds available to purchase the new technology as budgeted in May 20X6. **(5 marks)**

11/05

This information covers questions (d) to (g)

CK is an entity that sells computer spare parts and peripherals to computer retail stores. The entity's sales and purchases accrue evenly throughout the year and inventory is managed in such a way as to give a constant inventory level throughout the year.

CK had the following figures for the year ended 31 March 20X6:

	$'000
Revenue from credit sales during the year	6,192
Purchases on credit during the year	4,128
Trade receivables balance at 31 March 20X6	1,083
Trade payables balance at 31 March 20X6	344
Inventory balance at 31 March 20X6	1,020
Cash balance at 31 March 20X6	622

The directors wanted working capital management improved and commissioned a consultant to prepare a report on working capital management in CK. The consultant's report indicated that efficiency savings were possible and, if the recommendations were implemented, the following changes in outstanding days would be achieved:

Trade receivables reduced to 45 days.

Suppliers would be willing to wait a total of 40 days for payment.

Inventory could be reduced by 40% (from 31 March 20X6 $ value levels) without having an adverse impact on sales.

The budgets for the year to 31 March 20X7 have been commenced, but are incomplete. Budgeted revenue from credit sales is based on the year to 31 March 20X6 figure, plus a price increase of 10% from 1 April 20X6 and a reduction of an estimated 3% in volume caused by the price increase.

Cost of sales is budgeted at the same percentage of credit sales revenue as the year to 31 March 20X6.

	$'000	
Salaries and wages are budgeted at	620	for the year
Other operating expenses budget is	432	for the year
Budgeted capital expenditure is	2,500	

The consultant's report recommended that $1,500,000 of the proposed purchase of non-current tangible assets could be leased instead of purchased. The terms of the lease would be five payments of $400,000 each, payable in advance of 1 April each year, commencing on 1 April 20X6.

The lease would be classified as a finance lease by IAS 17 *Leases.*

The implicit interest rate is 16.875%.

Required

(d) Calculate the following for CK at 31 March 20X6:

- Trade receivables days outstanding;
- Trade payables days outstanding;
- Inventory days outstanding.

(*Note.* You should base your calculations on a 365 day year) **(3 marks)**

5/06

(e) Prepare a cash budget for the year to 31 March 20X7 based on the budgeted data and assuming CK implements the efficiency changes recommended by the consultant from 1 April 20X6. **(10 marks)**

5/06

(f) Explain the effect on CK's cash budget if it decides to lease $1,500,000 of the non-current assets, instead of purchasing them.

(*Note.* You are **not** required to recalculate CK's cash budget) **(2 marks)**

5/06

(g) Comment on any possible difficulties that CK may encounter when implementing the efficiency changes. **(5 marks)**

5/06

(*Note.* All workings should be to the nearest $'000)

(Total = 40 marks)

Answers

Extra guidance

Remember you can find additional guidance on a number of questions in this kit on BPP's website: www.bpp.com/cima/extra-question-guidance

1 Objective test answers: The regulatory framework

1 The three stages are:

1 Establishment of Advisory Committee
2 Discussion Draft issued
3 Exposure Draft issued

2 C Guidance on application and interpretation of IASs/IFRSs is provided by the International Financial Reporting Interpretations Committee (IFRIC).

3 A The priority given to different user groups in different countries (eg investor groups in the US and employees in Europe) is actually a **barrier** to harmonisation.

4 B Many of the older IASs permitted **two** accounting treatments for like transactions or events – the benchmark treatment and the allowed alternative. As these are revised allowed alternative treatments are being eliminated. This gives preparers of accounts **less** choice.

5 Expense and equity

6 C The *Framework* cites two underlying assumptions:

The accounts have been prepared on an accruals basis (accruals).
The business is expected to continue in operation for the foreseeable future (going concern).

7 B The elements of financial statements are assets, liabilities and equity in the balance sheet and income and expenses in the income statement. Profits and losses are not elements.

8 B The income statement measures **performance**. Financial position is measured in the balance sheet and financial adaptability in the cash flow statement.

9 D Accruals and going concern.

10 An asset is a resource controlled by an entity as a result of past transactions or events and from which future economic benefits are expected to flow to the entity.

11 D Generally accepted accounting practice

12 C International Accounting Standards Committee (IASC) Foundation Trustees

13 D Going concern and accruals

14 C IFRIC reports to the IASB. SAC advises the IASB.

15 Decreases in economic benefits during the accounting period in the form of outflows or depletions of assets or incurrences of liabilities that result in decreases in equity, other than those relating to distributions to equity participants.

[This is the IASB definition, which contains **36** words. You can choose which words to leave out.]

16 To provide information about the financial position, performance and changes in financial position of an entity that is useful to a wide range of users in making economic decisions.

17 D The IASC Foundation oversees and directs the work of the IASB.

18 Reliability and understandability.

2 Objective test answers: External audit

1 These matters can be subdivided into:

- Qualified opinion
- Adverse opinion
- Disclaimer of opinion

2 B The auditor has been prevented from obtaining sufficient appropriate audit evidence.

3 C No qualification is needed as the directors have made full disclosure.

4 D The auditors report covers all of these matters.

5 B This is a limitation on scope.

6 C The auditors will be unable to give an opinion in this case.

7 A This will be an 'except for' qualification.

8 A In order to state that the financial statements show a true and fair view the auditor must satisfy himself that the other three matters are valid.

9 D The auditors will begin by trying to persuade the directors.

10 Power to require access to all books and records
Power to require information and explanations from officers of the company
Power to attend meetings and address shareholders

11 C If the auditor believes that the financial statements do not show a true and fair view this should first be discussed with management. If management refuse to adjust the accounts, the auditor would give an adverse opinion in the audit report.

12 A ISA 700 describes the different audit opinions.

3 Section B answers: Regulation

(a)

Top tips. We have only given five answers here as this is all that is required for five marks.

Examiner's comments. The answers provided for this question were very weak. Many candidates did not know what the purpose of the Framework was and tried explaining the purpose of financial statements.

The purposes of the *Framework* are:

(i) To assist in the **review of existing IASs and IFRSs** and the **development of new IFRSs**

(ii) To promote **harmonisation** of accounting standards by reducing the number of allowed alternative accounting treatments

(iii) To **assist national standard-setting bodies** in developing national standards

(iv) To assist preparers of financial statements in **applying IFRSs** and dealing with topics not yet covered by an IFRS

(v) To **assist auditors** in determining whether financial statements comply with IFRS

Alternative answers

You would also have scored marks if you had identified any of the following purposes.

- To **assist users** of financial statements prepared under IFRS in interpreting the information contained in them
- To provide **general information on the approach** used in formulating IFRSs

(b) The IASB *Framework* lays out the elements of financial statements as follows.

(i) **Asset**

A resource controlled by an entity as a result of past events and from which future economic benefits are expected to flow to the entity.

An example of an asset is an item of machinery used in the business.

(ii) **Liability**

A present obligation of the entity arising from past events, the settlement of which is expected to result in an outflow of resources from the entity.

An example of a liability is an amount due to a supplier for goods received.

(iii) **Equity**

The residual interest in the assets of the entity after deducting all its liabilities.

Ordinary share capital is an example of equity.

(iv) **Income**

Increases in economic benefits during the accounting period in the form of inflows or enhancements of assets or decreases of liabilities that result in increases in equity, other than those relating to contributions from equity participants.

An example of income is income recognised on the sale of goods.

(v) **Expenses**

Decreases in economic benefits during the accounting period in the form of outflows or depletions of assets that result in decreases in equity, other than those relating to distributions to equity participants.

Depreciation is an example of an expense.

(c)

Examiner's comments. Candidates failed to include enough detail in their answers. Many answers identified a characteristic and then the explanation added nothing to it, for example, 'Relevance – information needs to be relevant'.

The four principal qualitative characteristics of financial information are as follows.

Relevance

Information is said to be relevant when it influences the economic decisions of users by helping them to evaluate past, present and future events or by confirming , or correcting their past evaluations. So relevant information has both a predictive and confirmatory role.

Reliability

Information is reliable when it is free from material error and bias, and can be depended upon by users to represent faithfully that which it either purports to represent or could reasonably be expected to represent.

Comparability

The importance of comparability is that users must be able to compare the financial statements of an entity over time and to compare the financial statements of different entities. For this to be possible users must be informed of the accounting policies employed in the preparation of the financial statements and any changes in those policies and their effects. The financial statements must also show corresponding amounts for the previous period.

Understandability

The financial statement information should be readily understandable to users. For this purpose users are assumed to have a reasonable knowledge of business and economic activities and accounting and a willingness to study the information with reasonable diligence.

(d)

Examiner's comments. Most candidates did well on this question, although some could not think of three alternatives. A common error was using bullet points or short notes to answer the question and as a result not providing sufficient detail for 5 marks.

C could pursue any of the following options:

(i) **Develop its own standards without reference to the IASB**. This would produce standards which reflected trading conditions in the country but, when it developed to the point of needing to attract foreign investment, investors may not be drawn to companies whose financial statements are not prepared under generally recognised standards.

(ii) **Adopt IFRS**. This would mean that C had adopted high-quality, generally recognised standards from the outset, and would have no future harmonisation process to undergo. However, it may find that time and expense has gone into implementing standards which may not be that relevant to its current economic situation.

(iii) **Adopt those IFRSs which are currently applicable**, such as IAS 41 *Agriculture*, and **develop additional standards of its own based on IFRS**. This would produce a set of standards which were theoretically high-quality and relevant to its own economy. However, the judgement and expertise required to carry this out may not be available and C will be resolving issues between local standards and IFRS on an ongoing basis.

(e)

> **Examiner's comments.** This question was very badly answered, Those candidates that did identify the correct IAS and the correct accounting treatment often omitted to explain why the items should be treated that way, as a consequence only partial marks could be awarded.

In order to decide how to treat these items of expenditure in its financial statements, EK must decide whether the expenditure gives rise to an asset or intangible asset which can be recognised on the balance sheet. Asset recognition criteria are dealt with in the IASB *Framework*. Intangible assets are covered by IAS 38 *Intangible assets*.

The IASB *Framework* defines an asset as **a resource controlled by an entity as a result of past events** and from which **further economic benefits are expected to flow** to the entity.

Both assets and intangible assets can only be recognised if both the following apply.

- It is probable that future economic benefits will flow to the entity.
- The cost of the asset can be measured reliably.

(i) **Book publishing and film rights**

If the book is profitable once it has been written and published, the $1m cost can be recognised as an intangible asset. If once published EK believe it is probable that the book is profitable and can also produce a profitable film, it can be classified as a non-current intangible asset. No amortisation is necessary until the book is actually published if the cost is recognised as an asset.

(ii) **Trade fair**

Since no new orders were taken as a direct result of the event and no estimate can be made of additional revenue, the cost of the trade fair cannot be recognised as an asset. Future economic benefits may not be probable and cannot be measured reliably. The cost of the trade fair does not meet the recognition criteria for an asset and should therefore be treated as an expense in the year incurred.

(iii) **Consultant**

Although the cost of the consultancy itself is known, it is virtually impossible to quantify any change in the value of the image of EK. Since the cost of the corporate image cannot be measured reliably, the consultancy fees should not be recognised as an asset and should be expensed in the year incurred.

4 Section B answers: External audit

(a) (i) **Qualified opinion** – an auditor will be unable to issue an unqualified audit report if he has disagreements with management regarding the treatment of one or more items in the accounts, or if the scope of his audit has been limited in some way, for instance certain records may not have been made available to him. When the auditor concludes that he cannot issue an unqualified report for one of these reasons, but that the effect of the disagreement or limitation of scope is not so material or pervasive as to require an adverse opinion or a disclaimer of opinion, then he will express a qualified opinion. The opinion will be expressed as being 'except for the effects of the matter to which the qualification relates'.

(ii) **Disclaimer of opinion** – where the possible effect of a limitation on scope is so material or pervasive that the auditor has not been able to obtain sufficient appropriate audit evidence and is therefore unable to express an opinion on the financial statements, a disclaimer of opinion will be expressed. This limitation may have arisen through circumstances, or may have been imposed by the client or may have arisen due to the inadequate nature of the company's accounting records. The auditor's report should give an explanation of the nature of the limitation of scope and quantify the effects on the financial statements where possible.

(iii) **Adverse opinion** – where the effect of a disagreement is so material or pervasive that the auditor concludes that a qualified opinion is insufficient to disclose the misleading or incomplete nature of the financial statements an adverse opinion will be expressed. Such a disagreement may concern the selection of accounting policies, the application of accounting standards or the inadequacy of disclosures. The report must fully describe the circumstances leading to the adverse opinion. The opinion will state that, because of the effect of these circumstances, the financial statements do not present fairly the financial position of the company and its results.

(b) **Right of access to records**

The auditor has a right of access at all times to the books, accounts and vouchers of the company.

Right to require information

The auditor has a right to require from the company's officers such information and explanations as he thinks necessary for the performance of his duties as auditor. It is an offence for a company's officer to make a statement to the auditor which is materially misleading, false or deceptive.

These rights make it possible for the auditor to carry out an audit. If these rights are violated, the auditor will qualify his report. If the situation is serious, for instance if the auditor believes the directors to be involved in a fraud, he has the following rights which enable him to communicate directly to the shareholders:

Right to attend/receive notice of general meetings

The directors cannot keep the auditor away from the AGMs by not informing him of when they are taking place.

Right to speak at general meetings

The auditor has a right to be heard at general meetings which he attends, on any part of the business that concerns him as auditor.

Right in relation to written resolutions

The auditor has the right to receive a copy of any written resolution proposed. This means that he must receive a copy of any resolution which is proposed to terminate his engagement.

In practice, an auditor would not expect to have to invoke these rights very often, but the fact that they exist establishes his status in relation to the directors and makes it possible for him to get the co-operation that he needs in order to carry out his engagement.

(c)

Examiner's comments. I was very surprised at the low quality of answers to this question. Many candidates clearly did not understand the objective of an audit and a large proportion of answers were unable to correctly identify the type of report or the information required.

(i) **The objective of an external audit** is to enable the auditor to express an opinion on whether the financial statements give a true and fair view (or present fairly) the financial position of the company and the results of its operations and its cash flows, in accordance with applicable Accounting Standards.

(ii) **EA & Co should issue a qualified opinion** based on disagreement on accounting policies under ISA 700. We have not been told that this issue is so material or pervasive that the financial statements are misleading or incomplete, so an adverse opinion is not indicated.

They will include in their report:

'Profit on long-term contracts has not been accounted for in accordance with IAS 11. Per the standard, a foreseeable loss on a long-term contract should be recognised immediately. In the financial statements for the year to 30 September 2006, only that portion of the loss which has been incurred to date has been included. $3.7m has been included in the income statement in respect of long-term contracts. This should be amended to $1.3m in order to recognise in full the expected loss.

In our opinion, except for the effect on the financial statements of the matter referred to in the preceding paragraph, the financial statements give a true and fair view...'

5 Objective test answers: Presentation

1 A Members do not inspect the accounting records – the auditors do this on their behalf.

2 A All of these items appear in the statement of changes in equity.

3 B Item (2) is no longer required to be disclosed after the revision of IAS 1.

4 D Authorised share capital is disclosed in the notes to the balance sheet, the other disclosures are made in the income statement or notes.

5 C 2 is a change of accounting estimate, 4 is specifically mentioned in IAS 8 as not constituting a change of accounting policy.

6 D Material errors are treated in the same way as changes of accounting policy, by the application of retrospective restatement.

7 B IAS 8 requires that a change in accounting policy is accounted for by retrospective application.

8 A Changing the method of depreciation is a change of estimation technique not a change of accounting policy and therefore retrospective application is not required. However the current year figures must be changed to reflect the change in estimation technique and the change must be disclosed.

9 C Provisions are covered by IAS 37.

10 B Capitalisation of borrowing costs represents a change of accounting policy

11 D Revenue and finance cost

12 B This is the most commonly seen form of the income statement, which includes cost of sales and distribution costs

6 Section B answers: Presentation

(a) Companies might be expected to publish accounts using standard formats so as to ensure **complete disclosure** of material and important items and to ensure **consistency between accounting periods and comparability between companies.**

In addition, in certain European and other countries where standard formats have been in use for many years their use provides governments with **consistent information for the preparation of national accounts** and other economic statistics.

The detail shown in each of the standard income statements would enable users of accounts to calculate certain key **ratios** such as gross margins, net margins, ratio of administration costs to sales or profit and to identify the proportion of the net income arising from operations separately to that arising from financing transactions.

This information would be of use to **shareholders** and stockholders' analysts who will wish to assess the **profitability** of a company and compare it with possible alternative investments.

(b)

> **Examiner's comments.** Candidates scored high marks on this question. This question was the most popular part of question 2 and was generally the best answer.
>
> The most common error was to incorrectly adjust for the change in inventory value and some candidates ignored the requirement to make a provision for compensation.

CE
INCOME STATEMENT FOR THE YEAR ENDED 31 MARCH 20X6

	$'000
Revenue	2,000
Cost of sales (W)	688
Gross profit	1,312
Distribution costs	200
Administrative expenses (260 + 500)	760
	352
Finance costs	190
Profit before tax	162

Working: Cost of sales

Per trial balance	480
Inventory adjustment	16
Depreciation ((1,500 – 540) × 20%)	192
	688

7 Objective test answers: Cash flow statements

1 A It is important to know which way round the additions and subtractions go when preparing a cash flow statement.

2 D Profit on disposal will be included in profit, so should be deducted.

3 C These items do not affect cash flow.

4 D The final figure in the cash flow statement is the increase or decrease in cash and cash equivalents.

5 B

	$'000
Retained earnings 31.12.X5	1,660
Retained earnings 31.12.X4	1,470
∴ Post tax profit for 20X5	190
Add back tax charge*	840
	1,030

* *Note.* This is the current liability at 31.12.X5, just as the 20X4 charge is the current liability at 31.12.X4.

6 A

PROPERTY, PLANT AND EQUIPMENT: COST

	$m		$m
Opening balance	40	Transfer disposal (balancing figure)	6
Cash – additions	16	Closing balance	50
	56		56

PROPERTY, PLANT AND EQUIPMENT: ACCUMULATED DEPRECIATION

	$m		$m
		Opening balance	10
Transfer disposal (balancing figure)	2	Income statement	6
Closing balance	14		
	16		16

PROPERTY, PLANT AND EQUIPMENT: DISPOSAL

	$m		$m
Transfer cost	6	Transfer depreciation	2
		Loss on sale	1
		Proceeds of sale (balancing figure)	3
	6		6

7 B Equity investments do not generally fulfil the description of cash equivalents

8 A All of these items involve movements of cash

9 C Depreciation and losses on disposal are added back.

10 A

	$'000
Cash from sales	
$3,600 + $600 – $700	3,500
Cash paid for purchases	
$2,400 + $300 – $450	(2,250)
Payments for expenses	(760)
	490

11 Property, plant and equipment purchases = $105,000

PROPERTY, PLANT AND EQUIPMENT

	$'000		$'000
Opening balance	180	Depreciation	40
Revaluation	20	Disposal (15 – 10)	5
Additions (bal fig)	105	Closing balance	260
	305		305

12 A Interest paid = $38,000

INTEREST PAYABLE

	$		$
Cash paid (bal fig)	38,000	Opening balance	12,000
Closing balance	15,000	Income statement	41,000
	53,000		53,000

8 Section B answers: Cash flow statements

Examiner's comments. A very large proportion of candidates prepared a cash flow statement according to IAS 7 indirect method rather than the direct method, thereby losing most of the marks.

FC

CASH FLOW STATEMENT FOR THE YEAR ENDED 31 MARCH 20X8

Cash flows from operating activities	$'000	$'000
Cash received from customers (W1)	440	
Rents received	45	
Cash paid to suppliers (W2)	(225)	
Cash paid to and on behalf of employees	(70)	
Other operating expenses	(15)	
Cash generated from operations		175

Workings

1 *Cash received from customers*

	$'000
Opening trade receivables	45
Revenue	445
Closing trade receivables	(50)
Cash received from customers	440

2 *Cash paid to suppliers*

	$'000
Cost of sales	220
Opening inventory	(25)
Closing inventory	40
Purchases	235
Opening payables	20
Closing payables	(30)
Cash paid to suppliers	225

9 Tex cash flow

Text references. Cash flow statements are covered in Chapter 8. The income statement and balance sheet formats are in Chapter 3.

Top tips. The key to this type of question is familiarity with the format of the statements. The best way to achieve this is through practising your question technique. This question gives you practice on all three financial statements.

Easy marks. There was some calculation to do on taxes, but there were a lot of easy marks in the cash flow statement. You should have been able to get most of the marks for the cash flow and scored well on the income statement and balance sheet as long as you proceeded methodically.

(a) TEX

CASH FLOW STATEMENT FOR THE YEAR ENDED 30 SEPTEMBER 20X1

	$'000	$'000
Cash flows from operating activities		
Profit before taxation	3,576	
Finance cost	124	
Depreciation	2,640	
Loss on disposal (2,600 – 900 – 730)	970	
Operating profit before working capital changes	7,310	
Increase in inventory (1,600 – 1,100)	(500)	
Increase in receivables (1,500 – 800)	(700)	
Decrease in payables (800 – 700)	(100)	
Cash generated from operations	6,010	
Interest paid	(124)	
Income taxes paid (W)	(485)	
Net cash from operating activities		5,401
Cash flows from investing activities		
Purchase of property, plant and equipment	(8,000)	
Proceeds of sale of property, plant and equipment	730	
Net cash used in investing activities		(7,270)
Cash flows from financing activities		
Dividend paid	(1,000)	
Repayment of interest-bearing borrowings	(1,200)	
Proceeds from issue of shares (10,834 – 7,815)	3,019	
Net cash from financing activities		819
Net decrease in cash and cash equivalents (1,200 – 150)		(1,050)
Cash and cash equivalents at 1 October 20X0		1,200
Cash and cash equivalents at 30 September 20X1		150

Working

Income taxes paid

INCOME TAXES

	$'000		$'000
Cash flow (bal fig)	485	Opening balance – current	685
Closing balance – current	1,040	Opening balance – deferred	400
Closing balance – deferred	600	Income statement	1,040
	2,125		2,125

(b) TEX

INCOME STATEMENT FOR THE YEAR ENDED 30 SEPTEMBER 20X2

	$'000
Revenue	18,000
Cost of sales (1,600 + 9,000 – 1,700)	(8,900)
Gross profit	9,100
Other operating expenses (3,000 + 2,000)	(5,000)
	4,100
Finance cost	(120)
Profit before tax	3,980
Income tax expense	(1,300)
Profit for the period	2,680

TEX

BALANCE SHEET AS AT 30 SEPTEMBER 20X2

	$'000	$'000
Non-current assets		
Property plant and equipment (18,160 – 3,000)		15,160
Current assets		
Inventory	1,700	
Trade receivables (W1)	2,800	
Bank (W3)	4,390	8,890
		24,050
Equity and liabilities		
Equity		
Share capital		10,834
Retained earnings (W4)		8,216
		19,050
Non-current liabilities		
Interest-bearing borrowing		1,700
Deferred tax		600
Current liabilities		
Trade payables (W2)	1,400	
Taxation	1,300	2,700
		24,050

Workings

1 TRADE RECEIVABLES

	$'000		$'000
Balance b/f	1,500	Cash received	16,700
Sales	18,000	Balance c/f	2,800
	19,500		19,500

2 TRADE PAYABLES

	$'000		$'000
Cash paid	8,300	Balance b/f	700
Balance c/f	1,400	Purchases	9,000
	9,700		9,700

3 BANK

	$'000		$'000
Balance b/f	150	Payments to suppliers	8,300
Received from customers	16,700	Expenses paid	2,000
		Tax paid	1,040
		Loan interest paid	120
		Dividend paid	1,000
		Balance c/f	4,390
	16,850		16,850

4 RETAINED EARNINGS

	$'000		$'000
Dividend paid	1,000	Balance b/f	6,536
Balance c/f	8,216	Profit for year	2,680
	9,216		9,216

10 AG

Text references. Cash flow statements are covered in Chapter 8. The issues you need to consider in redrafting the balance sheet are covered in Chapters 4, 5 and 6.

Top tips. Make sure you read Section C questions carefully in your reading time before the examination begins, noting the proformas and any unusual items. In the exam write out your proformas and insert the easy numbers first. Remember to tackle the parts you can confidently do first and deal with the other areas at the end.

Easy marks. Cash flows from operating activities is simple and logical and you can get most of it right. The working capital adjustments are easy marks and you will always have to adjust for depreciation and interest and to deduct tax and interest paid. Look out for any other adjustments. Cash flows from investing activities will always have property, plant and equipment transactions, which you can get right. Then look for any figures you do not have to calculate and put them in. Proceeds of a share issue are easy to work out – just take the movement on share capital and share premium. In (b), work out retained earnings first.

Examiner's comments. Some candidates gained full marks on this question. Errors included not using the correct format, mistakes in the property, plant and equipment calculations and errors in calculating tax and accruals. (Comments on part(a)).

(a) AG

CASH FLOW STATEMENT FOR THE YEAR ENDED 31 MARCH 20X5

Cash flows from operating activities	$'000	$'000
Profit before taxation	255	
Depreciation	720	
Profit on sale of non-current assets (98 – 75)	(23)	
Development expenditure amortised	80	
Increase in accrued expenses (W1)	10	
Interest expense	45	
		1,087
Increase in receivables	(95)	
Increase in inventories	(110)	
Increase in payables	130	
		(75)
Cash generated from operations		1,012
Interest paid (W2)	(120)	
Income taxes paid (W3)	(200)	
		(320)
Net cash from operating activities		692
Cash flows from investing activities		
Purchase of property, plant and equipment (W4)	(370)	
Sale of property, plant and equipment	98	
Development expenditure (W5)	(50)	
Net cash used in investing activities		(322)
Cash flows from financing activities		
Share issue (1.4m shares @ $0.75)	1,050	
Dividend paid (W6)	(100)	
Repurchase of loan notes	(1,000)	
Net cash used in financing activities		(50)
Net increase in cash and cash equivalents		320
Cash and cash equivalents at beginning of period		232
Cash and cash equivalents at end of period		552

Workings

1 *Accrued expenses*

	$'000	$'000
Balance at 31.3.20X4	172	
less interest payable	(87)	
		85
Balance at 31.3.20X5	107	
less interest payable	(12)	
		95
Increase in non-interest accruals		10

2 *Interest paid*

INTEREST PAYABLE

	$'000		$'000
Interest paid (balance)	120	31.3.20X4 Balance b/d	87
31.3.20X5 Balance c/d	12	Finance costs	45
	132		132

3 *Income taxes paid*

INCOME TAXES

	$'000		$'000
Deferred tax transfer	50	Balance b/d	190
Tax paid (balance)	200	Income tax expenses	140
31.3.20X5 Balance c/d	80		
	330		330

4 *Property, plant and equipment*

PROPERTY, PLANT AND EQUIPMENT

	$'000		$'000
31.3.20X4 Balance c/d	4,800	Disposals	75
Revaluation	125	Depreciation	720
Purchases (balance)	370	31.3.20X5 Balance c/d	4,500
	5,295		5,295

5 *Development*

DEVELOPMENT

	$'000		$'000
31.3.20X4 Balance b/d	400	Amortisation	80
Expenditure (balance)	50	31.3.20X5 Balance c/d	370
	450		450

6 *Dividends paid*

RETAINED EARNINGS

	$'000		$'000
Dividend paid (balance)	100	31.3.20X4 Balance b/d	1,415
31.3.20X5 Balance c/d	1,430	Profit for year	115
	1,530		1,530

(b) AG

REDRAFTED BALANCE SHEET AT 31 MARCH 20X5

	$'000	$'000
Non-current assets		
Property plant and equipment	4,500	
Development expenditure (370 + 25)	395	
		4,895
Current assets		
Inventories	685	
Receivables	515	
Cash and cash equivalents (552 – 250)	302	
		1,502
		6,397
Equity and liabilities		
Equity		
Share capital	2,600	
Share premium	750	
Revaluation surplus (425 – 5)	420	
Retained earnings (W)	1,192	
		4,962
Non-current liabilities		
5% loan notes	500	
Deferred tax (250 + 18)	268	
		768
Current liabilities		
Trade payables	480	
Income tax	80	
Accrued expenses	107	
		667
		6,397

Workings

RETAINED EARNINGS

	$'000		$'000
Prior period adjustment	120	Balance b/f	1,430
Misappropriated cash	250	Current year adjustment to cost of sales	120
Increase in deferred tax provision (60,000 × 30%)	18	Capitalise development expenditure	25
Balance c/f	1,192	Transfer from revaluation surplus – excess depreciation	5
	1,580		1,580

11 CJ

Text references. Cash flow statements are covered in Chapter 8: *IAS 7 Cash flow statements.* Construction contracts are in Chapter 10: *Inventories and construction contracts.*

Top tips. It would be a good idea to use the reading time before the exam to make a note of the proformas you need to produce and then analyse the additional information. Highlight any unusual items and try to decide on which order to tackle the adjustments. On tackling the question make sure you pick out the parts you can do first and deal with the other areas at the end. Always adopt a methodical approach as Section C questions can be quite time pressured.

Easy marks. 'Cash flows from operating activities' was easy apart from the tax and would have gained you a lot of marks. The only complication in the rest of the cash flow was the property, plant and equipment. The construction contract was easy if you knew how to deal with it. If nothing else, you could probably have arrived at attributable profit and added that to retained earnings.

Examiner's comments. This question was generally very well done, with many candidates obtaining full marks. Common errors included not using the correct IAS 7 format, mixing up sale proceeds and gain on disposal and failing to adjust for deferred tax.

(a) CJ

CASH FLOW STATEMENT FOR THE YEAR ENDED 31 MARCH 20X6

	$'000	$'000
Cash flows from operating activities		
Profit before tax	4,398	
Depreciation	4,055	
Finance cost	1,302	
Profit on sale of plant (118 – 95)	(23)	
Gain on disposal of investments	(20)	
Dividends received	(180)	
Increase in inventory	(214)	
Increase in receivables	(306)	
Increase in payables (excluding interest)	420	
Cash generated from operations	9,432	
Interest paid (1,302 – 350 + 650)	(1,602)	
Income tax paid (1,810 + 1,900 – 1,914)	(1,796)	
Net cash from operating activities		6,034
Cash flows from investing activities		
Payment to acquire property, plant and equipment (W)	(2,310)	
Receipt on disposal of plant	118	
Receipt on disposal of investments (2,100 – 1,500 + 20)	620	
Dividends received	180	
Net cash used in investing activities		(1,392)
Cash flow from financing activities		
Proceeds of share issue	10,000	
Borrowings repaid	(6,000)	
Dividends paid	(800)	
Net cash flow from financing activities		3,200
Increase in cash and cash equivalents		7,842
Cash and cash equivalents at 31.3.X5		(880)
Cash and cash equivalents at 31.3.X6		6,962

Workings

Property

PROPERTY

	$'000		$'000
Balance b/d	18,000	Depreciation	2,070
Revaluation	1,500	Balance c/d	19,160
Additions (balance)	1,730		
	21,230		21,230

Plant and equipment

PLANT AND EQUIPMENT

	$'000		$'000
Balance b/d	10,000	Disposal	95
Additions (balance)	580	Depreciation	1,985
		Balance c/d	8,500
	10,580		10,580

	$'000
Property additions	1,730
Plant additions	580
	2,310

(b) CJ

BALANCE SHEET AT 31 MARCH 20X6

	$'000	$'000
Non-current assets		
Property, plant and equipment	27,660	
Available for sale investments	1,500	
		29,160
Current assets		
Inventory and WIP (2,714 + 560(W))	3,274	
Trade receivables (2,106 + 500(W))	2,606	
Cash at bank	6,553	
Cash in hand	409	
		12,842
Total assets		42,002
Equity and liabilities		
Ordinary shares	12,000	
Share premium	10,000	
Revaluation reserve	4,200	
Retained earnings (3,009 + 360(W))	3,369	
		29,569
Non-current liabilities		
Interest bearing borrowings	7,000	
Provision for deferred tax	999	
		7,999
Current liabilities		
Trade and other payables (1,820 + 700)	2,520	
Income tax payable	1,914	
		4,434
Total equity and liabilities		42,002

Working

Long-term contract

	$'000
Total expected profit (5,000 – 2,500 – 700)	1,800
Profit to date (1,800 × 20%)	360

Adjustment to retained profit

	$'000
Revenue (5,000 × 20%)	1,000
Cost of sales	(640)
Profit	360

Adjustments to balance sheet

	$'000
Inventory – WIP	
Gross amount due from customers	
Costs to date	700
Profit to date	360
	1,060
Progress billings	(500)
Due from customers	560
Receivables – progress billings	500
Payables – due to suppliers	700

12 DN

Top tips. You need to be well organised to get the balance sheet done in this question. Make sure you know your proformas and can set them out accurately and quickly. As with all Section C questions, it is best to concentrate on the easy marks first and make an attempt at some of the harder workings at the end of the question time.

Easy marks. Nothing here was difficult, although part (b) was time pressured. If your workings were clear, there were plenty of easy marks available.

Examiner's comments. There were some excellent answers to this question. Common errors were:

- Not using the correct IAS 7 format
- Mixing up proceeds of sale and gain on disposal
- Not allowing for property revaluation
- Incorrectly calculating proceeds of share issue and cost of dividend

(a) DN

CASH FLOW STATEMENT FOR THE YEAR ENDED 31 OCTOBER 20X6

	$'000	$'000
Cash flows from operating activities		
Profit before tax		790
Adjustments for:		
Depreciation (230 + 100)		330
Interest expense		110
Profit on sale of plant (15 – 10)		(5)
		1,225
Increase in receivables		(110)
Increase in inventories		(50)
Increase in payables		20
Cash generated from operations		1,085
Interest paid (75 + 110 – 55)		(130)
Income taxes paid (50 + 140 – 70)		(120)
Net cash from operating activities		835
Cash flows from investing activities		
Proceeds from sale of plant	15	
Cost of acquiring new plant (W)	(677)	
Net cash used in investing activities		(662)
Cash flows from financing activities		
Repayment of loan	(2,000)	
Proceeds from new loan	1,500	
Proceeds of share issue (300 + 300)	600	
Equity dividend paid (2,000 × 0.20)	(400)	
Net cash used in financing activities		(300)
Net decrease in cash and cash equivalents		(127)
Cash and cash equivalents at beginning of period		45
Cash and cash equivalents at end of period		(82)

Working: plant and equipment

PLANT AND EQUIPMENT

	$'000		$'000
Balance b/d	1,405	Disposal (60 – 50)	10
Additions (balance)	677	Depreciation	230
		Balance c/d	1,842
	2,082		2,082

Note. There were no additions to properties, which is cost and revaluation surplus less depreciation.

(b) DN

BALANCE SHEET AT 31 OCTOBER 20X7

	$'000	$'000
Net current assets		
Property, plant and equipment (4,942 – 330)		4,612
Current assets		
Inventory	190	
Receivables (340 + 3,300 – 3,100)	540	
Cash (W1)	643	
		1,373
Total assets		5,985

	$'000	$'000
Equity and liabilities		
Equity		
Share capital	1,300	
Share premium	300	
Revaluation reserve	400	
Retained earnings (W2)	2,280	
		4,280
Non-current liabilities		
Bank loans		1,500
Current liabilities		
Trade payables (105 + 1,700 – 1,600)		205
Total equity and liabilities		5,985

Workings

1 *Cash*

CASH

	$'000		$'000
Receipts from customers	3,100	Balance b/d	82
		Supplier payments	1,600
		Expenses	500
		Interest 20X6	55
		Interest 20X7 ($1,500 × 6%)	90
		Tax 20X6	70
		Tax 20X7	60
		Balance c/d	643
	3,100		3,100

2 *Retained earnings*

RETAINED EARNINGS

	$'000		$'000
Balance c/d	2,280	Balance b/d	1,660
		Profit for year (W3)	620
	2,280		2,280

3 *Profit to 31 October 20X7*

	$'000
Revenue	3,300
Cost of sales	(1,700)
Gross profit	1,600
Depreciation	(330)
Expenses	(500)
Finance cost	(90)
	680
Tax	(60)
Profit for period	620

13 Lemming Inc

Text references. The income statement is covered in Chapter 3: *Presentation of published financial statements.* Cash flow statements are covered in Chapter 8: *IAS 7: Cash flow statements*

Top tips. Make sure you know how to calculate profit before tax from the movement on retained earnings. In this question you are not given the income statement. Interest expense and interest paid are the same here, as all interest to date has been paid. This will not always be the case.

(a) LEMMING
INCOME STATEMENT FOR THE YEAR ENDED 31 AUGUST 20X9

	$'000
Revenue	14,050
Cost of sales (W1)	(10,490)
Gross profit	3,560
Profit on sale of plant	50
Operating expenses (700 + 1,200)	(1,900)
	1,710
Finance costs (1,500 × 10%)	(150)
Profit before tax	1,560
Income tax expense	(500)
Profit for the period	1,060

Workings

1 *Cost of sales*

	$'000
Purchases	10,690
Opening inventory	1,200
Closing inventory	(1,400)
	10,490

2 *Retained earnings*

RETAINED EARNINGS

	$'000		$'000
Dividend paid	500	Balance b/f	2,400
Balance c/f	2,960	Profit for year	1,060
	3,460		3,460

(b) LEMMING

CASH FLOW STATEMENT FOR THE YEAR ENDED 31 AUGUST 20X9

	$'000	$'000
Cash flows from operating activities		
Profit before taxation		1,560
Depreciation		1,200
Profit on sale of property, plant and equipment		(50)
Interest expense		150
Increase in inventory		(200)
Decrease in receivables		100
Decrease in payables		(100)
Cash generated from operations		2,660
Interest paid		(150)
Income taxes paid (500 + 400 – 500)		(400)
Net cash from operating activities		2,110
Cash flows from investing activities		
Purchase of property, plant and equipment	(2,500)	
Proceeds of sale of property, plant and equipment	250	
Net cash used in investing activities		(2,250)
Cash flows from financing activities		
Dividends paid (W2)	(500)	
Issue of share capital	400	
Issue of loan notes	500	
Net cash from financing activities		400
Net increase in cash and cash equivalents		260
Cash and cash equivalents at beginning of period (200 – 360)		(160)
Cash and cash equivalents at end of period (300 – 200)		100

14 Objective test answers: Non-current assets, inventories and construction contracts I

1 C 780 + 117 + 30 + 28 + 100 = 1,055

2 D They are all correct

3 D Neither internally generated goodwill nor internally developed brands can be capitalised.

4 A Goodwill on acquisition is retained in the balance sheet and reviewed annually for impairment.

5 A Carriage outwards is charged to distribution, abnormal costs are not included in inventory.

6 D
1. Production overheads should be included in cost on the basis of a company's normal level of activity.
2. Trade discounts should be deducted but not settlement discounts.
3. IAS 2 does not allow the use of LIFO.

7 C

	$
Contract revenue recognised (900 × 60%)	540,000
Costs	(840,000)
Expected loss (900 – 1,200)	(300,000)
Costs incurred	720,000
Recognised loss	(300,000)
Progress billings	(400,000)
Due from customer	20,000

8 D None of these statements is correct.

Depreciation relating to a revaluation surplus can be transferred from the revaluation reserve to retained earnings, but there must still be a debit to the income statement.

9 C Recoverable amount is the higher of value in use and net realisable value.

10

Revenue	=	$40m × 45%	=	$18m
Profit	=	$6m × 45%	=	$2.7m

	$m
Contract price	40
Total costs (16 + 18)	(34)
Anticipated profit	6

11

	$
NBV (100,000 × 0.75^4)	31,640
Recoverable amount	28,000
Impairment loss	3,640

12 The contract is 70% complete. Revenue earned = $90m × 70% = $63m.

13 CN should recognise a loss of $20m (90m – 77m – 33m).

14 D An allocation of EW's administration costs would not be included as these do not relate specifically to the non-current asset.

15 Objective test answers: Non current-assets, inventories and construction contracts II

1 C

	$
Original purchase price	50,000
Depreciation 20X1: (50,000 – 5,000)/5	(9,000)
Depreciation 20X2	(9,000)
Upgrade	15,000
	47,000
Depreciation 20X3: (47,000 – 5,000)/5	(8,400)
Net book value 1 January 20X4	38,600
Disposal proceeds	(7,000)
Loss on disposal	31,600

2 B The impairment loss is applied first against the goodwill and then against the other non-current assets on a pro-rata basis. It will be allocated as follows:

	$m
Building	10
Plant and equipment	5
Goodwill	5
	20

The carrying value of the building will then become $10m (20 – 10)

3 A fall in the value of an asset, so that its recoverable amount is now less than its carrying value in the balance sheet.

4 B Low production or idle plant does *not* lead to a higher fixed overhead allocation to each unit.

5 The amount for which an asset could be exchanged between knowledgeable, willing parties in an arm's length transaction.

6 The publishing rights cannot be recognised as they have no reliable monetary value as they were a gift and had no cost. The expected future value cannot be recognised as an asset as the event has not yet occurred.

7 Value of goodwill = $130,000

	$'000	$'000
Fair value of consideration – shares (10,000 × $20)		200,000
Cash		20,000
		220,000
Fair value of net assets acquired:		
Tangible non-current assets	25,000	
Patents	15,000	
Brand name	50,000	
		(90,000)
Goodwill		130,000

8

Year ended:	*Cost/valuation*	*Depreciation*	*Acc depreciation*	*NBV*
March 20X2	100,000	10,000	10,000	90,000
March 20X3	100,000	10,000	20,000	80,000
March 20X4	95,000	(20,000)	–	95,000
March 20X4	95,000	11,875 (95,000/8)	11,875	83,125
March 20X5	**95,000**	**16,625** (83,125/5)	**28,500**	**66,500**

9 Depreciable amount is asset cost or valuation less residual value.

10 A This is replacement of a significant part of the asset. The carrying amount of the existing furnace lining must be derecognised. B, C and D refer to repairs and maintenance.

11 NBV of machine at 30 September 20X5 = 10,500

Remaining useful life = 2 years

Depreciation for year ended 30 September 20X6 (10,500/2) = 5,250

12 This question appears to refer to the criteria for recognising development expenditure, which are:

1 Technical feasibility of completing the intangible asset
2 Intention to complete and use or sell the asset
3 Ability to use or sell the asset
4 The asset will generate future economic benefits
5 Adequate resources exist to complete the project
6 Expenditure on the asset can be reliably measured

13

	$'000
Total contract value	3,000
Total costs (1,500 + 250 + 400)	(2,150)
Expected total profit	850

Percentage completed = 1,500/2,150 % = 70%

Income statement amounts:

	$'000
Revenue (3,000 × 70%)	2,100
Costs	(1,500)
Profit	600

16 Section B answers: Non-current assets, inventories and construction contracts

(a) (i) **Research costs**

IAS 38 does not allow the capitalisation of research costs.

Development costs

IAS 38 lays down strict **criteria** to determine when carry forward of development costs is permissible.

- The expenditure attributable to the intangible asset during its development must be measurable.
- The technical feasibility of completing the product or process so that it will be available for sale or use can be demonstrated.
- The entity intends to complete the intangible asset and use or sell it.
- It must be able to use or sell the intangible asset.
- There must be a market for the output of the intangible asset or, if it is to be used internally rather than sold, its usefulness to the entity, can be demonstrated.
- Adequate technical, financial and other resources must exist, or their availability must be demonstrated, to complete the development and use or sell the intangible asset.

(ii) IAS 1 has three basic accounting assumptions: going concern, accruals and consistency.

Each of these concepts is relevant in considering the criteria discussed above for carrying forward development expenditure.

Going concern. The business must be in a position to continue its operations at least to the extent of generating resources sufficient to complete the development project and therefore to market the end product.

Accruals. The purpose of deferring development expenditure at all is to comply with the accruals concept by matching such expenditure with the income expected to arise from it.

Consistency. IAS 38 states that the criteria for deferral of expenditure should be consistently applied.

(b) The general principle underlying IAS 2 is that inventories should be shown in financial statements at the **lower of cost and net realisable value**. This principle accords with both the matching concept, which requires costs to be matched with the relevant revenues, and the prudence concept, which requires that profits are not anticipated and any probable losses are provided for.

The **cost** of an item of manufactured inventory can include both external and internal costs and it is important that only correctly attributable costs are included. These are direct acquisition costs, direct inventory holding costs and production overheads based on a **normal** level of activity. General overheads are excluded.

Production overheads are usually incurred on a time basis and not in relation to the quantities of inventory produced. Most businesses, however, are assumed to continue to exist in the medium term and production overheads are part of the inevitable cost of providing production facilities in the medium term. Thus, so long as the scale of the overheads is not distorted by unusual levels of activity, it is reasonable to include them in the 'cost' of inventory produced in the period to which they relate. Identifying a 'normal' level of activity is more difficult where business is seasonal.

The establishment of NRV also poses a number of practical problems. For many intermediate products, and even for finished items, there may be a limited market and the inventory volumes may represent a significant proportion of the market especially if disposed of under distress conditions. Where a well-developed and liquid market does not exist, it is usually appropriate to base NRV on an orderly disposal after allowing for the reasonable additional costs of marketing and distribution.

(c)

MEMO

To: Transport manager
From: Trainee management accountant
Subject: Useful life

IAS 16 *Property, plant and equipment* requires that the useful lives of non-current assets should be regularly reviewed and changed if appropriate.

By 31 March 20X3 the delivery vehicle will have been depreciated for two years out of the original estimate of its useful life of four years:

	$
Cost	20,000
Depreciation ($20,000 × $^2/_4$)	(10,000)
Net book value at 31 March 20X2	10,000

The net book value at the start of the year ending 31 March 20X3 should now be written off over the remaining, revised useful life of four years giving an annual depreciation charge of $2,500 ($10,000/4).

In the income statement for the year ended 31 March 20X3 therefore the depreciation charge will be $2,500. In the balance sheet the delivery vehicle will appear at its net book value of $7,500 ($10,000 – 2,500).

(d)

Examiner's comments. Most candidates made a better attempt at the buildings part of the question then the brand name. Some candidates did not depreciate the buildings for enough years before revaluating. Despite the question saying that the brand name had been acquired for £500,000, many candidates treated it as internally generated.

Building

The building has previously been revalued upwards and the gain on revaluation taken to equity (a revaluation reserve). Therefore IAS 36 *Impairment of assets* states that the impairment loss of $200,000 ($1.7m – 1.5m) should be charged against the previous revaluation surplus of $900,000 leaving a revaluation surplus of $700,000 and a carrying value for the building of $1,500,000. The building is reported under property, plant and equipment.

Revaluation surplus at 30 Sept 20X4 = $1.8m – ($1.0 – ($1.0 × 2/20))
= $900,000

Carrying value of building at 30 Sept 20X5 = $1.8m – ($1.8m/18)
= $1.7m

Market value at 30 Sept 20X5 = $1.5m

Brand name

IAS 36 requires the brand to be written down to its recoverable amount, which is the higher of its fair value less costs to sell and value in use. Therefore the recoverable amount is the market value of $200,000 as this is higher than its value in use of $150,000.

The impairment loss of $50,000 (250,000 – 200,000) is recognised immediately in the income statement. The brand is measured at $200,000 in the balance sheet and reported as an intangible asset.

Carrying value = $500,000 – ($500,000 × 5/10)
= $250,000

Recoverable amount = higher of fair value and value in use
= $200,000

Impairment = $50,000 ($250,000 – 200,000) charged to the income statement

Brand in balance sheet = $200,000

(e)

> **Examiner's comments**. The most common error made by those who understood the concept of revaluing non-current assets was to miscount the number of years' depreciation, either using 4 or 6 years before the first revaluation in 2007.

Building A

	$
Cost	200,000
Depreciation to 31.8.01 (200,000/20 × 5)	(50,000)
NBV	150,000
Revaluation 31.8. 01 – to revaluation reserve	30,000
Carrying value	180,000
Depreciation to 31.8.06 (180,000/15 × 5)	(60,000)
	120,000
Valuation 31.8.06 – impairment loss	(20,000)
Carrying value	100,000

Building A has suffered an impairment loss of $7,500 at 31 August 2006 which can be debited to revaluation reserve reversing the previous revaluation gain.

Building B

	$
Cost	120,000
Depreciation to 31.8.01 (120,000/15 × 5)	(40,000)
NBV	80,000
Valuation 31.8.01 – impairment loss	(5,000)
Carrying value	75,000
Depreciation to 31.8.06 (75,000/10 × 5)	(37,500)
	37,500
Valuation 31.8.06 – impairment loss	(7,500)
Carrying value	30,000

Building B has suffered impairment losses totalling $7,500 at 31 August 2006, which will be charged to the income statement.

17 Geneva

> **Top tips.** Begin by working out for each contract whether a profit or a loss is forecast. If it is a profit, calculate how much can be recognised. If it is a loss, it is all recognised immediately.
>
> **Easy marks.** Note that all of these contacts started in the current year – so any attributable profit to date belongs to the current year. This makes the calculations easier.

Treatment of construction contracts in the balance sheet

	$'000
Contract Lausanne	
Asset (1,000 + 240 – 1,080)	
Gross amount due from customers for contract work	160
Contract Bern	
Liability (1,100 – 200 – 950)	
Gross amount due to customers for contract work	50
Contract Zurich	
Liability (640 + 70 – 800)	
Gross amount due to customers for contract work	90

Treatment of construction contracts in the income statement

	Lausanne	*Bern*	*Zurich*
	$'000	$'000	$'000
Revenue	1,200	1,000	700
Cost of sales	960	1,200	630
Gross profit/(loss)	240	(200)	70

18 Objective test answers: Capital transactions and financial instruments

1 C The premium is transferred from share capital to share premium

2 C $500,000 + $11,000 (990,000 × 50c + 10,000 × $1.60)

Note that the forfeited shares each brought in a total of $2.60

3 D Share capital $500,000 + $250,000 + $300,000 + $350,000
Share premium $800,000 – $250,000 + $900,000 + $910,000

4 A The called-up value will be debited to share capital and credited to a forfeited shares account.

5 D All four are permitted.

6 A $500,000 – $360,000 = $140,000

7 D If a shareholder fails to pay a call his shares are forfeited and the company is not obliged to return his money.

8 C Cumulative and redeemable preference shares are classified as financial liabilities under IAS 32.

9 B As a deduction from equity.

10 A Cash received on application and allotment

$1 × 5,000 = $5,000

Balance of share capital due = $2,500

Cash received on reissue of shares $1 × 5,000 = $5,000

Additional share premium:

INVESTMENT IN OWN SHARES ACCOUNT

	$		$
Call amount	2,500	Bank	5,000
Share premium	2,500		
	5,000		5,000

11 $3.8m

	$m
Receipt from issue ($10m - $0.5m)	9.5
Dividend payable over 4 years ($10m × 7% × 4)	(2.8)
Payable on redemption ($10m + 5%)	(10.5)
Total finance charge	(3.8)

12 $10.025m

	$m
Receipt from issue	9.5
Finance charge 10%	0.95
Dividend paid	(0.7)
Balance at 31 December 20X8	9.75
Finance charge 10%	0.975
Dividend paid	(0.7)
Balance at 31 December 20X9	10.025

19 Objective test answers: Accounting standards I

1 A $^{3}/_{10} \times$ \$3,000

2 D $^{2}/_{6} \times$ \$3,000

3 D Adjusting events are shown in the financial statements, not the notes.

4 C \$1,800,000 – \$116,000 – \$20,000 = \$1,664,000

5 B Discovery of fraud, error or impairment, which will have existed at the balance sheet date.

6 D These have all occurred after the balance sheet date.

7 C
1 Contingent liability that is possible, therefore disclose.
2 Contingent liability but remote, therefore no disclosure.
3 Non-adjusting post balance sheet event, material therefore disclose.

8 B IAS 37 excludes retraining and relocation of continuing staff from restructuring provisions.

9 A All three criteria must be present.

10 D This does not affect the position as at the balance sheet date

11 D The dividend will not be shown on the income statement or appear as a liability in the balance sheet.

12
1 An entity has a present obligation as a result of a past event.
2 It is probable that an outflow of resources embodying economic benefits will be required to settle the obligation.
3 A reliable estimate can be made of the amount of the obligation.

13 C

14 B A, C and D are changes of accounting estimate.

15 An **operating segment** is a component of an entity:

(a) that engages in business activities from which it may earn revenues and incur expenses

(b) whose operating results are regularly reviewed by the entity's chief operating decision maker to make decisions about resources to be allocated to the segment and assess its performance, and

(c) for which discrete financial information is available

16 B Revenue must be 10% or more of the total revenue of all segments

20 Objective test answers: Accounting standards II

1 C Item 1 is not correct – if it is probable and the amount can be estimated reliably, then it must be provided for.

2 C Customers, suppliers and providers of finance are not related parties.

3 C In a finance lease, the risks and rewards of ownership are transferred.

4 A

	$
Deposit	30,000
Instalments (8 × $20,000)	160,000
	190,000
Fair value	154,000
Interest	36,000

$$\text{Sum of the digits} = \frac{8 \times 9}{2} = 36$$

6 months to	June X1	$^8/_{36} \times \$36,000$		
	Dec X1	$^7/_{36} \times \$36,000$		
	June X2	$^6/_{36} \times \$36,000$		
	Dec X2	$^5/_{36} \times \$36,000$		
	June X3	$^4/_{36} \times \$36,000$	=	$4,000
	Dec X3	$^3/_{36} \times \$36,000$	=	$3,000
				$7,000

5 D The fire is non-adjusting as it does not clarify the 31 December value of the building. It is therefore only disclosed if it threatens the company's going concern status.

Again the customer is assumed to be insolvent at 31 December. We simply did not know this and therefore it is an adjusting event and it should be accrued for.

The answer would be B if the customer had become insolvent after the year end.

6 C

1 As the board decision had not been communicated to customers and employees there is assumed to be no legal or constructive obligation therefore no provision should be made.

2 As refunds have been made in the past to all customers there is a valid expectation from customers that the refunds will be made therefore the amount should be provided for.

3 There is no present obligation to carry out the refurbishment therefore no provision should be made under IAS 37.

7 B Members of the close family of any key management of an entity are presumed to be related parties.

8 An entity has a present obligation (legal or constructive) as a result of a past event.

It is probable that an outflow of resources embodying economic benefits will be required to settle the obligation.

A reliable estimate can be made of the amount of the obligation.

9 C A provision should be made for the claim against AP.

10 B Customers, suppliers and bankers are not normally related parties.

11 Finance cost = $2,160

	$
Total finance cost	
Total payments 12,000 × 5	60,000
Fair value	51,900
Finance cost	8,100

Payments being made over five year period:

To 30 Sept 20X4	5/15 × 8,100	
To 30 Sept 20X5	4/15 × 8,100	$2,160

12 C BW must provide for customer refunds.

13 Any four of the following:

- the seller has transferred to the buyer the significant risks and rewards of ownership
- the seller retains neither continuing managerial involvement to the degree usually associated with ownership nor effective control over the goods sold
- the amount of revenue can be measured reliably
- it is probable that the economic benefits associated with the transaction will flow to the seller
- the costs incurred or to be incurred in respect of the transaction can be measured reliably

14

	Cost	*Interest*	*Instalment*
	$	*$*	*$*
20X4	80,000	6,344	(20,000)
20X5	66,344	5,261	(20,000)
20X6	51,605	4,092	(20,000)
20X7	35,697	2,831	(20,000)
20X8	18,528	1,472	(20,000)

Current liability (20,000 – 4,092) = $15,908
Non-current liability (40,000 – 2,831 – 1,472) = $35,697

15

	$
Original cost	80,000
Depreciation 2004/2005 (80,000/12,000 × (2,600 + 2,350))	(33,000)
Net book value	47,000

16 D No sale has taken place, so DT must show that it is holding $90,000 which belongs to XX.

17 D Fair value less costs to sell ($740,000 - $10,000) is lower than carrying value ($750,000).

Note that non-current assets held for sale are not depreciated.

18 B Non-current assets held for sale are shown separately under the 'current assets' heading.

21 Section B answers: Accounting standards I

(a) **Asset**

IAS 17 is an example of economic substance triumphing over legal form. In legal terms, with a finance lease, the lessor may be the owner of the asset, but the lessee enjoys all the **risks and rewards** which ownership of the asset would convey. This is the key element to IAS 17. The lessee is deemed to have an asset as they must maintain and run the asset through its useful life.

Liability

The lessee enjoys the future economic benefits of the asset as a result of entering into the lease. There is a corresponding liability which is the obligation to pay the instalments on the lease until it expires. Assets and liabilities cannot be netted off. If finance leases were treated in a similar manner to the existing treatment of operating leases then no asset would be recognised and lease payments would be expensed through the income statement as they were incurred. This is '**off balance sheet finance**'. The company has assets in use and liabilities to lessors which are not recorded in the financial statements. This would be misleading to the user of the accounts and make it appear as though the assets which were recorded were more efficient in producing returns than was actually the case.

(b) **MEMO**

To: Production manager
From: Trainee management accountant
Subject: De-commissioning costs

Provision

The accounting question regarding the de-commissioning costs is whether or not a provision should now be set up in the accounts for the eventual costs. According to IAS 37 any future obligations arising out of past events should be recognised immediately. The de-commissioning costs are a future obligation and the past event is the granting of the licence and the drilling of the site.

Therefore a provision should be recognised immediately in the accounts for the year ended 31 March 20X3. This will be $20million discounted to present value.

Discounting

As this cost gives access to future economic benefits in terms of oil reserves for the next 20 years then the discounted present value of the de-commissioning costs can be capitalised and treated as part of the cost of the oil well in the balance sheet. However this total cost, including the discounted de-commissioning costs should be reviewed to ensure that the net book value does not exceed the recoverable amount. If there is no impairment then the total cost of the oil well and discounted de-commissioning costs should be depreciated for the next 20 years and a charge made to the income statement.

(c) Because the airline operation was sold before the balance sheet date and was a distinguishable component of the entity it is a **discontinued operation** as defined by IFRS 5 *Non-current assets held for sale and discontinued operations.* A separate line in the income statement for discontinued operations should be included after the profit after tax for continuing operations. IFRS 5 states that this should be made up of the post-tax profit or loss of the discontinued operation and the post-tax gain or loss on disposal of the airline assets. The loss on sale of the fleet of aircraft of $250m and the provision for severance payments of $20m will both be reported in this line.

	$m
Discontinued operations	(270)

IFRS 5 also requires an **analysis** of the amount into:

(i) the revenue, expenses and pre-tax profit of discontinued operations (to include the loss made by the airline for the year and the provision for the $20m severance payments); and

(ii) the gain or loss recognised on the disposal of the assets (the $250m loss on the sale of the fleet of aircraft).

This can be presented either on the face of the income statement or in the notes.

The **cash flows** attributable to the operating, investing and financing activities of the airline should also be disclosed, either in the notes to the financial statements or in the cash flow statement itself.

As the restructuring has been agreed and active steps have been taken to implement it a **provision** is required for $10m (because the entity has a constructive obligation to carry out the plan). This will be reported as part of the continuing activities, probably as part of administrative expenses.

(d)

Examiner's comments. Most candidates correctly identified that the customer was not a related party. Most candidates correctly identified that George was a related party but did not give sufficient explanation.

Some candidates correctly identified the provider of finance as not being a related party, but did not go on to identify that Arnold was a related party.

XC

XC is not a related party of CB. The discount represents no more than a normal commercial arrangement with a favoured customer.

Property

George is one of the key management personnel of the company and thus a related party, and the sale of the property to him at a discount of $250,000 must be disclosed in the financial statements.

FC

As a provider of finance, FC is not itself a related party. However, Arnold is close family of George and therefore a related party to CB, and the loan does not appear to have been advanced at normal commercial terms. The loan and the involvement of Arnold will need to be disclosed.

(e)

Examiner's comments. Few candidates did well on this question. Most candidates failed to include all three elements of the finance cost in the total cost. Some candidates used the straight line or sum of digits method to allocate the finance cost instead of the actuarial method, despite the discount rate of 10% being given.

(a)

	$
Receipt (2,000,000 – 192,800)	1,807,200
Costs:	
Dividends (100,000 × 5)	500,000
Redemption	2,300,000
	(2,800,000)
Finance cost	(992,800)

(b)

	Balance	Interest 10%	Dividend	Balance
20X6	1,807,200	180,720	(100,000)	1,887,920
20X7	1,887,920	188,792	(100,000)	1,976,712
20X8	1,976,712	197,671	(100,000)	2,074,383
20X9	2,074,383	207,438	(100,000)	2,181,821
20Y0	2,181,821	218,179	(100,000)	2,300,000

The balance at 31 March 20Y0 is $2,300,000, which is the amount needed to redeem the shares.

(f)

Examiner's comments. A large proportion of candidates seemed to have problems with the dates in this question. They said that the 20X5 accounts should be changed, despite the fact that the fraud was discovered more than 6 months after the year end and the accounts had been signed off by the directors two months earlier.

Fraud

The discovery of the fraud in April 20X6 would be an adjusting event after the balance sheet date, if it had occurred before the financial statements were authorised for issue. If the accounts were approved on 1 March, they would probably have been issued by April. So it is unlikely that this can be accounted for in the September 20X5 financial statements.

In the September 20X6 financial statements the overstatement of profit for the year ended 30 September 20X5 must be accounted for as a prior year adjustment. This will be shown in the Statement of Changes in Equity. The profit for the year ended 30 September will be reduced to $555,000. This will affect the retained earnings for the current year but not the current year profit.

Payment from new customer

The payment received in advance in September 20X6 cannot be treated as income because DF has not yet done anything to earn that income. It should be posted to current liabilities as 'deferred income' and released to the income statement when the goods are despatched.

(g)

> **Examiner's comments**. Most candidates correctly identified the factory closure as a discontinued activity but did not give sufficient explanation to gain more than a mark. Few candidates were able to explain how to deal with assets 'held for sale'.

The factory will be treated as a *discontinued operation* under IFRS 5 at 31 March 20X7, as all operations have ceased and sale of the land and buildings is 'highly probable'.

In the income statement **one figure** will be shown under *discontinued operations*, being the trading loss for the period from the discontinued operation (we are not told what this is), plus the loss on disposal of the plant and equipment ($70,000), plus the closure costs ($620,000), less any tax allowances. This single figure should then be analysed in the notes.

In the balance sheet, the net book value of the land and buildings ($750,000) should be moved out of non-current assets and shown under current assets as 'non-current assets held for sale'. The fair value less costs to sell would be higher, so the property is left at net book value. It is not depreciated.

(h) (i)

> **Examiner's comments**. A large proportion of answers did not refer to the asset values and costs given in the question. If a question asks for an explanation of the treatment in financial statements and provides figures it should be fairly obvious that the answer must include reference to costs and asset values given.

EK can treat the sale of its retailing division as a discontinued operation under IFRS 5 for the following reasons:

- It is classified as held for sale.
- It represents a separate major line of business, with clearly distinguishable cash flows.

The retailing division can be classified as 'held for sale' because it is available for immediate sale, the company expects to dispose of it within one year and negotiations are already proceeding with a buyer.

(ii) **Income statement**

EK should disclose a single amount on the face of the income statement comprising:

(a) The post-tax profit or loss of the retailing division up to 31 October 20X7; and

(b) The post tax gain or loss on measurement to fair value less costs to sell. A disposal group held for sale should be measured at the lower of its carrying amount and fair value less costs to sell. For EK this is the lower of $443,000 and $398,000 ($423,000 – $25,000). The impairment loss of $45,000 should be recognised.

Balance sheet

The assets of the retailing division should be removed from non-current assets and shown at their fair value under current assets, classified as 'non-current assets held for sale'. The impairment should all be taken from the goodwill balance.

22 Section B answers: Accounting standards II

(a) IAS 37 defines a provision as a liability of uncertain timing or amount. It goes on further to state that a provision should only be recognised when:

(a) There is a present obligation, either legal or constructive, arising as a result of a past event.

(b) It is probable that an outflow of resources embodying economic benefits will be required in order to settle the obligation.

(c) A reliable estimate of the amount of the obligation can be made.

This can be compared to the IASB's definition of a liability in its Framework for *Preparation and Presentation of Financial Statements:*

A liability is a present obligation of the entity arising from past events, the settlement of which is expected to result in an outflow of resources from the entity.

The key elements from the liability definition are all encompassed in the rules for recognising a provision.

(a) **Obligation**. A liability is a present obligation and a provision is only recognised if there is an obligation. This obligation can either be a legal or a constructive obligation. A constructive obligation arises out of past practice or as a result of actions which have previously taken place which have created an expectation that the organisation will act in such a way.

(b) **Past event.** A provision must arise out of a past event so the event must already have happened at the balance sheet date. If the event has not yet occurred then there is no provision as the entity may be able to avoid it.

(c) **Outflow of resources.** A provision will only be recognised if it is probably that there will be an outflow of resources to settle the obligation which ties in with the IASB's definition of a liability.

(b) INCOME STATEMENT (EXTRACTS)

	Year 1	*Year 2*
	$'000	$'000
Finance charge (W1)	5,567	4,453
Depreciation charge (W3)	17,660	17,660

BALANCE SHEET (EXTRACTS)

	Year 1	*Year 2*
	$'000	$'000
Non– current assets		
Property, plant and equipment (W3)	70,640	52,980
Non-current liabilities		
Amounts due under leases (W2)	56,320	38,660
Current liabilities		
Amounts due under leases		
(72,867 – 56,320) (W2)	16,547	
(56,320 – 38,660) (W2)		17,660

Workings

1 *Finance charge*

	$'000
Total lease payments (5 × $21,000)	105,000
Fair value of asset	(88,300)
Total finance charge	16,700

Finance charge allocation

		$
Year 1	5/15 × 16,700	5,567
Year 2	4/15 × 16,700	4,453
Year 3	3/15 × 16,700	3,340
Year 4	2/15 × 16,700	2,227
Year 5	1/15 × 16,700	1,113
		16,700

2 *Lease liabilities*

		Finance charge	*Repayment*	
	$	$	$	$
Year 1	88,300	5,567	(21,000)	72,867
Year 2	72,867	4,453	(21,000)	56,320
Year 3	56,320	3,340	(21,000)	38,660
Year 4	38,660	2,227	(21,000)	19,887
Year 5	19,887	1,113	(21,000)	–

3 *Non-current assets*

Annual depreciation charge $= \frac{\$88,300}{5} = \$17,660$

	$
Year 1	
Cost	88,300
Depreciation	(17,660)
Net book value	70,640
Year 2	
Depreciation	(17,660)
Net book value	52,980

(c)

Examiner's comments. Few candidate were able to produce a correct answer. Errors included:

- Not calculating overall profitability of the contract
- Ignoring the work in progress inventory

Income statement

	$'000
Sales revenue (W)	30,000
Cost of sales (balancing figure)	21,500
Recognised profit (W)	8,500
Balance sheet	$,000
Total costs to date	24,000
Recognised profit	8,500
Progress billings	(25,000)
Gross amount due from customer	7,500

Working

Revenue	60,000
Costs to date	(24,000)
Costs to completion	(19,000)
Total expected profit	17,000
Profit to date: 17,000 × 50%	8,500
Revenue to date: 60,000 × 50%	30,000

(d)

Examiner's comments. Most candidates were able to calculate the finance cost and the outstanding balances at each year end, but many were unable to produce correct income statement and balance sheet extracts.

Common errors included:

- Basing the calculation on 4 years instead of 5
- Applying the digit weightings in reverse order
- Applying the sum of the digits to the annual repayment instead of the finance charge

(i) The amount of finance cost charged to the income statement for the year ended 31 March 20X5 is $9,067.

Working

	$
Total lease payments	150,000
Fair value of asset	116,000
Finance charge	34,000

Using sum of the digits:

31.3.X4	34,000 ×5/15 =	11,333
31.3.X5	34,000 × 4/15 =	9,067
31.3.X6	34,000 × 3/15 =	6,800
31.3.X7	34,000 × 2/15 =	4,533
31.3.X8	34,000 × 1/15 =	2,267
		34,000

(ii) *Balance sheet extracts*

Property, plant and equipment	
Held under finance lease	116,000
Depreciation (2/5)	46,400
	69,600
Non-current liabilities	
Amounts due under finance leases (76,400 – 23,200)	53,200
Current liabilities	
Amounts due under finance leases (30,000 –6,800)	23,200

Working

Year ended	*Balance b/f*	*Finance charge*	*Payment*	*Balance c/f*
31.3.X4	116,000	11,333	(30,000)	97,333
31.3.X5	97,333	9,067	(30,000)	76,400
31.3.X6	76,400	6,800	(30,000)	53,200
31.3.X7	53,200	4,533	(30,000)	27,733
31.3.X8	27,733	2,267	(30,000)	–

(e)

Examiner's comment. Most candidates were able to score good marks on this question. Many had learnt a mnemonic to aid their recall of the six criteria. In Part (ii) some candidates failed to explain why the development costs should be treated as recommended.

(i) Under IAS 38 development costs will normally be recognised as an expense in the accounting period in which they are incurred. However, they may be capitalised if they meet *all* of the following criteria:

- It is **technically feasible** to complete the asset so that it is available for use or sale.
- The **intention** is to **complete** the asset so that it can be used or sold.
- The business is able to **use** or **sell** the asset
- It can be demonstrated that the asset will **generate future economic benefits**. For instance, a market must exist for the product.
- **Adequate technical, financial and other resources exist** to complete the development.
- The development expenditure can be **reliably measured**.

(ii) CD's development costs meet all of the above criteria. The development is complete, testing has confirmed the future economic benefits and the costs involved have been reliably measured. CD should capitalise $180,000 development costs at 30 April 20X6. Amortisation should begin on 1 May 20X6 and continue over the expected life of the process.

(f)

> **Examiner's comments.** Most candidates were able to correctly calculate the finance charges and balances for each of the three years, but many candidates could not select the correct figures from their workings to answer the question.

(i) Finance charge for the year ended 31 March 20X7: $72,000

(ii) Current liability: $228,000
Non-current liability: $378,000

Working

	$'000
Purchase price	900
Payment 1 April 20X5	(228)
	672
Interest 13.44%	90
Payment 1 April 20X6	(228)
	534
Interest 13.44%	72
Balance at 31 March 20X7	606
Payment due 1 April 20X7 (current liability)	228
Balance due (non-current liability)	378
	606

Note. As payments are made in advance, the payment due on 1 April 20X7 includes no interest relating to future periods.

(g)

> **Examiner's comments**. Most candidates were able to give most of the IAS 18 criteria but few were able to apply the criteria correctly to the scenario.

(i) The criteria in IAS 18 for income recognition are as follows.

- The **risks** and **rewards** of ownership of the goods have been **transferred to the buyer**.
- The entity **retains neither managerial involvement nor effective control** over the goods.
- The amount of **revenue** can be **measured reliably**.
- It is **probable** that the **economic benefits** associated with the transaction will **flow** to the entity.
- The **costs** incurred in respect of the transaction can be measured reliably.
- The **stage of completion** of the transaction at the balance sheet date can be measured reliably (rendering of services).

(ii) The $150,000 received on 1 September 20X7 cannot be recognised as income at that point because the risks and rewards of ownership have not yet been transferred.

The $150,000 should be credited to deferred income in the balance sheet and $25,000 should be released to income each month as the magazines are supplied. The estimated $20,000 each month cost of making the supply will be recognised as it arises – at which point it can be measured reliably.

Therefore at 31 October two months revenue can be taken into account and two months costs will be set against that as follows:

	$
Revenue	50,000
Cost of sales	(40,000)
Gross profit	10,000

(h) **Related party** – under the terms of IAS 24 a party is related to an entity if:

(i) directly or indirectly the party

- controls, is controlled by, or is under common control with, the entity
- has an interest in the entity that gives it significant interest over the entity; or
- has joint control over the entity

(ii) the party is a member of the key management personnel of the entity or its parent, such as a director

(iii) the party is a close member of the family of any individual referred to in (i) or (ii) above

(iv) the party is an entity that is controlled, jointly controlled or significantly influenced by, or a significant proportion of whose voting rights are held by, any individual referred to in (ii) or (iii)

Related party transaction – a transfer of resources, services or obligations between related parties, regardless of whether a price is charged.

23 AZ

Text references. Leases are covered in Chapter 7: *IAS 17 Leases.* Prior year adjustments are covered in Chapter 4: *Reporting financial performance.*

Top tips. Make sure that you approach this type of question methodically. Numerical questions can be time pressured so get as much practice as you can to perfect your technique. Always read the question carefully and then set out your proformas. Tackle the parts you can do first to secure the easy marks before moving on to the more difficult areas. You can use the reading time at the start of the exam to decide in which order to attempt the adjustments.

Easy marks. A number of the adjustments will affect more than one figure. Once you have done the balance sheet, the statement of changes in equity is very easy. The complications here are the lease and the prior year adjustments. Do the lease calculations first, but don't spend too long on them.

AZ

INCOME STATEMENT FOR THE YEAR ENDING 31 MARCH 20X3

	$'000	$'000
Revenue		124,900
Cost of sales (W1)		(100,835)
Gross profit		24,065
Distribution costs (9,060 + 513 (W2))	(9,573)	
Administrative expenses (W3)	(15,445)	
Other operating expenses	(121)	
		(25,139)
		(1,074)
Income from investments	1,200	
Finance cost (W8)	(1,432)	
		(232)
Loss before tax		(1,306)
Income tax expense		(15)
Net loss for the period		(1,321)

AZ

STATEMENT OF CHANGES IN EQUITY FOR THE YEAR ENDED 31 MARCH 20X3

	Share capital	*Share premium*	*Retained earnings*	*Total*
	$'000	$'000	$'000	$'000
Balance at 31 March 20X2	19,000	–	14,677	33,677
Prior year adjustment			500	500
Share issue	1,000	500		1,500
Share issue costs		(70)		(70)
Net loss for the period			(1,321)	(1,321)
Dividend			(1,000)	(1,000)
	20,000	430	12,856	33,286

AZ

BALANCE SHEET AS AT 31 MARCH 20X3

	$'000	$'000
Non-current assets		
Property, plant and equipment (W4)		21,229
Current assets		
Inventory (W6)	5,080	
Trade receivables (9,930 – 600)	9,330	
Bank and cash	26,250	
		40,660
		61,889
Equity		
Share capital		20,000
Share premium (500 – 70)		430
Retained earnings (W5)		12,856
		33,286
Non-current liabilities		
7% loan notes	18,250	
Amount due under finance lease (W7)	1,074	
Other provisions	25	
		19,349
Current liabilities		
Trade payables	8,120	
Amount due under finance lease (W7)	480	
Tax payable	15	
Accruals (18,250 × 7% – 639)	639	
		9,254
		61,889

Workings

1 *Cost of sales*

	$'000
Opening inventory (4,852 + 500)	5,352
Manufacturing cost	94,000
Depreciation of plant and equipment (W2)	6,563
Less closing inventory (W6)	(5,080)
	100,835

2 *Depreciation*

	$'000
Plant and equipment (20% × 30,315)	6,063
Leased equipment (2m/4)	500
Vehicles ((3,720 – 1,670) × 25%)	513

3 *Administrative expenses*

	$'000
Per trial balance	16,020
Provision for legal claim	25
Less leasing cost	(600)
	15,445

4 *Property, plant and equipment*

	Plant and equipment	*Vehicles*	*Total*
	$'000	$'000	$'000
Cost (30,315 + 2,000)	32,315	3,720	36,035
Accumulated depreciation			
(6,060 + 6,563) (W2)	(12,623)		
(1,670 + 513) (W2)		(2,183)	(14,806)
Net book value	19,692	1,537	21,229

5 *Retained earnings*

	$'000
Per trial balance	14,677
Prior year adjustment – inventory	500
Net loss for the year	(1,321)
Dividend (20,000 × 0.05)	(1,000)
	12,856

6 *Closing inventory*

	$'000
As stated	5,180
Cost of damaged goods	(1,200)
NRV of damaged goods	1,100
	5,080

7 *Finance lease*

	$'000
Original cost	2,000
Interest 7.7%	154
Payment	(600)
Balance 31.3.X3	1,554
Interest 7.7%	120
Payment	(600)
Balance 31.3.X4	1,074
Due within 1 year (600 – 120)	480
Due after 1 year	1,074
	1,554

8 *Finance cost*

Interest payable on finance lease	154
Loan note interest (18,250 × 7%)	1,278
	1,432

24 AF

Text references. Use of the revaluation reserve is covered in Chapter 5: *Accounting for non-current assets.* Operating leases are covered in Chapter 7: *IAS 7 Leases.*

Top tips. Begin by setting out the pro-formas for the income statement and balance sheet, then go methodically through the workings, making sure they are neat and easy for the marker to read and understand. You must show workings.

Easy marks. The property, plant and equipment calculations were straightforward and would have been worth a few marks, especially if you charged the depreciation to cost of sales as instructed. You may not have known how to deal with the operating lease, but the income statement was otherwise relatively simple. With a correct balance sheet format in place, you could have slotted in those figures which needed no calculation, plus your plant and equipment figure. The movements on revaluation reserve and retained earnings were easy to work out although you may have missed the transfer back to retained earnings of the excess depreciation, and the only tricky part was probably the accruals, for which you needed to have worked out the loan interest and the charge for the operating lease.

Examiner's comments. Many candidates achieved almost full marks on this question, but very few were able to correctly deal with the operating lease. Errors were also made in dealing with the investment, tax, loan interest, dividends and depreciation.

AF
INCOME STATEMENT FOR THE YEAR ENDED 31 MARCH 20X5

	$'000
Sales revenue	8,210
Cost of sales (W2)	3,960
Gross profit	4,250
Other income	68
Distribution costs	(1,590)
Administrative expenses	(1,540)
Finance costs (1,500 × 6%)	(90)
Profit before tax	1,098
Income tax expense (W4)	(350)
Profit for the period	748

AF
STATEMENT OF CHANGES IN EQUITY FOR THE YEAR ENDED 31 MARCH 20X5

	Share capital	*Share premium*	*Revaluation reserve*	*Retained earnings*	*Total*
	$'000	$'000	$'000	$'000	$'000
Balance at 31 March 20X4	4,500	1,380	330	388	6,598
Revaluation surplus on available for sale investments			110		110
Revaluation surplus on property			250		250
Transfer excess depreciation			(3)	3	–
Profit for the period				748	748
Dividend paid				(275)	(275)
	4,500	1,380	687	864	7,431

AF
BALANCE SHEET AS AT 31 MARCH 20X5

	$'000	$'000
Non-current assets		
Property, plant and equipment (W1)		5,234
Available-for-sale investment		1,750
Current assets		
Inventory	1,320	
Receivables	1,480	
Bank and cash	822	
		3,622
Total assets		10,606
Equity and liabilities		
Equity		
Share capital		4,500
Share premium		1,380
Revaluation reserve (W7)		687
Retained earnings (W5)		864
		7,431
Non-current liabilities		
6% loan notes	1,500	
Deferred tax (710 + 100)	810	
		2,310
Current liabilities		
Payables	520	
Accruals (W6)	95	
Taxation payable	250	
		865
Total equity and liabilities		10,606

Workings

1 *Property, plant and equipment*

	Property	*Plant and equipment*	*Total*
	$'000	$'000	$'000
Cost	5,190	3,400	8,590
Revaluation	100		100
Depreciation b/f	(1,500)	(1,659)	(3,159)
Eliminated on revaluation (500 × 3% × 10)	150		150
Charge for year:			
(5,290 – 2,000) × 3%	(99)		(99)
(3,400 – 1,659) × 20%		(348)	(348)
NBV	3,841	1,393	5,234

2 *Cost of sales*

	$'000
Per trial balance	3,463
Depreciation (99 + 348)	447
Operating lease (W3)	50
	3,960

3 *Operating lease*

Four years @ 62,500 = 250,000
Spread over five years = 50,000 pa

4 *Income tax expense*

	$'000
Tax charge for year	250
Transfer to deferred tax ((2,700 × 30%) – 710)	100
	350

5 *Retained earnings*

	$'000
Balance b/f	388
Profit for year	748
Add back excess depreciation ((600 – 500) × 3%)	3
Dividend paid	(275)
	864

6 *Accruals*

	$'000
Interest payable (90 – 45)	45
Operating lease (W3)	50
	95

7 *Revaluation reserve*

	$'000
Balance b/f	330
Movement on investments	110
Surplus on head office buildings (600 – 350 NBV)	250
Transfer to retained earnings – excess depreciation	(3)
	687

25 Murdoch Co

Text references. Discontinued operations are covered in Chapter 4: *Reporting financial performance.*

Top tips. In this type of question, always resist the urge to question spot. Make sure you read the question carefully so you are aware of all the information provided, circling or highlighting key points. Set out your proformas and complete the easier parts first.

Easy marks. This question was straightforward apart from the discontinued operation. Candidates should note that they can still earn full marks even if they present workings alongside the figures in the financial statements they produce. Problem areas in this question were:

- Treatment of the discontinued operation
- Inventory adjustment
- Accruals and prepayments in the balance sheet (ie the expense heading contained the accruals but the balance sheet did not)
- Note that any adjustment to sales revenue will also affect receivables.

It is good exam technique to leave the more difficult areas to the end and concentrate on the areas you find easy first.

MURDOCH CO

INCOME STATEMENT FOR THE YEAR ENDED 30 JUNE 20X9

Continuing operations

	$'000
Sales revenue (14,800 – 24) (W1)	14,776
Cost of sales (W1)	(10,248)
Gross profit	4,528
Distribution costs (1,080 + 268(W2) + 190 – 120)	(1,418)
Administrative expenses (1,460 + 268(W2) + 70 – 60)	(1,738)
Finance cost (2,000 × 10% × 3/12)	(50)
Profit for the period from continuing operations	1,322
Discontinued operation	
Loss for the period from discontinued operation	(800)*
Profit for the period	522

** Note*

	$'000
Loss on discontinued operation	500
Loss recognised on measurement to fair value less costs to sell of assets constituting discontinued operation	300
	800

MURDOCH CO

BALANCE SHEET AS AT 30 JUNE 20X9

	$'000	$'000
Non current assets		
Land and buildings (12,000 + 8,000 – 2,130 – 120(W2) – 1,800)		15,950
Plant and equipment (12,800 – 2,480 – 2,560(W2))		7,760
		23,710
Current assets		
Inventory (W1)	1,566	
Receivables (4,120 + 120 + 60 – 24)	4,276	
		5,842
Non-current assets classified as held for sale		1,500
		31,052
Equity		
Share capital		14,000
Share premium account		4,000
Revaluation reserve (3,000 + 1,500)		4,500
Retained earnings (3,140 + 522)		3,662
		26,162
Non-current liabilities		
10% loan notes 20Y8		2,000
Current liabilities		
Payables	2,240	
Accruals (190 + 70 + 50)	310	
Bank overdraft	340	
		2,890
		31,052

Workings

1 *Cost of sales*

	$'000
Opening inventory	1,390
Purchases	8,280
	9,670
Closing inventories ((1,560 + 16 – 10) see below)	(1,566)
	8,104
Depreciation (W2)	2,144
Cost of sales	10,248

Inventory adjustments

(i) Lower of cost ($80,000) and NRV ($90,000 – $20,000) = $70,000. Therefore $10,000 (80,000 – 70,000) adjustment.

(ii) Inventory understated by $16,000

Sales overstated by $24,000

2 *Depreciation*

	$'000
Buildings ((8,000 – 2,000) @ 2%)	120
Plant (12,800 @ 20%)	2,560
	2,680

80% to cost of sales: 2,144. 10% to distribution and 10% to administration: 268

26 BG

Text references. The statement of changes in equity is explained in Chapter 3: *Presentation of published financial statements.* Deferred tax is covered in Chapter 14: *IAS 12 Income taxes.* Finance leases are covered in Chapter 7: *IAS 17 Leases.*

Top tips. This is a straightforward set of financial statements. Do not be put off by the description 'available for sale investments'. Just deal with them according to the instructions. Set out the proformas and then go through the workings tackling the parts that you find easy first. Part (b) is easier than it looks. Note that the first instalment is a deposit. You must be able to deal with deferred tax.

Easy marks. The income statement down to tax is easy marks. You should have included the reversal of the provision. The assets section of the balance sheet should have been no problem and you should have scored marks on the statement of changes in equity – the closing balances simply show the equity section of the balance sheet.

Examiner's comments. Few candidates could correctly deal with the release of the provision. Many candidates are still following the old UK format, including the dividend paid as a deduction from the income statement. The IFRS requirement is to show it as a movement in the statement of changes in equity. Many candidates showed the available for sale investments as current rather than non-current assets and errors were made in calculating deferred and current tax.

(a) BG

INCOME STATEMENT FOR THE YEAR ENDED 30 SEPTEMBER 20X5

	$'000
Revenue	1,017
Cost of sales (W1)	(799)
Gross profit	218
Distribution costs	(61)
Administrative expenses	(239)
Reversal of provision	190
Finance costs (net) (15 – 11)	(4)
Profit before tax	104
Income tax expense (W2)	(88)
Profit for the year	16

BG

STATEMENT OF CHANGES IN EQUITY FOR THE YEAR ENDED 30 SEPTEMBER 20X5

	Share Capital	*Share premium*	*Revaluation reserve*	*Retained earnings*	*Total*
	$'000	$'000	$'000	$'000	$'000
Balance at 1 Oct 20X4	200	40	30	226	496
Revaluation of available-for-sale investments			20		20
Net profit for the year				16	16
Dividends paid				(60)	(60)
Balance at 30 Sept 20X5	200	40	50	182	472

BG

BALANCE SHEET AS AT 30 SEPTEMBER 20X5

	$'000	$'000
Assets		
Non-current assets		
Property, plant and equipment (W3)		232
Available-for-sale investments		225
		457
Current assets		
Inventories	37	
Trade receivables	141	
Bank and cash	147	
		325
Total assets		782
Equity and liabilities		
Equity		
Share capital		200
Share premium		40
Revaluation reserve		50
Retained earnings		182
		472
Non-current liabilities		
Long-term borrowings	150	
Deferred tax (50 + 15)	65	215
Current liabilities		
Trade and other payables (W4)	31	
Current tax payable	64	95
Total equity and liabilities		782

Workings

1 *Cost of sales*

	$'000
Cost of cleaning materials consumed	101
Direct operating expenses	548
Depreciation – equipment and fixtures (20% x 752)	150
	799

2 *Income tax expense*

	$'000
Tax due for year	64
Underprovision in previous year	9
Deferred tax	15
	88

3 *Equipment and fittings*

	$'000
Cost	752
Accumulated depreciation (370 + 150 (W1))	520
Net book value	232

4 *Trade and other payables*

	$'000
Trade payables	24
Accrued bond interest (15 – 8)	7
	31

(b)

	$'000
Retained earnings as stated	182
Add back rental payments (61 × 2)	122
Deduct finance lease interest (W)	(36)
Deduct depreciation (180,000 × 40%)	(72)
Retained earnings if finance lease option used	196

Working

	$
Original cost	180,000
Deposit (8,000 × 9) 1.10.X3	(72,000)
	108,000
Interest to 30.9.X4 @ 21.53%	23,252
Instalment 1.10.X4	(72,000)
	59,252
Interest to 30.9.X5 (rounded)	12,748
Instalment 1.10.X5	(72,000)
	–

27 DM

Text references. The financial statement formats are covered in Chapter 3. Finance leases are in Chapter 7: IAS 17 *Leases*, and construction contracts are in Chapter 10: *Inventories and construction contracts.*

Top tips. In the exam, you should always use your reading time wisely. Note the proformas you will need to produce and decide the best order to tackle the adjustments. Always remember there is no right order in which to attempt the adjustments and that this will largely come down to personal preferences. In a time pressured question do the easy parts first to secure the most marks.

Easy marks. You should have been able to score good marks on tax, non-current assets and proper formats. You should know how to deal with a finance lease by this stage – it will probably crop up somewhere. But don't spend too long on it. Do not be put off by the construction contract. It is quite simple.

Examiner's comments. Very few candidates gained full marks as they were unable to correctly deal with the finance lease liability. Deferred and current tax were often wrongly calculated and the statement of changes in equity was not very well done by most candidates.

DM

INCOME STATEMENT FOR THE YEAR ENDED 30 SEPTEMBER 20X6

	$'000
Revenue (602 + 180 (W5))	782
Cost of sales (W1)	(302)
Gross profit	480
Distribution costs (46 + 20 (W2))	(66)
Administrative expenses (91 + 9 (W2))	(100)
Finance costs (W3)	(18)
Profit before tax	296
Income tax expense (24 + 15)	(39)
Profit for the period	257

DM

STATEMENT OF CHANGES IN EQUITY FOR THE YEAR ENDED 30 SEPTEMBER 20X6

	Share capital $'000	Share Premium $'000	Retained earnings $'000	Total $'000
Balance at 30.9.20X5	200		32	232
Share issue	100	50		150
Profit for the period			257	257
Dividend paid	–	–	(25)	(25)
Balance at 30.9.20X6	300	50	264	614

DM

BALANCE SHEET AS AT 30 SEPTEMBER 20X6

	$'000	$'000
Non-current assets		
Property, plant and equipment (W2)		631
Current assets		
Inventory	93	
Construction contract: gross amount due from customer	155	
Receivables (6 + 25)	31	
Cash	43	
		322
Total assets		953

	$'000	$'000
LIABILITIES AND EQUITY		
Equity		
Share capital	300	
Share premium	50	
Retained earnings	264	
		614
Non-current liabilities		
Deferred tax (40 + 15)	55	
Amounts due under finance lease (W4)	66	
6% Loan	140	
		261
Current liabilities		
Payables	29	
Taxation	24	
Amounts due under finance lease (W4)	18	
Loan interest payable (W3)	7	
		78
		953

Workings

1 *Cost of sales*

	$'000
Opening inventory	84
Purchases	285
Depreciation (W2)	26
Closing inventory	(93)
	302

2 *Non-current assets*

	Land	*Buildings*	*Plant*	*Vehicles*	*Total*
	$'000	$'000	$'000	$'000	$'000
Cost	200	300	211	100	811
Accumulated depreciation b/f		(45)	(80)		(125)
Current year depreciation	–	(9)	(26)	(20)	(55)
Net book value	200	246	105	80	631

3 *Finance costs*

	$'000
Loan interest (140 × 6% × 10/12)	7
Interest on finance lease (W4)	11
	18

4 *Finance lease*

	$'000
Cost	100
Interest 10.92%	11
Instalment paid	(27)
Balance at 30.9.2006	84
Due within one year (27 – (84 × 10.92%))*	18
Due after one year	66
	84

* Note that because the instalments are paid *in arrears* the instalment due within one year contains interest applicable to a future period, which must be deducted from the liability.

5 *Construction contract*

	$'000
Contract value	240
Costs to date	(105)
Costs to complete	(35)
Expected profit	100

Profit to date:

$\frac{105}{140}$ % = 75%. Therefore the contract is 75% complete.

Income statement

	$'000
Revenue (240 × 75%)	180
Cost of sales (140 × 75%)	(105)
Profit	75

$105,000 has already been charged to cost of sales, but revenue needs to be added to the income statement.

Balance sheet

	$'000
Costs to date	105
Profit recognised	75
Less progress billings	(25)
Gross amount due from customer	155

28 DZ

Text references. Chapter 3 and 5.

Top tips. Non-current assets (tangible and intangible) figured heavily in this question and it was important to organise the material clearly. A good answer to part (a) makes part (b) much easier. But do not spend too long on part (a). Time management is vital. The best way to pass P7 is to make a good attempt at all parts of the exam and not spend too long on certain parts of a question.

Easy marks. There were quite a few marks available for the financial statements and any errors on non-current assets would only be penalised once, so if your workings were clear you could still have scored well.

Examiner's comments. Very few gained full marks as they were unable to correctly prepare a property, plant and equipment note. A significant number still have problems calculating basic depreciation and dealing with deferred tax and development expenditure.

(a) Property, plant and equipment

Cost	*Land at valuation*	*Land at cost*	*Buildings*	*Plant*	*Total*
	$'000	$'000	$'000	$'000	$'000
Balance 1 April 20X6	1,250	3,500	7,700	4,180	16,630
Disposal	(1,250)			(620)	(1,870)
Revaluation	-	600	(2,000)	-	(1,400)
	-	4,100	5,700	3,560	13,360
Depreciation					
Balance at 1 April 20X6	-	-	1,900	2,840	4,740
Disposals			-	(600)	(600)
			1,900	2,240	4,140
Charge for year:			385 *	330**	715
			2,285	2,570	4,855
Revaluation adjustment	-	-	(2,285)	-	(2,285)
	-	-	-	2,570	2,570
NBV 31 March 20X7	-	4,100	5,700	990	10,790
NBV 31 March 20X6	1,250	3,500	5,800	1,340	11,890

* 7,700 × 5%

** 3,560 – 2,240 × 25%

Depreciation charge:

	Cost of sales	*Admin*
Buildings	308	77
Plant	330	
	638	

(b) DZ

INCOME STATEMENT FOR THE PERIOD ENDED 31 MARCH 20X7

	$'000
Revenue	8,772
Cost of sales (W1)	(4,457)
Gross profit	4,315
Distribution costs	(462)
Administration costs (891 + 77)	(968)
Gain on disposal of land (1,500 - 1,250)	250
Finance cost (2,000 × 8%)	(160)
Profit before taxation	2,975
Income tax expense (811 + 25 – (773 – 665))	(728)
Profit for the period	2,247

DZ

STATEMENT OF CHANGES IN EQUITY FOR THE PERIOD ENDED 31 MARCH 20X7

	Share capital	*Revaluation surplus*	*Retained earnings*	*Total*
	$'000	$'000	$'000	$'000
Balance at 1 April 20X6	1,000	2,100	2,024	5,124
Revaluation surplus (2,285 – 1,400)		885		885
Transfer to retained earnings*		(750)	750	-
Profit for the period	-	-	2,247	2,247
Balance at 31 March 20X7	1,000	2,235	5,021	8,256

* The land which was sold had previously been revalued from $500,000 to $1,250,000. Upon sale, this revaluation gain can be recognised and so is transferred to retained earnings.

DZ

BALANCE SHEET AT 31 MARCH 20X7

	$'000	$'000
Non-current assets		
Capitalised development costs (W2)		198
Property, plant and equipment (see (a))		10,790
		10,988
Current assets		
Inventory	435	
Receivables	1,059	
Cash	103	
		1,597
Total assets		12,585
Equity and liabilities		
Equity		
Share capital		1,000
Revaluation reserve		2,235
Retained earnings		5,021
		8,256
Non-current liabilities		
8% loan note		2,000
Deferred tax		665
Current liabilities		
Payables	773	
Interest payable (160 × 6/12)	80	
Tax payable	811	
		1,664
Total equity and liabilities		12,585

Workings

1 *Cost of sales*

	$'000
Opening inventory (240 + 132)	372
Purchases	2,020
Production labour cost	912
Production overheads	633
Depreciation	638
Research costs	119
Amortisation of development costs ((867 + 48) × 20%)	183
Loss on disposal of plant (5 - (620-600))	15
Closing inventory (165 + 270)	(435)
	4,457

2 *Capitalised development costs*

	$'000
Balance per trial balance	500
Deduct research costs	(119)
Less current year amortisation (W1)	(183)
Balance at 31 March 20X7	198

29 EY

Text references. Chapter 3

Top tips. You were given a lot of information to deal with here but the question was much easier than it looked. It was important to be very methodical. Start by getting down the formats, then go through the notes cross-referencing to the entries in the cash book. Remember to tackle the parts of the question that you find easiest first.

Easy marks. You had to calculate revenue and cost of sales using movement on receivables and payables, so there would have been easy marks for this. Property, plant and equipment and the construction contract were also quite straightforward.

Examiner's comments. Overall this question was reasonably well done but few gained full marks. The statement of changes in equity was not done very well by most candidates. Very few candidates showed the bonus issue, those that did usually only showed one entry under share capital. The transfer of the realised gain on disposal from revaluation reserve to retained earnings was nearly always omitted from the statement. The format of this part was often poor, with no total column and headings omitted.

EY
INCOME STATEMENT FOR THE YEAR ENDED 31 OCTOBER 20X7

	$'000
Revenue (W4)	8,207
Cost of sales (W5)	(5,947)
Gross profit	2,260
Profit on sale of land (1,200 – 1,000)	200
Distribution costs	(730)
Administrative expenses (W7)	(686)
Finance costs (W9)	(173)
Profit before tax	871
Taxation (W8)	(482)
Profit for the year	389

EY
STATEMENT OF CHANGES IN EQUITY FOR THE YEAR ENDED 31 OCTOBER 20X7

	Share capital	*Revaluation surplus*	*Retained earnings*	*Total*
	$'000	$'000	$'000	$'000
Balance 1 November 20X6	3,000	600	1,625	5,225
Bonus issue (1 / 6)	500		(500)	
Realisation of revaluation surplus on land (1,000 – 600)		(400)	400	
Profit for the year			389	389
Dividend paid	–	–	(750)	(750)
Balance 31 October 20X7	3,500	200	1,164	4,864

EY

BALANCE SHEET AT 31 OCTOBER 20X7

Non current assets	$'000
Property, plant and equipment (W3)	7,729
Development costs (W2)	1,100
	8,829
Current assets	
Inventory	985
Trade receivables	620
Amount due on construction contract (W1)	840
	2,445
Total assets	11,274
Equity and liabilities	
Equity	
Share capital	3,500
Revaluation surplus	200
Retained earnings	1,164
	4,864
Non-current liabilities	
Loan notes (2,260 + 2,500)	4,760
Deferred tax (180 + 42)	222
	4,982
Current liabilities	
Trade payables	670
Interest payable	130
Tax payable	420
Overdraft	208
	1,428
Total equity and liabilities	11,274

Workings

1 *Construction contract*

	$'000
Total value	1,400
Costs to date	(600)
Costs to complete	(400)
Expected profit	400

Costs incurred to date are 60% of total. Income statement amounts are:

Revenue (1,400 × 60%)	840
Cost of sales (1,000 × 60%)	(600)
Attributable profit	240

Gross amount due from customers:

Costs to date	600
Attributable profit	240
	840

2 *R&D expenditure*

	$'000
Balance at 1 November 20X6	1,000
Additions: Laminate	500
	1,500

Note: The artificial wood and the research project do not meet the criteria for capitalisation and will be written off to the income statement. Production of the new laminate is expected from January 20X8 and so this balance should only be amortised next year (year ended 31 October 20X8).

	$'000
Amortisation:	
Balance at 1 November 20X6	200
Charge for year (1,000 × 20%)	200
	400
Carrying value (1,500 – 400)	1,100

3 *Property, plant and equipment*

	Land	*Premises*	*Plant*	*Total*
Cost	$'000	$'000	$'000	$'000
B/f 1 November 20X6	2,000	1,500	3,800	7,300
Additions	–	1,600	1,860	3,460
Disposal	(1,000)	–	–	(1,000)
Balance at 31 October 20X7	1,000	3,100	5,660	9,760
Accumulated depreciation				
B/f 1 November 20X6		350	760	1,110
Charge for year: (3,100 x 6%)		186		186
(5,660 – 760) x 15%)		–	735	735
		536	1,495	2,031
Carrying value	1,000	2,564	4,165	7,729

Note that the excess of the land disposal proceeds over the carrying value ($200,000) will be recognised as profit in the year. The balance held in revaluation surplus ($400,000) can now be treated as realised and so is transferred to retained earnings.

4 *Revenue*

	$'000
Cash received from customers	7,500
Opening receivables	(753)
Closing receivables	620
Revenue recognised on construction contract (W1)	840
	8,207

5 *Cost of sales*

Opening inventory	1,200
Purchases (W6)	3,097
Closing inventory	(985)
Plant depreciation (W3)	735
Amortisation of development expenditure (W2)	200
W/off of development projects (W2)	1,100
Cost of sales – construction contract (W1)	600
	5,947

6 *Purchases*

Payments to suppliers	3,000
Opening payables	(573)
Closing payables	670
	3,097

7 *Administrative expenses*

	$'000
Per cash book	500
Premises depreciation (W3)	186
	686

8 *Income tax charge*

Prior year underprovision (690 – 670)	20
Charge for year	420
Increase in deferred tax	42
Income statement charge	482

9 *Finance cost*

Interest paid during the year	160
Less balance due at 31.10.X6	(117)
Outstanding at 31.10.X7	130
Charge for year	173

30 FZ

Text references. Assets held for sale are dealt with in Chapter 4: *Reporting financial performance.* Provisions are covered in Chapter 9: *Miscellaneous standards.*

Top tips. In this question it is important to recognise that you are required to present financial statements under IFRS 5 *Non-current assets held for sale and discontinued operations.* Always read the question carefully so that you do not miss anything important. Make sure you know how to show discontinued operations on the income statement.

Easy marks. Write out the proforma income statement and balance sheet and slot in figures from the trial balance for some easy marks. The statement of changes in equity is also straightforward if you know the format.

Examiner's comments. A disappointing number of candidates were unable to correctly identify the sale of shops as a discontinued operation. Most candidates that correctly identified the discontinued operation did not apply their answer in part (a) to their workings in part (b).

A disappointing number of candidates wanted to create a provision for the reorganisation package, even thought the items constituting the package were all disallowed by IAS 37.

Very few students provided for a discontinued operation in calculating the profit for the year.

(a) (i) The newsagents' shops meet the criteria of an **asset held for sale** under IFRS 5 *Non-current assets held for sale and discontinued operations.*

- The shops are available for immediate sale in their present condition.
- The sale is highly probable.

Non-current assets held for sale should be **measured at the lower of carrying amount and fair value less costs to sell**. For the newsagents' shops this is the $5,000,000 fair value less $200,000 selling costs or $4,800,000. The carrying amount is the higher amount of $5,260,000.

Under IFRS 5, an **impairment loss** should be recognised when fair value less costs to sell is lower than carrying amount. Thus, the difference between the carrying amount and the fair value less costs to sell of $460,000 should be written off, with $300,000 being allocated to goodwill and the remaining $160,000 to the newsagents' shops.

The newsagents' shops should be **presented separately** from other assets in the balance sheet under the heading 'non-current assets classified as held for sale'. A single amount should be presented on the face of the income statement as 'loss for the period from discontinued operation'. This amount should be the total of:

- The post-tax profit or loss of discontinued operations and
- The post-tax gain or loss recognised on the measurement to fair value less costs to sell.

(ii) IAS 37 Provisions, *contingent liabilities and contingent assets* deals with the accounting treatment necessary for this item.

When a **restructuring** involves a sale of an operation, as is the case with the newsagents' shops, IAS 37 states that no obligation arises until the entity has entered into a binding sale agreement. Since at year-end the sale of the shops had not been concluded, a provision cannot be made.

It is worth noting that even if the sale was binding at year-end, a provision would still be prohibited under IAS 37. This is because staff retraining, staff relocation and development of new computer systems are **specifically excluded**.

(b) FZ

INCOME STATEMENT FOR THE YEAR ENDED 31 MARCH 20X8

Continuing operations

	$'000
Revenue (10,170 – 772)	9,398
Cost of sales (W1)	(4,363)
Gross profit	5,035
Distribution costs (W3)	(384)
Administrative expenses (W5)	(406)
Profit from operations	4,245
Finance cost (1,000 × 5%)	(50)
Profit before tax	4,195
Income tax expense (W6)	(1,080)
Profit for the period from continuing operations	3,115
Discontinued operation	
Loss for the period from discontinued operation (W7)	(301)
Profit for the period	2,814

FZ

STATEMENT OF CHANGES IN EQUITY FOR THE YEAR ENDED 31 MARCH 20X8

	Share capital	*Share premium*	*Revaluation Reserve*	*Retained earnings*	*Total*
	$'000	$'000	$'000	$'000	$'000
Balance at 1 April 20X7	4,000	2,500	190	5,808	12,498
Profit for the period				2,814	2,814
Dividends				(500)	(500)
Issue of share capital	1,000	500			1,500
Balance at 31 March 20X7	5,000	3,000	190	8,122	16,312

FZ

BALANCE SHEET AT 31 MARCH 20X8

	$'000	$000
Assets		
Non-current assets		
Property, plant and equipment (W8)		11,516
Current assets		
Inventory	900	
Trade receivables (929 – 62)	867	
Cash and cash equivalents	853	
		2,620
Non-current assets classified as held for sale		4,800
Total assets		18,936
Equity and liabilities		
Equity		
Share capital	5,000	
Share premium account	3,000	
Revaluation reserve	190	
Retained earnings	8,122	
		16,312

	$'000	$000
Non-current liabilities		
5% Loan notes		1,000
Deferred tax		237
Current liabilities		
Trade payables	417	
Tax payable	920	
Interest payable	50	
		1,387
Total equity and liabilities		18,936

Workings

1 *Cost of sales continuing operations*

	$'000
Cost of goods sold (4,120 – 580)	3,540
Depreciation (W2)	823
Cost of sales	4,363

2 *Depreciation continuing operations*

	$'000
Factory buildings (12,000 × 3%)	360
Plant and equipment (2,313 × 20%)	463
Depreciation	823

3 *Distribution costs continuing operations*

	$'000
Distribution costs (432 – 57)	375
Vehicles depreciation ((147 – 67 – 57 + 52) × 25%)	19
Gain on disposal vehicles (W4)	(10)
	384

4 *Gain on disposal*

	$'000
Disposed vehicle cost	(57)
Disposed vehicle depreciation	52
Cash received	15
Gain on disposal	10

5 *Administrative expenses continuing operations*

	$'000
Administrative expenses (440 – 96)	344
Bad debt from customer X	62
Administrative expenses	406

6 *Income tax expense continuing operations*

	$'000
Taxation due for year (920 + 120)	1,040
Increase in deferred tax provision (237 – 197)	40
Income tax expense	1,080

7 *Loss for the period on discontinued operation*

	$'000
Revenue	772
Cost of sales	(580)
Impairment of goodwill	(300)
Impairment of shops	(160)
Administrative expenses	(96)
Distribution costs	(57)
Tax credit	120
Loss for the period	(301)

Note that IFRS 5 allows the analysis of the discontinued operation to be provided on the Income Statement rather than in the notes. The answer did not take this approach as note (k) of the question stated that FZ wants to disclose the minimum information allowed by IFRSs.

8 *Property, plant and equipment*

	Buildings	*Plant and equipment*	*Vehicles*	*Total*
	$'000	$'000	$'000	$'000
Cost (147 – 57)	12,000	2,313	147	14,460
Disposal			(57)	(57)
Accumulated depreciation b/f	(720)	(1,310)	(67)	(2,097)
Depreciation disposal			52	52
Disposal charge for the year	(360)	(463)	(19)	(842)
NBV	10,920	540	56	11,516

31 Objective test answers: General principles of taxation

1 (a) Tax is deducted at source, so non-payment is not an issue
(b) The costs of collection are borne by employers
(c) The funds are received at the same time each month, which helps financial planning

2 C The company acts as a tax collector on behalf of the tax authority. Therefore any tax deducted is put in a payable account until the money is actually paid to the tax authority. The balance on the payable account represents the amount collected but not yet paid over.

3 B The tax authorities do not have the power to detain company officials. Their powers relate to documents and information (eg information held on computer).

4 Direct taxation is charged directly on the **person** or **entity** that is intended to pay the tax.

5 Accounting profit + disallowable expenditure – non-taxable income – tax allowable expenditure = taxable profit

6 C Equity

7 Tax evasion is manipulation of the tax system by illegal means to avoid paying taxes.

8 A The classical system

	$'000
Company income tax (400,000 × 25%)	100
Personal income tax (250,000 × 30%)	75
	175

9
- Domestic legislation and legal decisions
- Tax authority practice
- International treaties
- Supranational bodies

10 C Tax deducted at source before payment of interest or dividends.

11 B The person or entity that finally bears the cost of the tax.

12 The tax authority within whose area an entity is resident.

13 A Power of arrest

14 C Effective incidence

15 A A progressive tax

16 Any three of the following:

(1) To give a date from which penalties and/or interest can accrue
(2) To get funds in as quickly as possible for use by central government
(3) To reduce backlogs and extra work for the tax department
(4) To prevent entities deducting tax at source, eg employers collecting payroll tax, from spending it before it reaches the tax authority

17 C Naturally, tax authorities like to minimise the tax gap.

18 A An example of hypothecation is the 'congestion charge' levied on London motorists that can only be spent on London transport.

19 (a) Under group loss relief, it is possible to set the losses of a group member against the profits of another group member. If the profit-making group member pays tax at a higher rate than the one making the loss, the total tax liability of the group for the year can be reduced.

(b) Claiming group loss relief can help improve group cash flows as the loss is relieved more quickly.

32 Objective test answers: International tax

1 D The head office is located, and all board meetings take place in, the Cayman Islands. Therefore the place of management is in the Cayman Islands.

2 C International tax treaties (eg double taxation treaties) are a source of tax rules.

The other options are all sources of accounting rules.

3 The EU issues rules on sales taxes, which must be applied by all member states.

4 It is called the schedular system.

5
- Interest payments
- Dividends
- Royalties
- Capital gains accruing to non-residents

6
- Full deduction
- Exemption
- Credit

7 B Double taxable treaties deal with **overseas** income.

8 B A place of management, a workshop, a quarry

9 D The country where most of the entity's products are sold.

10 B

	$
50,000 × 12%	6,000
Less already paid	(5,000)
Balance due:	1,000

11 B Corporate income tax is due on all profits of the branch, not just those remitted.

12 $20,000

	$
Net dividend	90,000
Withholding tax	10,000
Gross dividend	100,000
Underlying tax (100,000 × 200,000/1,000,000)	20,000

13 C EA will be deemed resident in Country C, which is its place of management.

33 Objective test answers: Indirect taxes

1 A suitable commodity would have the following characteristics:

- A limited number of large producers
- Products that are easily defined
- A commodity produced in large volume

2 C Sales tax is an indirect tax, all the others are direct taxes.

3 B As long as they are registered for sales tax, options A, C and D merely act as tax collectors, it is the end consumer who suffers the tax.

4

		$
DA	Input tax (200 × 15%)	(30)
	Output tax (500 × 15%)	75
	Total due	45
DB	Input tax	(75)
	Output tax (1,000 × 15%)	150
	Total due	75
Total		120

5

	$
Sale by DA (500 × 7%)	35
Sale by DB (1,000 × 7%)	70
Total paid	105

6

	$'000
Output tax (15,000 × 15/115)	2,400
Input tax (10,000 + 4,000 × 15%)	(2,100)
VAT due from FE	300

Note that VAT is deductible on purchases relating to zero-rated outputs, but not on purchases relating to exempt outputs

7 D Sales taxes such as VAT are indirect

8 B $1,450

	$
VAT output tax (200 × 50 × 15%)	1,500
VAT input tax (200 × 35 × 15%)	(1,050)
VAT payable	450
Excise duty payable (200 × 5)	1,000
Total payable	1,450

9 Amount paid = $14,000

	$
Output VAT 120,000 × 20%	24,000
Input VAT 100,000 × 10%	(10,000)
Amount paid	14,000

10

		$			$
CU:	Output tax	37.5	CZ:	Output tax	90.0
	Input tax	(15.0)		Input tax	(37.5)
	Payable	22.5		Payable	52.5

34 Objective test answers: Company taxation

1 B

	$	$
Accounting profit		350,000
Add: depreciation	30,000	
disallowed expenses	15,000	
		45,000
		395,000
Less: non-taxable income	25,000	
tax allowable depreciation	32,000	
		(57,000)
Taxable profit		338,000

2 D

	$	$
Taxable profit		350,000
Less: depreciation	30,000	
disallowed expenses	15,000	
		(45,000)
		305,000
Add: non-taxable income	25,000	
tax allowable depreciation	32,000	
		57,000
Accounting profit		362,000

3 A

	$	$
Accounting loss		(350,000)
Add: depreciation	30,000	
disallowed expenses	400,000	
		430,000
		80,000
Less: non-taxable income	25,000	
tax allowable depreciation	32,000	
		(57,000)
Taxable profit		23,000

4 B

	$m	$m
Taxable profit		50
Less: depreciation	15	
disallowed expenses	1	
		(16)
		34
Add: non-taxable income	3	
tax allowable depreciation	4	
		7
Accounting profit		41

5 D

	$	$
Accounting profit		250,000
Add: depreciation	45,000	
disallowed expenses	20,000	
		65,000
		315,000
Less: tax allowable depreciation		(30,000)
Taxable profit		285,000

Tax payable = $285,000 × 30% = $85,500.

6

	$
Output tax (15,000 × 15/115)	2,400
Input tax (10,000 + 4,000 × 15%)	2,100
VAT due from FE	300

Note that VAT is deductible on purchases relating to zero-rated outputs, but not on purchases relating to exempt outputs.

7 B

	$	$
Accounting profit		500,000
Add: depreciation	50,000	
disallowed expenses	5,000	
		55,000
		555,000
Less: non-taxable income	25,000	
tax allowable depreciation	60,000	
		(85,000)
Taxable profit		470,000

Tax payable = $470,000 × 25% = $117,500.

8 D

	$	$
Accounting profit		250,000
Add: depreciation	40,000	
disallowed expenses	2,000	
		42,000
		292,000
Less: tax allowable depreciation		(30,000)
Taxable profit		262,000

Tax payable = $262,000 × 30% = $78,600.

9 D Direct tax and earnings tax. (This is the examiner's answer.)

10 Tax due = $22,500

	$
Accounting profit	95,000
Less non-taxable income	(15,000)
Add non– allowable expenditure	10,000
Taxable profit	90,000

Tax = $90,000 × 25%
= $22,500

11 $4,000

	$'000
Revenue	45
Operating costs	(23)
Finance costs	(4)
Taxable allowance	(2)
Taxable amount	16
Tax @ 25%	4

12

		$
30 September 20X3	Tax on trading profits = 200 × 20%=	40,000
30 September 20X4	Tax on trading profit = (150 – 120) × 20% =	6,000
30 September 20X5	Tax on capital gains = (130 – 100) × 20% =	6,000
		12,000

13 B The company income tax that has already been paid is **imputed** to the shareholder as a tax credit.

14 A $320,000 less prior year over-provision ($290,000 – $280,000)

15

	Accounting book value	*Tax basis*	*Difference*	*Deferred tax balance*
	$	$	$	$
Cost 1.4.X4	500,000	500,000		
Depreciation to 31.3.X5	(100,000)			
Capital allowance 50%	-	(250,000)	-	-
	400,000	250,000	150,000	45,000
Depreciation to 31.3.X5	(100,000)			
Capital allowance 20%	-	(50,000)	-	-
	300,000	200,000	100,000	30,000
Revaluation 1.4.06	120,000			
	420,000			
Depreciation (42,000/3)	(140,000)			
Capital allowance 20%	-	40,000	-	-
	280,000	160,000	120,000	36,000

Deferred tax balance 31.3.X6	30,000
Deferred tax balance 31.3.X7	36,000
Income statement charge X6/X7	6,000

[Note:
Strictly, some of the movement on deferred tax should go to the revaluation reserve, but this aspect is not examinable at P7.]

16 $42,900

	$
Purchase cost	630,000
Surveyors and legal fees (3,500 + 6,500)	10,000
Renovation costs	100,000
	740,000
Indexation of purchase cost (630,000 x 50%)	315,000
Indexation of renovation costs (100,000 x 50%)	50,000
Total costs	1,105,000
Sale less disposal costs (1,250,000 – 2,000)	1,248,000
Taxable profit on disposal	143,000
Tax due at 30%	42,900

35 Objective test answers: Deferred tax

1 A

	$
Over provision for prior period	(2,000)
Provision for current period	50,000
Increase in deferred tax charge	5,000
Charge to income statement	53,000

2 C

	$
Under provision for prior period	200
Provision for current period	30,000
Decrease in deferred tax charge	(5,000)
Charge to income statement	25,200

3 A Item 2 consists of permanent differences, all the rest are temporary differences.

4 D All four items have a carrying amount equal to their tax base.

5 B IAS 12 states that deferred tax assets and liabilities should not be discounted.

6 D

	$
Taxable temporary differences b/f	850,000
Depreciation for tax purposes	500,000
Depreciation charged in the financial statements	(450,000)
Revaluation surplus	250,000
Taxable temporary differences c/f	1,150,000
Deferred tax at 30%	345,000

7 D

	$
Over provision for prior period	(27,500)
Provision for current period	30,000
Decrease in deferred tax charge	(10,000)
Credit to income statement	(7,500)

8 It is an imputation system.

9 D

	$
Under provision for prior period	2,800
Provision for current period	28,000
Increase in deferred tax charge	5,000
Charge to income statement	35,800

10 Deferred tax balance = $66,750

Tax written down value:

	$
1 Oct 20X3 cost	900,000
20X4 tax allowance – 50% × 900,000	(450,000)
30 Sept 20X4 tax written down value	450,000
20X5 tax allowance – 25% × 450,000	(112,500)
30 Sept 20X5 tax written down value	337,500

Accounting carrying value:

	$
Cost	900,000
Depreciation 2 × (900-50)/5	(340,000)
30 Sept 20X5 accounting carrying value	560,000

Temporary difference = $560,000 – 337,500
= $222,500

Deferred tax balance = $222,500 × 30%
= $66,750

11

	Temporary difference	
B/f (12,500 – 5,000)	7,500	
20X3 (2,120 – 1,630)	490	
20X4 (1,860 – 1,590)	270	
20X5 (1,320 – 1,530)	(210)	
Balance at 31 December 20X5	8,050	× 25% = 2,012.50

12

	$
Taxable profit for the year	946,000
Tax at 22%	208,120
Prior year over-provision	(31,000)
Increase in deferred tax provision	117,000
Charge to income statement	294,120

13 Deferred tax balance at 31 March 20X7 = $34

Deferred tax balance at 31 March 20X8 = ($2)

Tax written down value:

	$ '000
1 Apr 20X5 cost	600
20X6 tax allowance (50% × 600,000)	(300)
31 Mar 20X6 tax written down value	300
20X7 tax allowance (25% × 300,000)	(75)
31 Mar 20X7 tax written down value	225
20X8 tax allowance (25% × 225,000)	(56)
31 Mar 20X8 tax written down value	169

Accounting carrying value:

	$
Cost	600
Depreciation (2 × (600/5))	(240)
31 Mar 20X7 carrying value	360
1 Apr 20X7 impairment review	(120)
1 Apr 20X7 carrying value	240
Depreciation X7/X8 (240/3)	(80)
31 Mar 20X8 carrying value	160

31 March 20X7

Temporary difference = $360 – $225 = $135

Deferred tax balance = $135 × 25% = $34

31 March 20X8

Temporary difference = $160– $169 = ($9)

Deferred tax balance = ($9) × 25% = ($2)

Note. The question specifies working to the nearest $1,000.

14 $200,250

	$
Accounting profits	822,000
Entertaining expenses	32,000
Political donation	50,000
	904,000
Government grant	(103,000)
Taxable profit	801,000
Tax at 25%	200,250

15 $49,500

	Carrying value	*Tax base*
	$	$
1 October 20X5	400,000	400,000
Depreciation 25%	(100,000)	–
First year allowance	–	(400,000)
Balance 30 Sept 20X6	300,000	–
Depreciation 25%	(75,000)	–
Balance 30 Sept 20X7	225,000	–

Difference between carrying value and tax base = $225,000

Deferred tax at 22% = $49,500

36 Section B answers: Taxation I

(a)

> **Top tips**. We have given three examples here as this is all that is needed. Other acceptable answers would be a trust fund, a partnership or any other body set up to carry out a trade for profit (eg the bar at a golf club).

The person liable to pay tax is called a **taxable person**.

Examples include the following.

- An individual
- An estate of a deceased person
- A limited company

A taxable person usually pays tax in the country where he or she is resident. The tax authority able to charge tax is called the **competent jurisdiction**.

(b) (i) **Indirect taxation** is charged indirectly on the final consumer of the goods or services. An example is a sales tax (eg VAT in the UK; TVA in France). As value is added, the tax increases cumulatively.

Indirect taxes are not actually paid by the business. Instead, the business acts as a tax collector on behalf of the tax authorities. For example, a business charges sales tax on its sales (output tax) and it pays sales tax on its purchases (input tax). The difference between output tax and input tax is paid over to the tax authorities.

(ii) **Unit taxes** are based on the number or weight of items, eg excise duties on the number of cigarettes or on the weight of tobacco.

Ad valorem taxes are based on the value of the items, eg a sales tax or value added tax.

(c)

	$
Output tax $\frac{(587,500 \times 80\%)}{117.5} \times 17.5$	70,000
Input tax (350,000 × 80%) × 17.5%	49,000
Tax payable	21,000

(d)

	$'000
INCOME STATEMENT (EXTRACT)	
Income tax expense (W1)	1,145
BALANCE SHEET (EXTRACT)	
Non-current liabilities	
Deferred tax (W2)	1,750
Current liabilities	
Income tax	1,000

Workings

1 *Income statement*

	$
Income tax for year	1,000,000
Over-provision in previous year	(5,000)
Increase in deferred tax	150,000
Income tax expense	1,145,000

2 *Deferred tax*

	$
Opening balance	1,600,000
Increase in year	150,000
Closing balance	1,750,000

(e)

> **Examiner's comments.** Most candidates were able to explain the meaning of avoidance and evasion, with fewer highlighting the difference between them. Some candidates gave odd examples of tax avoidance, such as 'claiming capital allowances' or 'claiming loss relief'. These are not examples of tax avoidance, they are proper application of the tax legislation and are not 'loopholes'.
>
> Several candidates stated that giving double taxation relief on overseas profits was a means of preventing tax avoidance, which is incorrect.
>
> Many candidates did not give enough examples or sufficient detail within the examples to earn full marks.

(i) **Tax avoidance** is successful tax planning. It is arranging the financial affairs of an individual or an entity in such a manner as to minimise tax liability. It is perfectly legal.

Tax evasion is the use of illegal means to avoid paying tax, such as not declaring income, claiming deduction for non-deductible expense, or contravening tax legislation.

(ii) Although only evasion is illegal, avoidance is just as much of a problem for government. Methods that governments can use to reduce avoidance and evasion are:

- Anti-avoidance legislation. This outlaws specific avoidance schemes.
- Deducting tax at source such as the PAYE system in the UK.
- Keeping the tax system as simple as possible to minimise the number of factors that can be manipulated.
- Making sure that penalties for evasion are high enough to act as a deterrent.
- Increasing the efficiency of the tax collection and investigation machinery.
- Having a tax system which is not generally perceived as unfair. An unfair system makes people feel justified in avoiding tax.

(f)

> **Examiner's comments.** Most candidates could define withholding tax whilst many candidates found difficulty defining underlying tax. A common error Part (ii) was not grossing up the amount received before calculating withholding tax. As many candidates did not know what underlying tax was they could not calculate it.

(i) **Withholding tax** is deducted at source by the tax authority before a payment is made. This occurs most commonly when dividends are paid to non-residents. The tax authority has no power to tax the non-resident, so it taxes the dividend at source.

Underlying tax is the tax which has already been suffered by the profits from which a dividend is paid. When the recipient pays tax on his dividend income, this means that the dividend has effectively been taxed twice. To mitigate this, some tax authorities operate an imputation system, by which the recipient obtains relief for the underlying tax.

(ii) $45,000 represents 9/10 of the amount prior to withholding tax, so withholding tax is therefore $45,000/9 = $5,000.

(iii) The amount of dividend prior to withholding tax was $50,000. This has already been taxed at 20% (100/500). Therefore $50,000 is 80% and the other 20% is the underlying tax - $12,500.

(g)

> **Examiner's comments**. It was surprising how many candidates could not correctly calculate VAT when the figure inclusive of VAT was given.

(i)

		$
Revenue (40,250 × 100/115)		35,000
Cost of sales:		
Purchases plus excise duty	12,000	
Repackaging (6,900 × 100/115)	6,000	
		(18,000)
Net profit		17,000

(ii)

	$
VAT output tax (35,000 × 15%)	5,250
VAT input tax (18,000 × 15%)	(2,700)
Due to VAT authorities	2,550

37 Section B answers: Taxation II

(a) **Power to review and query filed returns**

The tax authorities usually have the power to ask for further information if they are not satisfied with a filed return. These queries must be answered or there may be legal penalties.

Power to request special reports or returns

The special report may take the form of asking for details of pay and tax deducted from an individual employee, where there are indications that the tax rules have been broken. There have been instances of casual employees having a number of jobs but using a number of false names, so that the tax authority has been defrauded.

Power to examine records

Most tax authorities have the power to inspect business records to ensure compliance. If mistakes in returns have been made, the tax authority may be able to re-open earlier years and collect back taxes owed.

Powers of entry and search

Where the tax authority believes fraud has occurred, it can obtain warrants to enter a business's premises and seize the records.

Exchange of information with tax authorities in other jurisdictions

This has become very important as a counter-terrorism measure in recent years. One tax authority may become aware of funds being moved to another country in suspicious circumstances. It will then warn the tax authority in that other jurisdiction. Exchange of information is also useful in dealing with drug smuggling and money laundering.

(b) If a company makes payments to an individual or another company resident in a different tax jurisdiction, it may have to pay **withholding tax** to the tax authority of its own jurisdiction.

The reason for this is to stop companies paying all their earnings abroad and then stopping trading without paying any tax to the tax authorities of the country where they are resident. Therefore the local tax authority will take a payment on account of the final tax liability by deducting at source a withholding tax from all payments sent abroad. The withholding tax can be as low as 5% or as high as 40%.

Payments affected are usually interest payments or dividends.

Alternative answers. You would also have scored marks for stating royalties or capital gains accruing to non-residents.

(c) **Double taxation treaties**

In order to establish more clearly which tax authority has jurisdiction, countries enter into **double taxation treaties**. These treaties seek to avoid a business having to pay tax twice on its income simply because it deals with two tax authorities.

A double taxation treaty (eg that between the UK and the USA) sets out which tax authority has jurisdiction. So a company incorporated in the UK that trades with the USA will be taxed primarily in the UK. The treaty defines a **permanent establishment** and directs that the business will be taxed in the country where it has its permanent establishment.

Where a double taxation treaty exists, provisions are usually made to reduce withholding taxes, or even to avoid paying withholding tax at all.

Another feature of a double taxation treaty is that where a company pays tax in Country A, but is resident in Country B, the tax authorities of Country B will give relief for the tax paid in Country A.

Methods of giving relief

One way is to give full **deduction** for foreign taxes paid. However this is not always appropriate, particularly if the country where the tax is paid has a high tax rate and the other has a low rate.

Relief may be given by **exemption**. In this case, if income is taxed in Country A, then it will not be taxed in Country B.

Another way of giving relief is by **credit**. This usually occurs where the tax rate in Country A is higher than that in Country B. Instead of deducting the full amount of tax paid in Country A, Country B credits the amount it would have paid in Country B. For example, the income is $10,000 and the tax rate in Country A is 30%, while that in Country B is 20%. The tax paid in Country A will be $3,000 but the double tax relief allowed in Country B will be $2,000 (20% × $10,000).

38 Section B answers: Taxation III

(a) **Deferred tax – balance sheet disclosure and note**

	$m
Temporary differences on non-current assets	0.56
Provision at 30 April 20X3	0.69
Deferred tax credit in income statement	(0.13)
Provision at 30 April 20X4	0.56

Working

Deferred tax

	$m
Temporary difference at 30 April 20X3	2.30
Temporary difference at 30 April 20X4	2.00
Deferred tax at 30 April 20X3 (2.30 × 30%)	0.69
Deferred tax at 30 April 20X4 (2.00 × 28%)	0.56
Reduction in deferred tax provision	0.13

Alternative approach

The reduction in provision is made up of two elements.

	$m
Reversal of temporary differences ((2.30 – 2.00) × 30%)	0.09
Change in tax rate (2.00 × (30% – 28%))	0.04
	0.13

(b) **Tax on profit on ordinary activities – note to income statement**

	$m
Current tax	
Tax on profit for the period	1.40
Overprovision for previous period ($750,000 – $720,000)	(0.03)
Deferred tax	
Increase in provision ($300,000 – $250,000)	0.05
Total tax charge	1.42

Balance sheet

	$m
Payables	
Current tax	1.40
Deferred tax	0.30

(c)

Examiner's comments. Part (i) was fairly well done; most candidates seem to be getting the idea of temporary differences and deferred tax balances. However, some had trouble with the dates. The asset had been owned for three years but many candidates calculated four or even five years before working out the temporary difference.

	Accounting value	*Tax value*
	$	$
Cost	200,000	200,000
Depreciation 20X3 – 20X5	(120,000)	(131,400)*
Balance 30 September 20X5	80,000	68,600
Disposal proceeds	(60,000)	(60,000)
Loss	20,000	8,600

(i) Timing difference at 30 September 20X5 (80,000 – 68,600) = 11,400

Tax at 20% = 2,280

(ii) The NBV of the asset at 30 September 20X6 is $80,000. Disposal at $60,000 will give rise to an accounting loss of $20,000.

(iii) At the date of disposal the tax WDV of the asset is $68,600. Disposal at $60,000 gives rise to a balancing allowance of $8,600.

* (60,000 + 42,000 + 29,400)

(d)

Examiner's comments. Most candidates gained reasonable marks for this question. The majority of candidates were able to calculate the adjusted profit before tax relief for non-current assets although the tax depreciation was often calculated incorrectly.

		$
Profit before tax		33,950
Local government tax		950
Entertaining		600
Depreciation		21,600
		57,100
Capital allowances:		
Buildings (70,000 × 4%)		(2,800)
Plant and equipment	- existing (80,000 × 73% × 27%)	(15,768)
	- addition (20,000 × 50%)	(10,000)
Taxable profit		28,532

	$
Tax due:	
$10,001 - $25,000 @ 15%	2,250
$25,001 - $28,532 @ 25%	883
Total due for 20X6	3,133

(e)

Examiner's comments. Very few candidates provided a fully correct answer to this question, and some demonstrated very little knowledge of deferred tax.

Some candidates used the wrong periods, some failed to apply the tax rate to the year end balances and some described the credit to the income statement as a charge.

Year ended	*Cost*	*Depreciation*	*Tax allowance*
31.3.X4	250,000	50,000	125,000
31.3.X5	250,000	50,000	31,250
		100,000	156,250

(i) Deferred tax balance: 31.3.X4: (125,000 – 50,000) × 30% = $22,500

(ii) Deferred tax balance: 31.3.X5: (156,250 – 100,000) × 30% = $16,875

(iii) Income statement credit: year ended 31.3.X5 = (22,500 – 16,875) = $5,625

(f)

Examiner's comments. Some candidates filled a page or more with calculations but did not show how the results would be used. You must answer the question asked, in this case the question asked for tax payable so the answer must state the taxable profits and tax payable otherwise the question has not been answered.

		$
Profit before tax		29,800
Gain on disposal		(4,000)
Depreciation		14,200
		40,000
Capital allowances:		
Buildings (80,000 × 5%)		(4,000)
Plant and equipment	– first year (30,000 × 50%)	(15,000)
	– disposal balancing allowance (11,812 – 5,000)	(6,812)
Taxable profit		14,188
Tax due for year ended 30 April 20X8 at 20%		2,838

39 Objective test answers: Short-term finance I

1 7.8%

We will take 7% and 9% as the rates.*

7%:	6 × 7.024	42.14
	100 × 0.508	50.80
		92.94
9%:	6 × 6.418	38.51
	100 × 0.422	42.20
		80.71

Extrapolating:

$$7\% + \frac{92.94 - 88.00}{92.94 - 80.71} \times 2 = 7\% + \frac{4.94}{12.23} \times 2 = 7.8\%$$

* You can choose different rates – you should still get the same answer. We would expect the yield to maturity to be slightly above the coupon rate.

2 D A property mortgage is generally for a term longer than five years, and this is therefore a long-term source of finance.

3 D Interest is only paid on the amount borrowed, not on the full facility.

4 D This is also known as a documentary credit.

5 B Although the level of return is a factor in the decision, it is more important to minimise the risk to the original capital invested.

6 C Deciding what credit limits customers should be given.

7 A Short-term cash surpluses will not normally be invested in equities owing to the risks associated with achieving a return over a short period.

8 9.88%

Taking 7% and 9% as the interest rates:

		$
7%:	Interest (6×4.100)	24.6
	Repayment (100×0.713)	71.3
		95.9
9%:	Interest (6×3.890)	23.34
	Repayment (100×0.65)	65.00
		88.34

Extrapolating:

$$7\% + \left(\frac{95.9 - 85.00}{95.9 - 88.34} \times 2\right) = 7\% + \left(\frac{10.9}{7.56} \times 2\right) = 7\% + 2.88 = 9.88\%$$

9 A This is an example of an aggressive working capital policy.

10 Effective annual interest rate = 14.78%

$$\text{Annual cost} = \left(\frac{100}{98.5}\right)^{\frac{365}{40}} - 1$$

$$= \left(\frac{100}{98.5}\right)^{9.125} - 1 = 14.78\%$$

11 Using rates of 7% and 9% from the tables:

$(4 \times 5.389) + (100 \times 0.623) = 21.556 + 62.3 = 83.856$
$(4 \times 5.033) + (100 \times 0.547) = 20.132 + 54.7 = 74.832$

$$7 + \left(\frac{83.856 - 83.000}{83.856 - 74.832} \times 2\right) = 7 + \left(\frac{0.856}{9.024} \times 2\right) = 7.19\%$$

12 D Cash budgets ensure that sufficient funds will be available when they are needed to sustain the activities of an entity.

13 9.21%

Using rates of 9% and 11% from the tables:

$(1{,}000 \times 0.708) + (120 \times 3.240) = 1{,}097$
$(1{,}000 \times 0.659) + (120 \times 3.102) = 1{,}031$

$$9 + \left(\frac{1{,}097 - 1{,}090}{1{,}097 - 1{,}031} \times 2\right) = 9 + \left(\frac{7}{66} \times 2\right) = 9.21\%$$

14 $869

	$
Capital at maturity (1,000 x 0.564*)	564
Interest (70 x 4.355**)	305
	869

* Discount factor year 6 @ 10%
** Cumulative discount factor 6 years @ 10%

40 Objective test answers: Short-term finance II

1 B Treasury bills are issued by the Central Bank on behalf of the government, to raise short-term cash (mostly for 90 days). They are traded 'second hand' on the discount market, and carry a low rate of interest because they are risk free. Other money market instruments carry slightly higher rates of interest.

2 Optimal transfer amount $= \sqrt{\frac{(2 \times 30 \times 240{,}000)}{0.05}}$

= $16,970

= $17,000 rounded

3 A The company will be retaining the majority of its delivery vehicles, and it is safe to assume that reasonably priced contracted-out alternatives are available. This sale should not damage the long-term profitability of the company.

B is not correct. It can be assumed that the blending of pigments to go into the china products is a core activity of the business. This plant should not be sold in these circumstances.

C is not correct. Such a patent is likely to be a key to securing the long-term future profitability of the company. It should not be sold to meet short-term needs.

D is not the most appropriate option. A 60% stake constitutes a controlling interest in a company. It could therefore be unsafe to sell this shareholding.

4 Any four of:

- Bank loan
- Bank overdraft
- Factoring
- Invoice discounting
- Use of trade credit

5 10.5%

Taking 10% as the discount factor:

100×0.467	46.70
7×5.335	37.35
	84.05

Taking 11% as the discount factor:

100×0.434	43.40
7×5.146	36.02
	79.42

Extrapolating:

$$10\% + \left(\frac{84.05 - 82.00}{84.05 - 79.42}\right) = 10\% + \left(\frac{2.05}{4.63}\right) = 10.44\%$$

This can be rounded to 10.5%.

6 C The interest yield is the **gross yield** divided by the **market value of the stock** expressed as a percentage, in this case (11,000 × 10%) ÷ 10,000.

7 The time lag between a payment being initiated and the funds becoming available in the recipient's bank account.

8 Spread $= 3\left[\dfrac{(0.75 \times 30 \times 300{,}000)}{0.00025}\right]^{1/3}$

$= 3 \times 3{,}000 = \$9{,}000$

Return point = 2,500 + 9,000/3 = $5,500

Upper limit = 2,500 + 9,000 = $11,500

9 A It is a method of providing medium-term export finance.

10 C Certificates of deposit are negotiable instruments.

11 D Preference shares. Shares are generally higher risk than loan stock.

12 The rate of interest at which the total of the discounted values of any future payments of interest and capital is equal to the current price of a security.

13 A The date of payment will be specified on the bill of exchange.

14 $10{,}000 \times \left(1 - \dfrac{0.06 \times 40}{365}\right) = \$9{,}934.25$

15 B Treasury shares have been repurchased but not cancelled.

16 Forfaiting has the following advantages for the exporter:

(i) He obtains immediate cash payment
(ii) The forfaiting bank has no recourse to the exporter, so the exporter carries no liability
(iii) The exporter has transferred all risks to the forfaiting bank
(iv) Forfaiting enables transactions to be entered into which may not otherwise be possible.

41 Section B answers: Short-term finance

(a) **Expected cash balance/overdraft**

	$'000
Balance at 1 December	+ 175
December cash flow ((+700 × 0.7) + (-300 × 0.3))	+ 400
	+ 575
January	– 900
Expected overdraft	– 325

Using expected values and probabilities the expected value of the overdraft at the end of January is $325,000.

However this outcome will never actually occur. Given the two possibilities for the cash flow in December the reality is that there will be either an overdraft of $25,000 (+ 175 + 700 – 900) or an overdraft of $1,025 (+ 175 – 300 – 900).

The expected value of $325,000 is only of relevance for a situation that is happening time after time. For a one-off situation such as this there is therefore little point in basing any decision-making on the expected value. Instead the short-term cash planning should be based upon both possible overdraft requirements rather than the expected value.

(b) **Features of an overdraft**

An **overdraft** is a negative balance on a current account at a bank. This constitutes borrowing and, because the balance will vary daily, the **interest** on the borrowing is normally computed on a **daily basis** at an **agreed rate**. A **maximum limit** to the overdraft is agreed with the bank and above this limit penalty **charges** will apply. In theory, the overdraft can be **cancelled immediately** if the bank is not happy with the company's **creditworthiness**. An overdraft can be **unsecured**, or **secured** on company assets or the personal assets of the proprietors.

The major advantage of an overdraft is that the company only pays interest when the overdraft is being used, in contrast to a bank loan.

Importance of overdraft

The overdraft is a key source of finance for working capital because of its **flexibility:** the finance varies automatically up to the agreed limit, enabling the company to handle peaks and troughs in cash flows without incurring excess interest charges. The potential disadvantage for an expanding company is that the **overdraft limit** may have to be **frequently renegotiated**. There is also a tendency for expanding companies to ignore the need to underpin their growth with longer term finance.

(c) **Alternatives to overdraft**

When considering alternatives to the bank overdraft, it is essential to consider the need for longer term funds (loans or equity funds) to **finance** the **permanent element** of working capital. Although such funds may be more expensive than short term finance, they provide a longer term stability for planning.

Short-term bank loans

A short-term bank loan (eg six months) can be arranged to **cover** a **forecast cash deficit**. The disadvantage compared with the overdraft is that the **interest is chargeable** on the **full amount** of the loan even if the finance is not required for part of the period.

Debt factoring

A **specialist organisation** will **collect the company's debts** and **advance cash**, effectively on the security of the company's receivables. The effective cost of the finance is sometimes difficult to compute but, for an expanding company, an advantage over overdrafts is that the source of finance effectively grows with the receivables ledger.

Discounting of invoices and bills of exchange

The company **presents invoices** or **bills of exchange** to the bank in return for immediate cash, slightly less than the face value (ie discounted). When the customers pay, the cash goes direct to the bank. The discount represents the **effective interest** on the funds advanced.

Supplier finance

Some suppliers will provide **extended credit periods** on inventory, or alternatively finance can be raised from finance houses on the security of inventory. Alternatively the company may exploit its relationships with suppliers by taking longer periods of credit. Unlike with an overdraft, the supplier may not charge any interest, but the company may lose **early payment discounts** and **supplier goodwill**.

Evaluation of different sources

The key to evaluating these different sources of finance is to **compute the true annual percentage interest rate** implicit in each arrangement and to quantify other **relevant cash flows**, such as administration costs, variations to selling prices and the likely effect on bad debts. Other issues which are less easy to quantify include the effect on customer, supplier and lender loyalty.

(d)

Examiner's comments. Some candidates took 30 days credit to mean that customers paid within the month of sale instead of in the following month and made the same error in relation to purchases.

Some failed to give any conclusion regarding the likelihood of AM being able to pay for the equipment

		May	June	July
		$'000	$'000	$'000
Receipts				
Cash sales		35	40	40
Credit sales:	30 days	66	66	72
	60 days	30	33	33
	90 days	5	5	6
Total receipts		136	144	151
Payments				
Purchases:	70%	35	39	39
	30%	15	15	16
Expenses		50	50	50
Equipment purchase		–	–	250
Total payments		100	104	355
Net movement		36	40	(204)
Cash balance b/f		96	132	172
Cash balance c/f		132	172	(32)

It is clear that AM will not have sufficient funds to pay for the equipment when the payment falls due.

(e)

Examiner's comments. Many candidates were unable to explain the terms 'coupon rate' and 'yield to maturity' satisfactorily. The vast majority of candidates were unable to calculate the yield to maturity. Very few candidates even got the formula correct.

(i) The coupon rate of a security is the actual amount of interest that is paid on the security based upon its face value. In the case of the bond illustrated this is $70 ($1,000 × 7%).

The yield to maturity however is the overall return that the security holder achieves over the period of holding the security to maturity. This is the interest receivable on the security together with the repayment at maturity compared to the original cost of the bond.

(ii) Yield to maturity = internal rate of return

Year	*Cash flow*	*Discount factor* @ 8%	*Present value* $	*Discount factor* @ 12%	*Present value* $
0	(850)	1.00	(850.00)	1.00	(850.00)
1-5	70	3.993	279.51	3.605	252.35
5	1,000	0.681	681.00	0.567	567.00
			110.51		(30.65)

$$\text{Internal rate of return} = 8\% + \frac{110.51}{110.51 + 30.65}(12\% - 8\%)$$

$$= 8\% + \left(\frac{110.51}{141.16} \times 4\right)\%$$

$$= 8\% + 3.13\%$$

Yield to maturity = 11.13%

(f)

Examiner's comments. The number of candidates who completely ignored this question was quite surprising. There were some easy marks to be had on this question, for example general knowledge comments on the risk of investing in the stock market.

To: Management Accountant
From: Assistant Management Accountant
Re: Investment of cash surplus

In the case of this cash surplus the issues are as follows:

1 This cash is needed to **pay for the factory**. Therefore the risk of loss must be minimised, even at the cost of lower returns during the period of investment.

2 The cash will be needed in **3-4 months**. Therefore it cannot be tied up for a longer period.

I have looked at the three possible investment opportunities and found the following:

(i) **Treasury bills.** These are virtually risk free and have an annual yield of 4% (1% over 3 months × 4). Purchased now and held for 91 days, they will give us a return of 1% over the three months.

(ii) **Equities** are higher yield (10%) but with a far higher level of risk. We have no way of knowing how the share index will perform over three months and we may end up selling at a loss in order to release the cash. If the shares are sold before the dividend is declared we will lose the dividend.

(iii) **A bank deposit account** will pay 3.5% per annum. This is slightly less than Treasury bills but is also virtually risk-free and only requires 30 days notice. If notice is not given, a month's interest will be lost.

The best option would appear to be the Treasury bills for 91 days. If at the end of that time the cash is not needed for another month it could be put into a bank deposit account.

(g)

Examiner's comments. Most candidates were able to identify possible sources of funding but most gave only superficial explanations. Very few candidates used the information provided to calculate trade payable/receivable days outstanding. A large proportion of the answers did not give realistic solutions and ignored the data provided in the question.

DF has the following sources available:

(i) **Short-term loan**. This would be easy to arrange and DF will probably be able to repay it in 6 months.

(ii) **Overdraft**. This will be more expensive but more flexible. With a turnover of $240m an additional $2m on the overdraft should not be a problem.

(iii) **Delaying payment to suppliers**. DF has a gross margin of 50% on $240m, so its cost of sales is $120m. With $16m trade payables outstanding, DF is taking 49 days (16/120 × 365) to pay suppliers. Increasing the amount outstanding by $2m will mean that suppliers are being paid after 55 days (18/120 × 365). This is still less than 60 days, so DF may not get too much protest from suppliers as the change may not be apparent from looking at their receivables ageing reports. However, for those suppliers who do become aware of it, DF's trading relationship may be adversely affected.

(iv) **Accelerating collection from customers**. DF's customers are currently paying after 30 days (20/240 × 365). These are normal trade terms and it is unreasonable to think that this period can be reduced without offering customers some incentive, such as a discount.

(h)

Examiner's comments. The majority of candidates were able to allocate a finance charge to periods using the sum of digits method. However, comparatively few were able to calculate the closing balances and even fewer were able to prepare correct accounting entries.

(i) As per IAS 32 redeemable preference shares are classified as a financial liability. The finance charge is calculated as follows.

Receipt from issue (10,000,000 – 601,500)	9,398,500
Dividend payable over 4 years (10,000,000 × 5% × 4)	(2,000,000)
Payable on redemption (10,000,000 × 110%)	(11,000,000)
Finance charge	(3,601,500)

Sum of the digits = 4 + 3 + 2 + 1 = 10

The $3,601,500 finance charge can then be apportioned over the four years.

30 April 20X7	$3,601,500 × 1/10	360,150
30 April 20X8	$3,601,500 × 2/10	720,300
30 April 20X9	$3,601,500 × 3/10	1,080,450
30 April 20Y0	$3,601,500 × 4/10	1,440,600
		3,601,500

(ii) The allocation of the finance charge is as follows.

Year	*Balance sheet liability*	*Finance charge for year*	*Dividends paid*	*Balance sheet liability*
	$	$	$	$
30 April 20X7	9,398,500	360,150	(500,000)	9,258,650
30 April 20X8	9,258,650	720,300	(500,000)	9,478,950
30 April 20X9	9,478,950	1,080,450	(500,000)	10,059,400
30 April 20Y0	10,059,400	1,440,600	(500,000)	11,000,000

The balance at 30 April 20Y0 is $11,000,000 which is the amount needed to redeem the shares.

FG
INCOME STATEMENT FOR THE YEAR ENDED 30 APRIL 20X8 (EXTRACTS)

	$
Finance charge	720,300

FG
BALANCE SHEET AS AT 30 APRIL 20X8 (EXTRACTS)

	$
Non-current liabilities	
5% preference shares	9,478,950

(i)

Examiner's comments. The compound interest required for the internet bank caused many candidates problems, many ignored compounding.

(i) In the case of the fixed term bonds, we calculate the yield to maturity.

This is an internal rate of return calculation, for which we will use 10% and 9%.

(Note: we are using rates below 12.5% to allow for the premium on acquisition ($2) and the commission on purchase)

10%

Cash flow (102 × 1.01)	(103.02)	(This includes the commission cost)
Interest (100 × 12.5% × 0.909)	11.36	
Repayment (100 × 0.909)	90.90	
	(0.76)	

9%

Cash flow	(103.02)
Interest (12.5 × 0.917)	11.46
Repayment (100 × 0.917)	91.70
	0.14

IRR = 9% + (0.14 / (0.14 + 0.76)) %

= 9% + 0.15% = 9.15%

(ii) To work out the interest paid by the internet bank over the 12 months, we compound the interest over 12 periods using the formula $(1 + r)^n = 1 + R$

Where: r = monthly interest rate
n = number of periods
R = annual interest rate

$(1.008)^{12} = 1.1003$

The interest rate is therefore 10.03%

The deposit account at the internet bank is offering a higher return and is therefore the most appropriate investment for the year.

42 Objective test answers: Working capital management I

1 A Short-term finance is matched to fluctuating current assets. B is a conservative policy, while C and D are aggressive policies.

2 D This is the ratio of current assets excluding inventories to current liabilities. C is wrong as the loan stock would normally be included with long-term liabilities. B is the current ratio.

3 A The credit cycle begins with the receipt of the customer's order. Price negotiations take place prior to this point.

4 A 365 × year end receivables ÷ credit sales. B is calculated adding bad debts to total receivables. D is calculated using total sales, not credit sales. C makes both mistakes.

5 D (Total sales × 2%) + $5,000. 'Without recourse' means that the factor carries the risk of the bad debts.

6 A C ignores the effect of the changes on the level of inventories and payables. B and D are wrong because they assume that the financing cost will increase not decrease.

Current level of receivables = $2m × $^{90}/_{365}$ = $493,151
New level of receivables = $2m × 80% × $^{30}/_{365}$ = $131,507

Current financing requirement = $500,000 + $493,150 – $30,000 = $963,150
New financing requirement = $400,000 + $131,507 – $24,000 = $507,507

Reduction in financing requirement = $963,150 – $507,507 = $455,643
Reduction in financing cost = $455,643 × 10% = $45,564 (round to $46,000)

7 B Return on discount = $\left(\frac{100}{100 - d}\right)^{\frac{12}{m}}$

where d = % size of the discount
m = reduction in payment period in months necessary to achieve discount

(see Formulae to learn in front pages)

Return on X's discount = $\left(\frac{100}{97}\right)^4 - 1 = 12.96\%$

Return on Y's discount = $\left(\frac{100}{96}\right)^3 - 1 = 13.02\%$

(Note that the formula here uses months rather than days. In this case, months is more accurate.)

8 Cost of discount = $(100/98)^{365/30} - 1$
= 27.86%

9 A As the current ratio is 2:1 the reduction of cash and payables by the same amount will increase the ratio. Payable days reduce the cash operating cycle, so if these are reduced, the cycle increases.

10 A Administrative costs, postage and quality control cost.

11 Optimal order size = 500 units

$$EOQ = \sqrt{\frac{2 \times \text{order cost} \times \text{demand}}{\text{holding cost}}}$$

$$EOQ = \sqrt{\frac{2 \times 200 \times 10{,}000}{\$4 + (3\% \times \$400)}}$$

EOQ = 500

12 $\sqrt{\frac{2 \times 15 \times 95{,}000}{3}} = \sqrt{950{,}000} = 975$

No. of orders = 95,000/975 = 98 orders

13 B Receivables at 31.3.X7 = 290,510/365 × 49 = 39,000

	$
Cash received is therefore:	
Opening receivables	22,000
Credit sales	290,510
Closing receivables	(39,000)
Cash received	273,510

14 B (70,000 + 10,000)/(88,000 + 7,000) = 0.84

15 D This option will reduce payables by more than the cash paid.

16 C

	$
Balance per TB	82,000
Irrecoverable debt	(12,250)
	69,750
3% impairment	(2,093)
Balance at 31 October 20X7	67,657

43 Objective test answers: Working capital management II

1

	$
90 days (345 + 150 – 200)	295
60 days	–
30 days (Invoice 420)	231
Current (Invoice 556)	319
Total	845

2 88 days

Inventory days ((360/1,400) × 365)	94
Receivables days ((290/2,400) × 365)	44
Payables days ((190/1,400) × 365)	(50)
	88

3 44 days

RECEIVABLES CONTROL ACCOUNT

	$		$
Opening balance	68,000	Returns	2,500
Sales	250,000	Cash received	252,100
		Write off*	3,400
	–	Balance	60,000
	318,000		318,000

* (68,000 × 5%)

Receivables days: 60/(500 –5) × 365 = 44.2
(Or you could use 60/(250 – 2.5) × 182.5)

4 B

		$
Cash sales	February 220,000 × 1.1 × 25%	60,500
Credit sales	December 220,000 × $\frac{1}{1.1}$ × 75% × 48%	72,000
	January 220,000 × 75% × 50%	82,500
		215,000

5 D The EOQ model can be used:

$$EOQ = \sqrt{\frac{(2C_oD)}{C_h}}$$

where EOQ = the reorder quantity
C_o = cost of making one order
C_h = holding cost per unit of inventory per year
D = usage in units per year

In this case:

$$EOQ = \sqrt{\frac{(2 \times 25 \times 10{,}000)}{0.50}}$$

= 1,000

6 D $$EOQ = \sqrt{\frac{(2 \times 100 \times 40{,}000)}{2}}$$

= 2,000

Since 40,000 wheels are required each year, 20 orders will be placed.

7 A $$EOQ = \sqrt{\frac{(2 \times 400 \times 160{,}000)}{8}}$$

= 4,000

Since 160,000 wheels are required each year, 40 orders will be placed.

Orders will therefore be placed every 52 ÷ 40 = 1.3 weeks.

8 D Although the purchasing manager may sanction payments to suppliers, the payment will normally be raised by the finance department.

9 B A standing order is the simplest method to use for regular fixed payments. It is preferred to a direct debit because the person making the payment retains control over the amount paid.

10 D A banker's draft cannot be stopped or cancelled once it is issued, and is effectively a cheque drawn on the bank. It is accepted by most people as being as good as cash, but has none of the inconvenience that cash would involve in a payment of this size.

11 172.7 days

Inventory days ((79 /139) × 365)	207.4
Receivables days ((52/270) × 365	70.3
Payables days ((40/139) × 365)	(105.0)
	172.7

12

	$
April credit sales (60,000 × 50% × 20%)	6,000
May credit sales (60,000 × 102% × 50% × 75%)	22,950
June cash sales (60,000 × 102% × 102% × 50%)	31,212
	60,162

13 C The entity will have **more** cash available but may have damaged its creditworthiness.

14 D A conservative policy makes the greatest use of long-term finance.

15 B The receivables will be sold at a profit to the selling company.

16 $540,000

	$'000
Expected cost of minor repairs ($3m x 14%)	420
Expected cost of major repairs ($12m x 1%)	120
Total expected cost	540

44 Objective test answers: Working capital management III

1 D Say current assets are $75,000

Current liabilities are $50,000

30% decrease in both will be $15,000. Current assets will then be $60,000, current liabilities $35,000, and current ratio will be 60:35 = 1.71. This is an increase of less than 30%.

2 D No cash movements have taken place, and inventory levels are the same.

3 D Greater inventory levels lessen the risk of running out of inventory.

4 B Change in payables = Purchases – Cash paid

15,000 = 360,000 – Cash paid
Cash paid = $345, 000

5 B The annual cash requirement is $120,000.

The interest cost of holding cash is 3% (5% – 2%)

$$\text{Optimum amount to transfer} = \sqrt{\frac{2 \times 120{,}000 \times 50}{0.03}} = 20{,}000$$

So $20,000 should be transferred in each transaction.

6 C Cash cycle = Inventory turnover + Receivables turnover – Payables turnover

$$= \left(\left(\frac{6}{36 \times 0.8}\right) \times 365\right) + \left(\left(\frac{8}{36}\right) \times 365\right) - \left(\left(\frac{3}{36 \times 0.8}\right) \times 365\right)$$

$$= 119 \text{ days}$$

7 A

$$\text{EOQ} = \sqrt{\frac{2C_0D}{C_h}}$$

$$= \sqrt{\frac{2 \times 10 \times 36{,}000}{2}}$$

$$= 600 \text{ units}$$

$$\text{No of orders} = \frac{36{,}000}{600}$$

$$= 60$$

8 C Non-current assets are sold. The other answers may have limited or no effect on working capital.

9 C Non-current assets are not part of working capital.

10 D $$\text{Spread} = 3\left[\frac{\frac{3}{4} \times \text{transaction cost} \times \text{variance of cash flows}}{\text{Interest rates}}\right]^{\frac{1}{3}}$$

$$= 3 \times \left(\frac{\frac{3}{4} \times 20 \times 250{,}000}{0.00025}\right)^{\frac{1}{3}}$$

$$= \$7{,}400$$

$$\text{Maximum level} = 7{,}400 + 1{,}000$$

$$= 8{,}400$$

11 B Inventory shortages are the most likely problem with JIT.

12 40.4%

Using the formula $(100/98.5)^{(365/16)} - 1$

$1.015^{22.813} - 1 = 40.4\%$

13 $$\text{EOQ} = \sqrt{\frac{2 \times 15}{1.2} \times 32{,}000} = \sqrt{800{,}000} = 894 \text{ units}$$

14

	$
Capital at maturity: 10,000 × 0.621* =	6,210
Interest: 700 over 5 years = 700 × 3.791 =	2,654
Market price	8,864

* Discount rate for 5 years at 10%

15 A EX will take into account the **cash received** on the disposal, the gain is not relevant.

16 $340,300

As purchases and sales accrue evenly over the year, we can take 60 days as the average inventory days and 50 days as the average payables days and use these to work out the closing inventory and closing payables as follows:

$$\text{Closing inventory: } \frac{(56 + \text{Closing inventory}) / 2}{350} \times 365 = 60$$

Closing inventory is therefore 59.

This gives cost of sales as follows.

	$'000
Opening inventory	56
Purchases (balancing figure)	353
Closing inventory	(59)
Coct of caloc	350

$$\text{Closing payables: } \frac{(42 + \text{Closing payables}) / 2}{353} \times 365 = 50$$

Closing payables are therefore 54.7

We can now calculate the amount paid.

PAYABLES

	$		$
Paid (balancing figure)	340,300	Opening balance	42,000
Closing balance	54,700	Purchases	353,000
	395,000		395,000

45 Section B answers: Working capital management I

(a) **Length of operating cycle** $= 365\left(\frac{\text{Average raw materials}}{\text{Purchases}} + \frac{\text{Average finished goods}}{\text{Cost of sales}} + \frac{\text{Average receivables}}{\text{Sales}} + \frac{\text{Average payables}}{\text{Purchases}}\right)$

$$= 365\left(\frac{0.5(55+80)}{850} + \frac{185}{1{,}830} + \frac{0.5(114+200)}{1{,}996} - \frac{0.5(50+70)}{850}\right)$$

= 29.0 days + 36.9 days + 28.7 days –25.8 days

= 68.8 days

(b)

Top tips. Make sure that you always read the question carefully. Note that sales are invoiced at the **end** of the month.

	October $'000	*November* $'000	*December* $'000	*January* $'000	*Total* $'000
Class A customers (W1)					
October sales			50	30	80
November sales				75	75
			50	105	155
Class B customers (W2)					
October sales		36	15	6	57
November sales			48	20	68
December sales				24	24
		36	63	50	149
Total cash received		36	113	155	304

Workings

1 *Class A customers*

October sales

50% received December $100,000 × 50% = $50,000

30% received January $100,000 × 30% = 30,000

November sales

50% received January $150,000 × 50% = $75,000

2 *Class B customers*

October sales

60% received November $60,000 × 60% = $36,000

25% received December $60,000 × 25% = $15,000

10% received January $60,000 × 10% = $6,000

November sales

60% received December $80,000 × 60% = $48,000

25% received January $80,000 × 25% = $20,000

December sales

60% received January $40,000 × 60% = $24,000

(c) (i) **Working capital management**

The **net working capital** of a business can be defined as its **current assets less** its **current liabilities**. The management of working capital is concerned with ensuring that **sufficient liquid resources** are **maintained** within the business. For the majority of businesses, particularly manufacturing businesses, trade payables will form the major part of the current liabilities figure.

Trade credit period

It follows that the **trade credit period** taken will be a major determinant of the working capital requirement of the company. This is calculated (in days) as the total value of **trade payables divided** by the level of **credit purchases** × 365.

Cash conversion cycle

A link can be made between working capital and liquidity by means of the **cash conversion cycle**. This measures the length of time that elapses between a firm **paying** for its **various purchases** and **receiving payment** for its **sales**. It can be calculated as the receivable days plus the inventory period less the trade credit period, and it measures the length of time for which net current assets must be financed.

(ii) **Use of trade credit**

For many firms, trade payables provide a very **important source** of **short-term credit**. Since very few companies currently impose interest charges on overdue accounts, taking extended credit can appear to be a very cheap form of short-term finance. However, such a policy entails some risks and costs that are not immediately apparent, as follows.

(1) If discounts are being forgone, the **effective cost** of this should be evaluated – it may be more beneficial to shorten the credit period and take the discounts.

(2) If the company gains a reputation for slow payment this will **damage its credit standing** and it may find it difficult to obtain credit from new suppliers in the future.

(3) Suppliers who are having to wait for their money may seek recompense in other ways, for example by raising prices or by placing a lower priority on new orders. Such actions could do **damage** to both the **efficiency and profitability** of the company.

(4) Suppliers may place the company **'on stop'** until the account is paid. This can jeopardise supplies of essential raw materials which in turn could cause production to stop: this will obviously provide the company with a high level of unwanted costs.

(d)

> **Examiner's comments.** Most candidates did well on this question. The most common error was not separately identifying the different categories of inventory, and including each in the correct calculation. A few candidates failed to deduct payables days.

154.5 days

Inventory days – raw materials = 111/641 × 365	63.2
Inventory days – WIP and finished goods = 165/898 × 365	67.0
Receivables days = 216/992 × 365	79.5
Payables days = 97/641 × 365	(55.2)
	154.5

(e)

Examiner's comments. Almost every candidate correctly calculated the Economic Order Quantity.

When calculating the likely extra cost/savings of increasing the order quantity to take advantage of the discount, almost all candidates omitted to calculate (or even consider) the increased inventory holding cost. Very few were able to correctly calculate the savings and advise accordingly. Most candidates advised not to accept the discount. Other candidates tried to advise BF without any calculation at all.

(i) $$\text{EOQ} = \sqrt{\frac{2\text{CoD}}{\text{Ch}}}$$

$$= \sqrt{\frac{2 \times 25 \times 65{,}000}{3}}$$

= 1,041 units

(ii) Total cost at order quantity 1,041 units

	$
Purchase price 65,000 × \$10	650,000
Order costs 65,000/1,041 × \$25	1,561
Holding costs 1,041/2 × \$3	1,562
	653,123

Total cost at order quantity of 2,000 units

	$
Purchase price 65,000 × \$10 × 98%	637,000
Order costs 65,000/2,000 × \$25	813
Holding costs 2,000/2 × \$3	3,000
	640,813

BF should accept the offer of the 2% discount as this decreases the total annual inventory cost.

(f)

Examiner's comments. The formulae for both models are given in the examination paper but many candidates found difficulty substituting the information in the question into the formulae. Candidates should be properly prepared for these simple mathematical calculations and should ensure they have a calculator which is capable of providing these functions.

(i) Optimal amount of bills to be sold under the Baumol model:

$$\sqrt{\frac{2 \times 420{,}000 \times 25}{0.073}} = 16{,}961$$

(ii) Optimal amount to sell under the Miller Orr model:

$$\text{Spread} = 3\left[\frac{75\% \times 25 \times 90{,}000}{0.0002}\right]^{1/3} = 6{,}107$$

$$\text{Amount to sell} = \frac{6{,}107}{3} = 2{,}036$$

(g)

> **Examiner's comments.** A significant number of candidates were able to correctly calculate the rate of interest being offered but came to the incorrect conclusion, assuming that it would cost DN more to accept the offer as the rate was higher than the overdraft.

We will calculate the value of the discount using the formula

$$\frac{100^{\frac{365}{t}}}{(100-d)}-1$$

This gives us 100/98 to the power of 365/30, minus 1

100/98 = 1.0204
365/30 = 12.1667

1.0204 ^ 12.1667 = 1.2786

Minus 1 gives 27.86%

The discount is therefore worth 27.86%

It is therefore to DN's advantage to pay 30 days earlier and obtain the discount, unless it has other investment opportunities yielding more than 27.86%. As it is only paying 10% on its overdraft, it would even be advantageous to borrow on overdraft, if necessary, in order to pay this supplier in 10 days.

(h)

> **Examiner's comments.** Many candidates spent too long on the question, writing far more than required for five marks.

Benefits

Possible benefits of a JIT purchasing system are as follows.

(i) Reduction of inventory holding costs.
(ii) Reduced manufacturing lead times.

Limitations

A JIT purchasing system has the following limitations.

(i) Not always appropriate. For example, running out of inventory in a hospital could prove fatal.
(ii) Large up-front costs of a full study of production methods.
(iii) Access to sizeable funds is required to run a JIT purchasing system.

Note. The examiner has stated that any other valid benefits or limitations would be given credit.

> **Alternative Answers**
>
> We have given five points here as the question is for five marks. You would also have scored marks for the following.
>
> **Benefits**
>
> - Improved labour productivity.
> - Reduced scrap/rework/warrant costs.
> - Elimination of poor quality production as scrapping work in progress and producing additional units can lead to time delays. Higher quality products will result in improved customer satisfaction.
> - Increased flexibility to supply small batches as production matches ultimate demand.
> - May help with the identification of weaknesses such as unreliable suppliers.

Limitations

- A JIT purchasing system requires long-term commitment to suppliers and so reduces flexibility in supplier choice.
- For JIT to work, suppliers must be able to regularly deliver materials of appropriate quality on time and at short notice.

(i)

Examiner's comments. Most candidates did not seem to know what an age analysis was or how to prepare one.

(i) Customer X – age analysis

	Current	*30 days*	*60 days*	*90 days*	*Total*
	$	$	$	$	$
Invoice AC913	233				233
Invoice AC690		204			204
Invoice AC112				160	160
	233	204	–	160	597

(ii)

- It highlights overdue amounts which the credit controller needs to chase up
- It highlights particular customers who may have a large outstanding balance and to whom no further goods should be delivered until the account is settled. If there is a possibility of a debt becoming irrecoverable, the credit controller will seek to minimise the size of the debt.

Alternative answers.

You would also have been given credit for the following.

- It draws attention to items which may be in dispute. For instance customer X above has only part paid invoice AC112 and the balance is now 90 days. This suggests that the balance of the invoice may be in dispute.
- It provides useful information for management accounting. For instance, if the cash flow forecast has been prepared on the basis of goods being paid for in the month following the month of sale and the age analysis shows that 70% of sales are paid after 60 days, the cash flow forecast will need to be revised.

46 Section B answers: Working capital management II

Top tips. These questions required little specialised knowledge, but you do have to be methodical and well-organised in your approach. You are given a lot of information so make sure you remember to underline or highlight key points as you read through.

Easy marks. The proforma for (b) is very simple here. In order to keep it simple, you should do separate workings, as we have. But show all the workings in full. The marker must be able to understand what you are doing. You can get the full 10 marks here and you should be able to get at least 3 marks on (c). So don't get bogged down in (a).

Examiner's comments. Part (a) was well done, but few candidates were able to calculate the forecast balance at 30 June. Part (b) was very well done. The main problem was with short course income calculation and remembering to include the cash balance brought forward. In Part (c) many students did not identify enough options for five marks or give sufficient detail for each option.

(a) (i) Trade receivables days outstanding = $\frac{34,100}{125,000} \times 365$

= 100 days

(ii) Trade receivables budgeted for 30 June 20X6

	$
Receivables at 31 December 20X5	34,100
6 months income (130,000/2)	65,000
Less: receipts (5 + 8 + 10 + 11 + 12 + 6)	(52,000)
Trade receivables at 30 June 20X6	47,100

Trade receivables days outstanding = $\frac{47,100}{65,000} \times 183$

= 133 days

(b) **Cash budget for January to June 20X6**

	Jan	Feb	Mar	Apr	May	June	Total
	$	$	$	$	$	$	$
Receipts							
Short training courses (W1)	667	2,533	3,600	4,267	5,466	5,467	22,000
In house courses	5,000	8,000	10,000	11,000	12,000	6,000	52,000
	5,667	10,533	13,600	15,267	17,466	11,467	74,000

	Jan	Feb	Mar	Apr	May	June	Total
	$	$	$	$	$	$	$
Expenditure							
Part time wages	0	2,500	4,000	4,000	5,000	6,000	21,500
Full time salaries	4,000	4,000	4,200	4,200	4,200	4,200	24,800
Rent	625			625			1,250
Short course expenses (W2)	0	300	450	450	600	600	2,400
In house course expenses	100	100	100	100	100	100	600
Overheads	1,500	600	600	1,500	600	600	5,400
Furniture				5,000			5,000
Computers					40,000		40,000
	6,225	7,500	9,350	15,875	50,500	11,500	100,950
Bank balance b/f	12,460	11,902	14,935	19,185	18,577	(14,457)	12,460
Net income/(expenditure)	(558)	3,033	4,250	(608)	(33,034)	(33)	(26,950)
Bank balance c/f	11,902	14,935	19,185	18,577	(14,457)	(14,490)	(14,490)

Workings

1 *Short training course receipts*

	Jan	*Feb*	*Mar*	*Apr*	*May*	*June*
Number of courses	0	2	3	3	4	4
Number of students per Course	0	10	12	12	14	13
Total number of students	0	20	36	36	56	52
	$	$	$	$	$	$
Income	0	2,000	3,600	3,600	5,600	5,200
Receipts – month in advance	667	1,200	1,200	1,867	1,733	2,000
Receipts – in month	–	1,333	2,400	2,400	3,733	3,467
	667	2,533	3,600	4,267	5,466	5,467

2 *Short course expenses*

	Jan	*Feb*	*Mar*	*Apr*	*May*	*June*	*July*
Number of courses	0	2	3	3	4	4	4
	$	$	$	$	$	$	$
Cost $150 per course	0	300	450	450	600	600	0

(c) The cash budget currently indicates that if the new technology is purchased in April and paid for in May as planned BB will exceed its agreed overdraft limit by $9,490. There are a variety of possible actions that BB could take in order make sufficient funds available for this purchase.

(i) An **increase in the overdraft facility** could be negotiated with the bank.

(ii) Negotiations could take place with the computer supplier to **spread the $40,000 payment** over a number of instalments.

(iii) BB could consider **leasing the computer equipment** rather than purchasing it

(iv) BB could take out a **short term loan** for the purchase of the computer equipment

(v) Purchase of the managing director's furniture could be **delayed** to free up $5,000 more funds

(vi) A strict policy of payment for short courses in the month before the course could be introduced in order to speed up cash receipts

(vii) Clearly slow paying receivables for in-house courses are a problem and a **cash discount** for payment within say one month compared to the budgeted position of 100 days in December and 133 days in June could be introduced.

(d)

Top tips. There is a lot of information provided in this question. Make sure you read through carefully, highlighting key or unusual items. Always be careful you answer the requirements in the narrative parts of the question.

Examiner's comments. Part (d) was generally well done as was part (g). Part (e) was not done at all well. Most candidates were not aware of the adjustments required to the cash flows as a result of the changes in the working capital policies.

Trade receivables days = 1,083/6,192 × 365 = 64 days
Trade payables days = 344/4,128 × 365 = 30 days
Inventory days = 1,020/4,128 × 365 = 90 days

(e) CK – CASH BUDGET FOR YEAR TO 31 MARCH 2007

	$'000	$'000
Receipts		
Revenue (6,192 × 97% × 110%)	6,607	
Additional receivables collection (1,083 – 815(W1))	268	
Total receipts		6,875
Payments		
Purchases (4,128/6,192 × 6,607)	4,404	
Reduction in inventory (1,020 × 40%)	(408)	
Increase in payables (437(W2) – 344)	(93)	
Purchase payments		(3,903)
Salaries and wages		(620)
Other operating expenses		(432)
Capital expenditure		(2,500)
Net payments		(580)
Cash balance at 31 March 20X6		622
Cash balance at 31 March 20X7		42

Workings

1 New receivables = 6,607 ÷ 365 × 45 = 815

2 New payables = (4,404 – 408) ÷ 365 × 40 = 437

(f) If CK decides to lease $1.5m of the non-current assets, there will be an immediate improvement in its cash budget for 20X7. As the payments are due prior to 1 April, it appears likely that it will have to pay two instalments in the year ending 31 March 20X7, but this will still be a saving of $700,000 (1,500 – 800). However, it will pay an additional $500,000 in financing over the term of the lease, which must be taken into consideration.

(g) **Customer relationships**

We are not told how the efficiency changes are to be achieved. However we can assume that the reduction in receivables days will be achieved by more energetic credit control. Any new or additional discounts offered would impact on the amount collectable, so we presume this is not the case. CK is in a market where there are plenty of competitors, and its customers are retail stores, who will also be seeking to maximise their payables days. Depending on the relationship it has with its customers, CK will be able to push tighter credit control just so far. It does not want customers deserting it for another supplier who will allow more liberal payment terms.

Supplier relationships

At the same time, CK is seeking to increase its payables days, so it is dealing with the same situation in reverse. There is no mention of loss of discounts, so we have to assume that is not an issue. If CK's suppliers are *willing* to wait 40 days for payment, then its relationship with them will not be affected by the change. It is important that CK retains the goodwill of its suppliers, as lower inventory levels will make it more dependent on suppliers delivering quickly.

Stock out

An inventory reduction of 40% will need to be carefully managed. If CK's customers require parts that it does not have in inventory, they are likely to go elsewhere. Computer spare parts will usually be required on an immediate basis – people want their systems to keep running. CK will need to have close supplier relationships in order to deal with this. It does not seem likely that suppliers will be willing to give this sort of service *and* wait longer to get paid.

Mock Exams

CIMA

Paper P7 (Managerial)

Financial Accounting and Tax Principles

Mock Exam 1

Question Paper		
Time allowed:	Reading time Answering question paper	**20 mins** **3 hours**
This paper is divided into three sections		
Section A	**Answer ALL sub-questions in this section**	
Section B	**Answer ALL of the six short answer questions**	
Section C	**Answer this ONE question**	

DO NOT OPEN THIS PAPER UNTIL YOU ARE READY TO START UNDER EXAMINATION CONDITIONS

SECTION A – 40 marks

Answer ALL sub-questions in this section

Question 1

1.1 A has a taxable profit of $100,000. The book depreciation was $10,000 and the tax allowable depreciation was $25,000. What was the accounting profit? **(2 marks)**

1.2 Company W makes an accounting profit of $300,000 during the year. This includes non-taxable income of $10,000 and depreciation of $35,000. In addition, $5,000 of the expenses are disallowable for tax purposes. If the tax allowable depreciation totals $30,000, what is the taxable profit?

A $290,000
B $295,000
C $300,000
D $310,000 **(2 marks)**

1.3 Which of the following is a source of tax rules?

A International accounting standards
B Supranational tax agreements
C Local company legislation
D Domestic accounting practice **(2 marks)**

1.4 In no more than 15 words, complete the following sentence:

'An indirect tax is one that ….' **(2 marks)**

1.5 Company E has sales of $230,000, excluding sales tax, in a period. Its purchases total $151,000, including sales tax. Purchases of $10,000 are zero rated. Sales tax is 17.5%. What is the sales tax payable for the period?

A $7,830
B $9,580
C $13,825
D $19,250 **(2 marks)**

1.6 A company is resident in Country A. It has a branch in Country B. The branch has taxable profits of $100,000, on which tax of $15,000 is paid. The tax rate in Country A is 20% and there is a double taxation treaty between Countries A and B that allows tax relief on the credit basis. If the company has total taxable profits, including those of the branch of $150,000, how much tax will it pay in Country A?

A $10,000
B $15,000
C $20,000
D $30,000 **(2 marks)**

1.7 A committee of the International Accounting Standards Board (IASB) is known as the IFRIC.

What does the IFRIC stand for?

A International Financial Reporting Issues Committee
B International Financial Recommendations and Interpretations Committee
C International Financial Reporting Interpretations Committee
D International Financial Reporting Issues Council **(2 marks)**

1.8 The IASB's *Framework for the Preparation and Presentation of Financial Statements (Framework)* lists the qualitative characteristics of financial statements.

Which THREE of the following are NOT included in the principle qualitative characteristics listed by the Framework?

1	Comparability	5	Understanding
2	Relevance	6	Matching
3	Prudence	7	Consistency
4	Reliability		

A 1, 3 and 7
B 1, 2 and 5
C 3, 6 and 7
D 3, 4 and 6 **(2 marks)**

1.9 Which of the following is NOT regarded as a related party of an entity by IAS 24 *Related party disclosures?*

A Directors of the entity
B A bank providing a loan to the entity
C The entity's employee pension fund
D A close relative of a director of the entity **(2 marks)**

1.10 IAS 10 *Events after the balance sheet date* distinguishes between adjusting and non-adjusting events.

Which of the following is an adjusting event?

A One month after the year end, a customer lodged a claim for $1,000,000 compensation. The customer claimed to have suffered permanent mental damage as a result of the fright she had when one of the entity's products malfunctioned and exploded. The outcome of the court case cannot be predicted at this stage.

B There was a dispute with the workers and all production ceased one week after the year end.

C A fire destroyed all of the entity's inventory in its furnished goods warehouse two weeks after the year end.

D Inventory valued at the year end at $20,000 was sold one month later for $15,000. **(2 marks)**

1.11 X signed a finance lease agreement on 1 October 20X2. The lease provided for five annual payments, in arrears, of $20,000. The fair value of the asset was agreed at $80,000.

Using the sum of digits method, how much should be charged to the income statement for the finance cost in the year to 30 September 20X3?

A $4,000
B $6,667
C $8,000
D $20,000 **(2 marks)**

1.12 D purchased a non-current asset on 1 April 20X0 for $200,000. The asset attracted writing down tax allowances at 25% on the reducing balance. Depreciation was 10% on the straight-line basis. Assume income tax is at 30%.

The deferred tax balance for this asset at 31 March 20X3 is:

A $9,000
B $16,688
C $27,000
D $55,625 **(2 marks)**

1.13 C started work on a contract to build a dam for a hydro-electric scheme. The work commenced on 24 October 20X1 and is scheduled to take four years to complete. C recognises profit on the basis of the certified percentage of work completed. The contract price is $10 million.

An analysis of C's records provided the following information:

Year to 30 September	*20X2*	*20X3*
Percentage of work completed and certified in year	30%	25%
	$'000	$'000
Total cost incurred during the year	2,900	1,700
Estimated cost of remaining work to complete contract	6,000	3,900
Total payments made for the cost incurred during the year	2,500	2,000

How much profit should C recognise in its income statement for the years ended:

	30 September 20X2	*30 September 20X3*
	$'000	$'000
A	100	375
B	330	375
C	330	495
D	500	825

(2 marks)

1.14 F's year end is 30 June. F purchased a non-current asset for $50,000 on 1 July 20X0.

Depreciation was provided at the rate of 20% per annum on the straight-line basis. There was no forecast residual value.

On 1 July 20X2, the asset was revalued to $60,000 and then depreciated on a straight-line basis over its remaining useful life which was unchanged. On 1 July 20X3, the asset was sold for $35,000.

In addition to the entries in the non-current asset account and allowance for depreciation account, which TWO of the following statements correctly record the entries required on disposal of the non-current asset?

1 Debit income statement with a loss on disposal of $5,000.
2 Credit income statement with a gain on disposal of $25,000.
3 Transfer $60,000 from revaluation reserve to retained earnings as a movement on reserves.
4 Transfer $30,000 from revaluation reserve to retained earnings as a movement on reserves.
5 Transfer $30,000 from revaluation reserve to income statement.
6 Transfer $60,000 from revaluation reserve to income statement.

A 1 and 4
B 2 and 3
C 1 and 5
D 2 and 6

(2 marks)

1.15 S announced a rights issue of 1 for every 5 shares currently held, at a price of $2 each. S currently has 2,000,000 $1 ordinary shares with a quoted market price of $2.50 each. Directly attributable issue costs amounted to $25,000.

Assuming all rights are taken up and all money paid in full, how much will be credited to the share premium account for the rights issue?

A $200,000
B $308,333
C $375,000
D $400,000

(2 marks)

1.16 A company has a current ratio of 2.3 and a quick ratio (or acid test) of 0.8.

If it increases its overdraft in order to buy more inventory as a cash purchase, what will happen to the company's current ratio and quick ratio as a result of this transaction?

	Current ratio	*Quick ratio*
A	Increase	Increase
B	Increase	Decrease
C	Decrease	Increase
D	Decrease	Decrease

(2 marks)

1.17 Which of the following is LEAST LIKELY to characterise overtrading?

A Increased borrowing

B Increased cash balances

C Increased turnover

D Reduced working capital

(2 marks)

1.18 Which of the following is LEAST RELEVANT to the simple economic order quantity (EOQ) model for inventory?

A Safety inventory

B Annual demand

C Holding costs

D Order costs

(2 marks)

1.19 Which of the following most appropriately describes *forfaiting*?

A It is a method of providing medium-term export finance.

B It provides short-term finance for purchasing non-current assets which are denominated in a foreign currency.

C It provides long-term finance to importers.

D It is the forced surrender of a share due to the failure to make a payment on a partly paid share.

(2 marks)

1.20 Which of the following is likely to have the LOWEST expected rate of return?

A Unsecured bank loan.

B Preference shares.

C Secured loan stock.

D Equity shares.

(2 marks)

(Total for Section A = 40 marks)

SECTION B – 30 marks

Answer ALL six sub-questions

Question 2

(a) At the beginning of the accounting period, D had a credit balance of $40,000 on its current tax account, which was paid during the period. The opening balance on the deferred tax account was $250,000 credit.

The provision for tax for the current period is $50,000 and the balance on the deferred tax account is to be reduced to $225,000.

Required

Prepare extracts from the income statement, balance sheet and notes to the accounts.

(Total for sub-question (a) = 5 marks)

(b) IAS 12 *Income taxes* requires entities to publish an explanation of the relationship between taxable income and accounting profit. This can take the form of a numerical reconciliation between the tax expense and the product of the accounting profit and the applicable tax rate. Explain why this explanation is helpful to the readers of financial statements.

(Total for sub-question (b) = 5 marks)

(c) Discuss the usefulness of the audit report to a potential investor.

(Total for sub-question (c) = 5 marks)

(d) K Co has a minimum cash balance of $20,000. The variance of its daily cash flows is $2,250,000. It has a transaction cost of $100 for each purchase or sale of securities and the interest rate is 0.025 per cent per day.

Using the Miller-Orr model, calculate the upper limit for cash balances and the return point.

(Total for sub-question (d) = 5 marks)

(e) What are the advantages of (i) centralised and (ii) decentralised purchasing?

(Total for sub-question (e) = 5 marks)

(f) IAS 8 *Accounting policies, changes in accounting estimates and errors* distinguishes between accounting policies and accounting estimates. Explain the distinction between accounting policies and accounting estimates, give an example of each and explain their treatment under IAS 8.

(Total for sub-question (f) = 5 marks)

(Total for Section B = 30 marks)

SECTION C – 30 marks

Answer this ONE question

Question 3

HI, listed on its local stock exchange, is a retail organisation operating several retail outlets. A reorganisation of the entity was started in 20X2 because of a significant reduction in profits. This reorganisation was completed during the current financial year.

The trial balance for HI at 30 September 20X3 was as follows:

	$'000	$'000
10% preference shares of $1 each fully paid		500
10% loan notes (redeemable 20Y0)		1,000
Retained earnings at 30 September 20X2		1,390
Administrative expenses	615	
Bank and cash	1,359	
Buildings	11,200	
Preference shares: issue costs	50	
Cash received on disposal of equipment		11
Cost of goods sold	3,591	
Distribution costs	314	
Equipment and fixtures	2,625	
Interest paid on loan notes – half year to 31 March 20X3	50	
Interim ordinary dividend paid	800	
Preference dividend paid	50	
Inventory at 30 September 20X3	822	
Investment income received		37
Available-for-sale investments at market value 30 September 20X2	492	
Ordinary shares of $1 each, fully paid		4,000
Provision for deferred tax		256
Provision for reorganisation expenses at 30 September 20X2		1,010
Allowances for depreciation at 30 September 20X2		
Buildings		1,404
Equipment and fixtures		1,741
Reorganisation expenses	900	
Revaluation reserve		172
Sales revenue		9,415
Share premium		2,388
Trade payables		396
Trade receivables	852	
	23,720	23,720

Additional information provided

(a) The reorganisation expenses relate to a comprehensive restructuring and reorganisation of the entity that began in 20X2. HI's financial statements for 20X2 included a provision for reorganisation expenses of $1,010,000. All costs had been incurred by the year end, but an invoice for $65,000, received on 2 October 20X3, remained unpaid and is not included in the trial balance figures. No further restructuring and reorganisation costs are expected to occur and the provision is no longer required.

(b) Available for sale investments are carried in the financial statements at market value. The market value of the available-for-sale investments at 30 September 20X3 was $522,000. There were no movements in the investments held during the year.

(c) On 1 November 20X3, HI was informed that one of its customers, X, had ceased trading. The liquidators advised HI that it was very unlikely to receive payment of any of the $45,000 due from X at 30 September 20X3.

(d) Another customer is suing for damages as a consequence of a faulty product. Legal advisers are currently advising that the probability of HI being found liable is 75%. The amount payable is estimated to be the full amount claimed of $100,000.

(e) The income tax due for the year ended 30 September 20X3 is estimated at $1,180,000 and the deferred tax provision needs to be increased to $281,000.

(f) During the year, HI disposed of old equipment for $11,000. The original cost of this equipment was $210,000 and accumulated depreciation at 30 September 20X2 was $205,000. HI's accounting policy is to charge no depreciation in the year of the disposal.

(g) Depreciation is charged using the straight-line basis on non-current assets as follows.

Buildings	3%
Equipment and fixtures	20%

Depreciation is regarded as a cost of sales.

(h) The preference shares were issued on 1 October 20X2 and are redeemable at par on 30 September 20X5. Issue costs were $50,000 and the effective interest rate is 14.4%.

Required

Prepare the income statement and a statement of recognised income and expense for HI for the year to 30 September 20X3 and a balance sheet at that date, in a form suitable for presentation to the shareholders, in accordance with the requirements of International Accounting Standards.

Notes to the financial statements are **not** required. **(30 marks)**

(Total for Section C = 30 marks)

Answers

DO NOT TURN THIS PAGE UNTIL YOU HAVE COMPLETED MOCK EXAM 1

A plan of attack

As you turned the page to start this exam any one of a number of things could have been going through your mind. Some of them may have been quite sensible, some of them may not.

The main thing to do is take a deep breath and do not panic. It's best to sort out a plan of attack before the actual exam so that when the invigilator tells you that you can begin and the adrenaline kicks in you are using every minute of the three hours wisely.

Your approach

This paper has three sections. The first section contains 16–20 multiple choice questions which are compulsory. The second has six short compulsory questions. The third has one compulsory question 30 marks.

OTs first again

However you find the paper, chances are you should **start with the objective test questions**. You should be able to do at least a few and answering them will give you a boost. **Don't even look at the other questions before doing Section A**. Remember how long to allocate to the OTs? That's right, 72 minutes.

You then have a **choice**.

- Read through and answer Section B before moving on to Section C
- Read the question in Section C, answer it and then go back to Section B

Time spent at the start of each Section B and the Section C question confirming the requirements and producing a plan for the answers is time well spent.

Doing the exam

Actually doing the exam is a personal experience. There is not a single *right way.* As long as you submit complete answers to the MCQs in Section A, the six Section B questions and the one question in Section C, your approach obviously works.

One approach

Having done or guessed at the MCQs, I would work straight through Section B. The possible pitfall would be getting sucked too deeply into Section B and leaving insufficient time for Section C.

So lets look at the Section B questions in the paper:

- Question (a) is a straightforward calculation of income tax liability. It would be a good idea to begin by putting the information into T accounts. Then the information just needs to be correctly presented. This can easily be done in 9 minutes.
- Question (b) is a discussion question on the relationship of accounting profit to taxable profit. Make a few notes before you start.
- Question (c) is a trap. You can probably think of lots of things to say about this and the worst thing you can do is to start writing them all down. You have 9 minutes for this, no more. Your plan (and you must have one) should be something like: 1. Limitations on its usefulness 2. Ways in which its usefulness is overestimated. Then think of the valid points you want to make in these two areas and make them briefly. Our answer does not use bullet points, but that would have been an equally valid approach.
- Question (d) is a gift. You are given the formula. Set your calculation out neatly and double-check your workings.
- Question (e) is crying out for bullet points and your answer will probably be similar to ours. The use of bullet points will save you from dangerous waffling.

- Question (f) is difficult and requires a good knowledge of IAS 8. If you had trouble with it, do revise this, as it could well come up.

Having hacked your way through Section B, taking no more than 9 minutes per question, you should now be left with 54 minutes to do your Section C question. This is worth 30 marks and you must aim to secure as many of them as possible. Read the question **twice** if you need to.

For the Section C Question you must proceed in a methodical way. Set out your format and then work through the question requirements, doing neat, readable calculations and fill out the figures. Even if you do not finish, you will get marks for what you have done, so do the easy bits first.

Time allocation

Be disciplined. Allocate your time according to the marks available but never go over the time allocation. The last few marks in a question are the hardest to earn.

Be sure to follow the requirements. If four advantages are required, give four. No extra credit will be given for five. Two advantages will only get you half marks.

Answer all of the question. Having a go at every part of all the Section B questions you are required to do will put you in a better position to pass than, say, only doing five questions. However difficult that sixth question seems at first there are marks to be earned.

If you have time left at the end of the exam ensure that you have attempted every part of every question. If you have, then scan through and ensure you complete any part of an answer you left earlier. Use the full three hours working towards a pass.

Marking the exam

When you mark your exam, be honest. Don't be too harsh though. Give yourself credit for the things you did well, but don't kid yourself with 'I would have done that in the real exam'. It may be worth your while making two lists; strengths and weaknesses.

Strengths will be areas of the syllabus you are confident with and also good exam technique. (Maybe you produced correct income statement and balance sheet formats.)

Weaknesses will be holes in your knowledge and poor exam technique (maybe you ran out of time and couldn't answer all the requirements of the last question).

Making this list will help you focus your last days of revision on the areas which require attention whilst reminding you of the areas you excel in.

SECTION A

Question 1

1.1

	$
Taxable profit	100,000
Less: depreciation	10,000
	90,000
Add: tax allowable depreciation	25,000
Accounting profit	115,000

1.2 The correct answer is C.

	$	$
Accounting profit		300,000
Add: depreciation	35,000	
disallowed expenses	5,000	
		40,000
		340,000
Less: non-taxable income	10,000	
tax allowable depreciation	30,000	40,000
Taxable profit		300,000

1.3 The correct answer is B. Supranational tax agreements (eg the EU rules on sales tax) are a source of tax rules. The other options are all sources of accounting rules.

1.4 An indirect tax is one that charges tax indirectly on the final consumer of the goods or services.

1.5 The correct answer is D.

	$
Output tax (230,000 x 17.5%)	40,250
Input tax ((151,000 – 10,000)/117.5 × 17.5)	21,000
Payable	19,250

1.6 The correct answer is B.

Total tax due is $30,000 ($150,000 x 20%) less double taxation relief of $15,000 (less than $100,000 x 20%), leaves $15,000 to pay.

1.7 C International Financial Reporting Interpretations Committee

1.8 C Qualitative characteristics

- Relevance
- Reliability
- Understandability
- Comparability

1.9 B IAS 24 specifically states that 'providers of finance' are not related parties 'simply by virtue of their normal dealings with an entity'.

1.10 D The subsequent sale provides evidence of the net realisable value of the inventory as at the year end.

1.11 B $\$(100{,}000 - 80{,}000) \times \frac{5}{5+4+3+2+1} = \$20{,}000 \times \frac{5}{15}$

$= \$6{,}667$

1.12 B *WDA*

	$	*Capital allowance* $
Cost 1.4 X0	200,000	
WDA 25%	50,000	50,000
WDV 31.3 X1	150,000	
WDA 25%	(37,500)	37,500
WDV 31.3 X2	112,500	
WDA 25%	(28,125)	28,125
WDV 31.3 X3	84,375	
Capital allowances claimed		115,625
Depreciation w/off 3 yrs @ 10% straight line		60,000
Accelerated allowances		55,625
Tax rate		× 30%
		16,688

1.13 C

	20X2 $'000	*20X3* $'000
Costs to date	2,900	4,600
Costs to complete	6,000	3,900
Estimated total cost	8,900	8,500
Projected profit	1,100	1,500
Contract price	10,000	10,000
Completed	30%	55%
Cumulative profit	330	825
Profit recognised	330	495

1.14 A

	Non-current asset $	*Revaluation reserve* $
Cost 1.7.X0	50,000	
Depreciation to 1.7.X2 20% × 2 yrs	20,000	
Book value 1.7.X2	30,000	
Revaluation increase	30,000	30,000
New carrying value 1.7.X3	60,000	
Depreciation: 1/3	20,000	
Value at 1.7.X3	40,000	
Disposal proceeds	35,000	
Loss on disposal	5,000	

1.15 C Number of shares issued:

$$\frac{2,000,000}{5} = 400,000 \text{ shares}$$

	$
Issue price	2
Nominal value	1
Premium	1

	$
∴ Total premium	400,000
Less issue costs	25,000
Net to share premium	375,000

1.16 D Say current assets are $230, current liabilities are $100 and inventory is $150 (hence current assets excluding inventory are $80).

Say overdraft is increased by $20 to pay for $20 inventory

New current ratio = 230 + 20: 100 + 20 = 2.08. Current ratio has decreased.

New quick ratio = 80: 100 + 20 = 0.67. Quick ratio has decreased.

1.17 B Increased cash balances, Overtrading will generally result in a shortage of cash.

1.18 A Safety inventory. B – D are all terms in the EOQ formula.

1.19 A Forfaiting is a method of providing medium-term export finance.

1.20 C Secured loan stock will have the lowest return, because it has the lowest risk due to the security.

SECTION B

Question 2

(a)

	$
Income Statement (extract)	
Tax expense (Note 1)	25,000
Balance Sheet (extract)	
Current liabilities	
Tax payable	50,000
Non-current liabilities	
Deferred tax (Note 2)	225,000

Notes to the financial statements

1 *Tax expense*

	$
Provision for the current period	50,000
Decrease in deferred tax provision	(25,000)
	25,000

2 *Deferred tax*

	$
Balance brought forward	250,000
Decrease in provision	(25,000)
Balance carried forward	225,000

(b) In many sets of financial statements, there **may appear to be little relationship** between the figure reported as the profit before tax and the actual tax charge that appears in the income statement. In a simple tax system, the tax charge would be the reported profit multiplied by the tax rate. However this will not normally be the case in real life, due to the complexities of the tax system and the estimates and subjective decisions that the directors must make in estimating the tax charge for the year.

The purpose of the reconciliation between the actual tax charge and the reported profit multiplied by the standard rate of tax is to highlight to the users of the financial statements these estimates and judgements. This reconciliation should **clarify the effect of adjustments** such as changes in tax rates, estimated tax charges differing from final agreed tax liabilities and other factors that have affected the amount that appears as the tax charge in the income statement.

(c) **Types of report**

Any potential investor will of course examine a company's latest set of audited accounts and will expect to see an unqualified audit report. If the report is **qualified** she/he will ask further questions. If it is a disclaimer or an adverse report, he will probably decide to invest elsewhere.

Unqualified reports

So, assuming that the report is unqualified, how useful will it be to him? The audit report is the expression of the auditor's **opinion**. The auditor has given his opinion that the accounts present fairly the financial position of the company and comply with the relevant legislation and accounting standards. The report will state that he has sought to obtain 'reasonable assurance' that the accounts are free from 'material misstatement'.

The reason he auditor feels able to give nothing more than 'reasonable assurance' is that he did not prepare the accounts and he will not have had time to examine all of the transactions. The auditor will begin by testing the internal control system. If the internal controls appear to be effective, he will reduce the time spent on substantive testing. If fraud or errors are well-hidden, and the auditor's suspicions have not been aroused, the chances of him stumbling across the discrepancy are not that high.

Other matters

While the auditor will certainly give attention to any going concern issues, the audit report cannot be taken as any guarantee of the future viability of the entity. Nor does it assure the effectiveness or efficiency of management. These are probably the two factors which most interest an investor. The audit report is a **useful addition** to whatever other information the investor is able to obtain, but the above points mean that it cannot be used to frame an investment decision.

(d) Using the Miller-Orr model, the spread between the upper and lower cash limits will be:

$$3\left(\frac{\frac{3}{4}\times 100\times 2{,}250{,}000}{0.00025}\right)^{\frac{1}{3}} = \$26{,}314$$

As the minimum cash balance is $20,000, the maximum balance will be $46,314.

$$\text{Return point} = \text{lower limit} + {}^{1}/_{3} \times \text{spread} = \$20{,}000 + \left(\frac{26{,}314}{3}\right) = \$28{,}771$$

(e) (i) **Centralised purchasing**

- The firm will be buying in larger quantities and so will be able to negotiate more substantial discounts.
- The organisation as a whole should be able to arrange more favourable credit terms than an individual branch
- Inventory handling functions will be mainly centralised, which should save costs.
- It should be possible to hold lower overall levels of inventory than if inventory was being held at each branch. This will reduce holding costs.
- Only one buying department will be needed, which will save staff costs.

(ii) **Decentralised purchasing**

- Local branches will be more in control of their production and sales if they have local control of purchasing.
- The purchasing requirements of individual branches may vary. For instance, some lines of inventory may sell better in some areas than others.
- Local branches will be able to form their own relationships with suppliers. There may be a higher level of co-operation between a smaller organisation and its supplier.
- A local branch can be made more accountable for its own profitability and cash if it has control of its own purchasing function.

(f) **Accounting policies**

Accounting policies are defined in IAS 8 as the 'specific principles, bases, conventions, rules and practices adopted by an entity in preparing and presenting financial statements'. In practice, accounting policies are formulated by reference to the appropriate IAS or IFRS. They should be applied consistently from one period to the next and for all similar transactions within a period.

An example of an accounting policy would be that non-current assets are held at historical cost and depreciated over their useful lives.

Accounting estimates

In applying an accounting policy, it is often necessary to make estimates. When a non-current asset is purchased, its expected life can only be estimated. An entity may have to estimate the expected level of bad debts, the possibility of some of its inventory becoming obsolescent, the fair value of assets and liabilities.

An example of an accounting estimate would be the method by which an asset was depreciated – this is the means by which the accounting policy of depreciation is applied. So a change from straight-line to reducing balance depreciation would be accounted for as a change of accounting estimate.

Changes

Changes of accounting policy are relatively rare and should be accounted for using **retrospective restatement**. The corresponding figures for previous periods are restated, so that the new policy is applied to transactions and events as if it had always been in use. Changes of accounting estimate are accounted for using **prospective restatement** – the change of estimate is applied to the current period and to future periods if they are affected.

SECTION C

Question 3

> **Text references.** The treatment of preference shares is covered in Chapter 11: *Distributable profits and capital transactions*. Provisions are dealt with in Chapter 9: *Miscellaneous standards*.
>
> **Top tips**. As with all Section C questions, read the requirements carefully. Notes to the accounts are not required, so you should not have wasted time preparing them. However workings need to be clear and almost a substitute for notes, for example non-current assets. The preference shares may have worried you – if so, you should have left them to the end and concentrated on the areas where you felt most confident first.
>
> **Easy marks**. Property, plant and equipment workings are important as they affect both the income statement and balance sheet, so do these carefully. You may have had trouble with the reorganisation costs and the tax but, once you had handled property, plant and equipment, the rest of the income statement and balance sheet would give you plenty of easy marks. The statement of recognised income and expense was very easy if you know the format – remember it is basically gains/losses recognised directly in equity plus profit/loss for the period.

HI

INCOME STATEMENT FOR THE YEAR ENDED 30 SEPTEMBER 20X3

	$'000
Revenue	9,415
Cost of sales (W2)	(4,410)
Gross profit	5,005
Distribution costs	(314)
Administrative expenses (W3)	(760)
Reorganisation costs overprovision (W4)	45
Profit on disposal of asset (W1)	6
Finance cost (W5)	(165)
Investment income	37
Profit before tax	3,854
Income tax expense (W6)	(1,205)
Profit for the period	2,649

HI

STATEMENT OF RECOGNISED INCOME AND EXPENSE FOR THE YEAR ENDED 30 SEPTEMBER 20X3

	$'000
Available-for-sale investments:	
Valuation gain taken to equity	30
Net profit for the period	2,649
Total recognised income and expense for the period	2,679

HI

BALANCE SHEET AS AT 30 SEPTEMBER 20X3

	$'000	$'000
Assets		
Non current assets		
Property, plant and equipment (W1)		9,856
Available-for-sale investments (W7)		522
		10,378
Current assets		
Inventory	822	
Receivables (852 – 45)	807	
Cash at bank and in hand	1,359	
		2,988
		13,366

	$'000	$'000
Equity and liabilities		
Equity		
Ordinary shares of $1 each	4,000	
Share premium	2,388	
Revaluation reserve (W7)	202	
Retained earnings (1,390 + 2,649 – 800)	3,239	
		9,829
Non current liabilities		
Interest bearing borrowing	1,000	
Amount due on preference shares (W8)	415	
Deferred tax	281	
Other provisions (W3)	100	
		1,796
Current liabilities		
Trade payables	396	
Taxation	1,180	
Amount due on preference shares (W8)	50	
Accruals: restructuring (W4)	65	
loan note interest (W5)	50	
		1,741
		13,366

Workings

1 *Property, plant and equipment*

	Buildings $'000	*Equipment and fixtures* $'000	*Total* $'000
Cost			
Opening balance	11,200	2,625	13,825
Additions			–
Disposals		(210)	(210)
	11,200	2,415	13,615
Accumulated depreciation			
Opening balance	1,404	1,741	3,145
On disposals		(205)	(205)
Charge for year			
• $11,200 × 3%	336		} 819
• $2,415 × 20%		483	
Closing balance	1,740	2,019	3,759
Net book value	9,460	396	9,856

Profit on disposal:

	$'000	$'000
Sale proceeds		11
Net book value		
Cost	210	
Accumulated depreciation	205	
		5
Profit		6

2 *Cost of sales*

	$'000
Per trial balance	3,591
Depreciation (W1)	819
	4,410

3 *Administrative expenses*

	$'000
Per trial balance	615
Bad debt written off (Note 1)	45
Provision for legal claim re faulty product (Note 2)	100
	760

Notes

1 Although the customer went into liquidation after the year end, this provides additional evidence of conditions existing at the balance sheet date. It is thus an adjusting event under IAS 10.

2 The obligation is probable, therefore a provision must be made.

4 *Reorganisation costs*

	$'000	$'000
Provision in 20X2 accounts		1,010
Reorganisation expenses	900	
Invoice received after y/e	65	
		965
Provision surplus		45

5 *Finance cost*

Loan notes:

	$'000
Per trial balance: half year to 31 March 20X3	50
Accrual for six months to 30 September 20X3: 10% × $1m × 6/12	50
Preference shares – finance cost (W8)	65
	165

6 *Taxation*

	$'000	$'000
Income tax payable		1,180
Deferred tax		
Provision b/fwd	256	
Provision required	281	
∴ Increase required		25
Charge to income statement		1,205

7 *Investments and revaluation reserve*

	Investments	*Revaluation reserve*
	$'000	$'000
Per trial balance	492	172
Revaluation of investments to market value	30	30
	522	202

8 *Preference shares*

	$'000
Cash received 1.10.X2 (500 – 50)	450
Interest to 30.9.X3 @ 14.4%	65
Dividend paid	(50)
Balance at 30.9.X3	465
Interest to 30.9.X4	67
Dividend paid	(50)
Balance at 30.9.X4	482
Interest to 30.9.X5 (rounded)	68
Dividend paid	(50)
Redemption amount	500
Current liability	
Amount due on preference shares	50
Non-current liability	
Amount due on preference shares (465 – 50)	415
Finance charge to 30.9.X3	65

CIMA

Paper P7 (Managerial)

Financial Accounting and Tax Principles

Mock Exam 2

Question Paper		
Time allowed:	Reading time Answering question paper	**20 mins** **3 hours**
This paper is divided into three sections		
Section A	**Answer ALL sub-questions in this section**	
Section B	**Answer ALL of the six short answer questions**	
Section C	**Answer this ONE question**	

DO NOT OPEN THIS PAPER UNTIL YOU ARE READY TO START UNDER EXAMINATION CONDITIONS

SECTION A – 40 marks

Answer ALL sub-questions in this section

Question 1

1.1 Sometimes interest payments may be treated for tax purposes as if they were dividends. What is the name of this rule? **(2 marks)**

1.2 Which of the following statements most closely defines double taxation relief?

A The group is treated as one entity for tax purposes
B Losses of one group member can be offset against the profits of another.
C Capital gains tax is deferred until an asset is sold outside the group.
D Tax paid by a company in one country is offset against the tax due in another country. **(2 marks)**

1.3 Company T has sales of $230,000, including sales tax, in a period. Its purchases, excluding sales tax, total $180,000, of which $20,000 are zero-rated. Sales tax is 15%. What is the sales tax payable for the period?

A $6,000
B $6,522
C $10,500
D $11,022 **(2 marks)**

1.4 Company P makes an accounting loss of $320,000 during the year. This includes non-taxable income of $20,000 and depreciation of $33,000. In addition, $40,000 of the expenses are disallowable for tax purposes. If the tax allowable depreciation totals $45,000, what is the taxable amount?

A $182,000 loss
B $300,000 loss
C $312,000 loss
D $328,000 loss **(2 marks)**

1.5 Which of the following items are taxable temporary differences, according to IAS 12 *Income taxes?*

1 Capitalised development costs being amortised in the income statement, but deducted in full from taxable profit as incurred

2 Interest received in arrears and time apportioned for accounting purposes, but included in taxable profit on a cash basis

3 Tax allowances for capital expenditure exceeding depreciation charged in accounts

A All three items
B 1 and 2 only
C 1 and 3 only
D 2 and 3 only **(2 marks)**

1.6 An asset has to meet two recognition criteria before being recognised in financial statements. One of these is the probability that future economic benefits will flow to the entity. The other criterion is:

A The asset has a cost or value that can be measured reliably
B The future economic benefits will be received within the current accounting period
C The future economic benefits can be reliably measured
D The asset has an open market value **(2 marks)**

1.7 Which of the following are covered by the auditors' report?

1 Cash flow statement
2 Statement of recognised income and expense
3 Notes to the income statement and balance sheet

A All three are covered.
B 1 and 2 only
C 2 and 3 only
D 1 and 3 only **(2 marks)**

1.8 IAS 1 *Presentation of financial statements* defines the classification of liabilities as current or non-current.

Which of the following liabilities should be included within current liabilities in the balance sheet?

1 Loan notes issued five years ago, due for repayment within one year, which have been agreed to be refinanced on a long-term basis before the financial statements are approved

2 Trade payables due for settlement more than twelve months after the balance sheet date, within the normal course of the operating cycle

3 Trade payables due for settlement within twelve months after the balance sheet date, within the normal course of the operating cycle

4 Bank overdrafts

A All four items
B 1, 3 and 4 only
C 1 and 2 only
D 2, 3 and 4 only **(2 marks)**

1.9 Which of these items may appear in a company's statement of total recognised income and expense, according to IAS 1 *Presentation of financial statements?*

1 Profit for the financial year
2 Dividends paid
3 Unrealised revaluation gains and losses
4 New share capital subscribed

A 1, 2 and 4
B 1, 3 and 4
C 1 and 3 only
D All four items **(2 marks)**

1.10 Which one or more of the following statements about IAS 38 *Intangible assets* are correct?

1 Research expenditure, other than capital expenditure on buildings and equipment for research purposes, must be written off as incurred.

2 All companies must disclose in their financial statements the total amount spent on research and development and recognised as an expense during the period.

3 If development expenditure is capitalised, it must be amortised over a period not exceeding five years.

A 1 only
B 1 and 2
C 2 and 3
D 1 and 3 **(2 marks)**

1.11 The following figures apply to a construction contract at the end of the first year:

	$'000
Total contract price	36,000
Costs to date	10,000
Expected costs to completion	20,000
Cash received from customer	24,000

What amounts will be included as attributable profit in the income statement and shown under *amounts due to customers* in the balance sheet?

	Profit	*Amounts due to customers*
	$'000	$'000
A	16,000	14,000
B	6,000	14,000
C	2,000	12,000
D	6,000	12,000

(2 marks)

1.12 Which of the following statements about IAS 17 *Leases* are correct?

1. A finance lease is one which transfers substantially all the risks and rewards of the ownership of an asset to a lessee.
2. A leased asset should be depreciated over the shorter of the lease term and the useful life of the asset.
3. All obligations under finance leases will appear in the balance sheet under the heading of 'Current liabilities'.
4. An asset held on an operating lease should appear in the lessee's balance sheet as a non-current asset and be depreciated over the term of the lease.

A 1 and 3 only
B 1 and 2 only
C 2 and 4 only
D All four statements are correct **(2 marks)**

1.13 An asset with a fair value of $15,400 is acquired under a finance lease on 1 January 20X1 with a deposit on that date of $4,000 and four further annual payments in arrears of $4,000 each. The interest rate implicit in the lease is 15%.

What figure would appear in the balance sheet at 31 December 20X1 under the heading of current liabilities?

A $2,634
B $4,000
C $6,476
D $9,110 **(2 marks)**

1.14 Which of the following is a non-adjusting post balance sheet event in accordance with IAS 10 for financial statements prepared to 30 June 20X6 and approved on 3 October 20X6?

A Final agreement of the price for the sale of a building which had been under contract since 28 June 20X6

B Receipt of the financial statements for the year ended 31 May 20X6 of an unlisted company in which the business owns 10% of the share capital showing that it is going into liquidation

C A decision made on 1 July 20X6 to close a division of the business which made significant losses in the year ending 30 June 20X6

D Information showing that a long-term contract on which profit had been taken in the year ending 30 June 20X6 will in fact not be profitable due a defect in materials used in January 20X6 **(2 marks)**

1.15 According to IAS 24 *Related party disclosures*, which of the following would not be a related party of Garo?

A An associated undertaking of Garo
B The managing director of Garo's parent company
C A company in which Garo holds a 10% investment
D Garo's pension fund for its employees **(2 marks)**

1.16 Which of the following factors would a bank be LEAST LIKELY to take into account when deciding whether to lend money to a company?

A The purpose of the loan
B The amount of the loan
C The duration of the loan
D The currency in which the loan is denominated **(2 marks)**

1.17 Which of the following investments would not be appropriate for a company with a temporary cash surplus of approximately one week?

A Local authority deposits
B Money market lending arranged directly
C Treasury bills
D Convertible loan stock **(2 marks)**

1.18 A 9% bond has a face value of $100 and its current market price is $120. What is the interest yield? **(2 marks)**

1.19 The following figures are taken from the balance sheet of GEN:

	$m
Inventories	2
Receivables	3
Cash	1
Payables	3
5 year bank loan	3

What is the current ratio?

A 1.33
B 2.00
C 1.00
D 0.33 **(2 marks)**

1.20 A company has a current ratio of 1:5. It has decided to offer credit customers 60 days credit rather than 30 days.

What will be the effect of this change on the company's current ratio, assuming the policy does not involve any interest cost?

A Increase
B Decrease
C Neither increase nor decrease
D Either increase or decrease **(2 marks)**

(Total for Section A = 40 marks)

SECTION B – 30 marks

Answer ALL six sub-questions

Question 2

(a) Tax rules arise from four main sources. List the sources and describe two of these in detail.

(Total for sub-question (a) = 5 marks)

(b) Discuss briefly the problems encountered in attempting to regulate financial reporting in the absence of a conceptual framework.

(Total for sub-question (b) = 5 marks)

(c) Jedders Co has three long leasehold properties in different parts of the region each of which had an original life of 50 years. As at 1 January 20X0, their original cost, accumulated depreciation to date and carrying (book) values were as follows.

	Cost	*Depreciation*	*Carrying value 1.1.20X0*
	$'000	$'000	$'000
Property in North	3,000	1,800	1,200
Property in Central	6,000	1,200	4,800
Property in South	3,750	1,500	2,250

On 1 January an independent surveyor provided valuation information to suggest that the value of the South property was the same as book value, the North property had fallen against carrying value by 20% and the Central property had risen by 40% in value against the carrying value.

The directors wish to show all their properties at a revalued amount in the accounts as at 31 December 20X0.

Required

Calculate the income statement charges and the non-current asset balance sheet extracts for all the properties for the year ended 31 December 20X0. You should follow the requirements of IAS 16 *Property, plant and equipment.*

(Total for sub-question (c) = 5 marks)

(d) IAS 10 distinguishes between 'adjusting' and 'non-adjusting' events.

Required

Explain what is meant by 'adjusting events' and 'non-adjusting events' and give three examples of each.

(Total for sub-question (d) = 5 marks)

(e) The treasurer of a local government department is reviewing her cash management procedures. The following information is available.

(i) The department has agreed with its bank that it will maintain a minimum daily cash balance of $15,000. Severe financial penalties will apply if this balance is not maintained.

(ii) A forecast of daily cash movements for the next twelve months shows a standard deviation of daily cash flows of $3,000.

(iii) The daily interest rate is at present 0.0236% and this is not expected to change for the foreseeable future.

(iv) The transaction cost for each sale or purchase is $25.

Required

Using the Miller-Orr model calculate the spread between the upper and lower cash balance limits. Explain what is meant by the **return point** and calculate what it will be in this case.

(Total for sub-question (e) = 5 marks)

(f) Discuss the main factors that a company should consider when determining the appropriate mix of long-term and short-term debt in its capital structure.

(Total for sub-question (f) = 5 marks)

(Total for Section B = 30 marks)

SECTION C – 30 marks

Answer this ONE question

Question 3

The balance sheets of YZ are given below:

BALANCE SHEET AT

	30 September 20X3		*30 September 20X2*	
	$'000	$'000	$'000	$'000
Assets				
Property, plant and equipment		634		510
Current assets				
Inventory	420		460	
Trade receivables	390		320	
Interest receivable	4		9	
Short term Investments	50		0	
Cash in bank	75		0	
Cash in hand	7		5	
		946		794
Total assets		1,580		1,304
Equity and liabilities				
Equity				
Ordinary shares $0.50 each	363		300	
Share premium account	89		92	
Revaluation reserve	50		0	
Retained earnings(loss)	93		(70)	
		595		322
Non-current liabilities				
10% loan notes	0		40	
5% loan notes	329		349	
		329		389
Current liabilities				
Bank overdraft	0		70	
Trade payables	550		400	
Income tax	100		90	
Accruals	6		33	
		656		593
Total equity and liabilities		1,580		1,304

Additional information

(a) On 1 October 20X2, YZ issued 60,000 $0.50 ordinary shares at a premium of 100%. The proceeds were used to finance the purchase and cancellation of all its 10% loan notes and some of its 5% loan notes, both at par. A bonus issue of one for ten shares held was made on 1 November 20X2; all shares in issue qualified for the bonus.

(b) The current asset investment was a 30 day government bond.

(c) Property, plant and equipment include certain properties which were revalued in the year.

(d) Property, plant and equipment disposed of in the year had a net book value of $75,000; cash received on disposal was $98,000. The balance on the disposal account has been added to sales revenue.

(e) Depreciation charged for the year was $87,000.

(f) The accruals balance is interest payable of $33,000 at 30 September 20X2 and $6,000 at 30 September 20X3.

(g) Interim dividends paid during the year were $23,000.

(h) Sales revenue for the year was reported as $2,900,000 and purchases were $1,694,000. Other expenses (not including depreciation) were $775,000. YZ earned investment income of $5,000 and finance costs for the year were $19,000. The tax charge is estimated at $104,000.

Required

Prepare the following for YZ for the year ended 30 September 20X3:

(a)	An income statement	**(11 marks)**
(b)	A cash flow statement, using the indirect method	**(17 marks)**
(c)	An analysis of cash and cash equivalents	**(2 marks)**

(Total for Section C = 30 marks)

Answers

DO NOT TURN THIS PAGE UNTIL YOU HAVE COMPLETED MOCK EXAM 2

A plan of attack

This is the second mock exam, so you will now have some feel of what you have to get done in the exam.

Your approach

This paper has three sections. All sections, and all questions, are compulsory. The first section contains 20 multiple choice questions. The second has six short questions. The third has one accounts preparation question which carries 30 marks.

OTs first again

However you find the paper, chances are you should **start with the objective test questions**. You should be able to do a good number of them and answering them will give you a boost. Remember how long to allocate to the OTs? That's right, 72 minutes.

You then have a **choice**.

- Read through and answer Section B before moving on to Section C
- Answer the question in Section C, and then go back to Section B

Time spent at the start of each Section B and C question confirming the requirements and producing a plan for the answers is time well spent.

Doing the exam

Actually doing the exam is a personal experience. There is not a single *right way.* As long as you submit complete answers to the MCQs in Section A, the six Section B questions and the one question from Section C, your approach obviously works.

One approach

Having done or guessed at the MCQs, I would work straight through Section B. The possible pitfall would be getting sucked too deeply into Section B and leaving insufficient time for Section C.

So lets look at the Section B questions in the paper:

- Question (a) is fairly easy but to score marks you must do exactly as specified in the question – list **four** and describe **two** (not one or three).
- Question (b) looks easy but is not. It is very easy to write off the point in a question like this. So before you start, list out the problems, and then briefly discuss each one.
- Question (c) is more straightforward that it looks, but you must read it carefully so that you know exactly what to do. Then write your answer out methodically.
- Question (d) should have given you no trouble as long as you were clear about what constitutes an 'adjusting event'. You are asked for three examples of each – six altogether – so do exactly that.
- Question (e) is on Miller Orr and you are given the formula. You also need to know that the variance of cash flows is the square of the standard deviation.
- Question (f) needs tight planning to ensure that you do not spend too long on it. You are asked for the "main factors". Identify what they are first.

Having worked your way through Section B, taking no more than 9 minutes per question, you should now be left with 54 minutes to do your Section C question.

For the Section C Question you must proceed in a methodical way. Set out your format and then work through the question requirements, doing neat, readable calculations and fill out the figures. Even if you do not finish, you will get marks for what you have done, so do the easy bits first.

Time allocation

Be disciplined. Allocate your time according to the marks available but never go over the time allocation. The last few marks in a question are the hardest to earn.

Be sure to follow the requirements. If four advantages are required, give four. No extra credit will be given for five. Two advantages will only get you half marks.

Answer all of the question. Having a go at every part of all the Section B questions you are required to do will put you in a better position to pass than, say, only doing five questions. However difficult that sixth question seems at first there are marks to be earned.

If you have time left at the end of the exam ensure that you have attempted every part of every question. If you have, then scan through and ensure you complete any part of an answer you left earlier. Use the full three hours working towards a pass.

Marking the exam

Marking the MCQs is not too difficult. You only have 2-4 marks to award. In the longer questions, give yourself credit where you used the correct method, even if your answer was wrong.

Most important, list out all the items you did not know or got wrong, and make sure you revise them.

SECTION A

Question 1

1.1 This is called the recharacterisation rule.

1.2 D Option A is the definition of group relief and options B and C show aspects of group relief.

1.3 A

	$
Output tax $\left(\frac{230{,}000}{115} \times 15\right)$	30,000
Input tax ((180,000 – 20,000) × 15%)	24,000
Payable	6,000

1.4 C

	$	$
Accounting loss		(320,000)
Add: depreciation	33,000	
disallowed expenses	40,000	
		73,000
		(247,000)
Less: non-taxable income	20,000	
tax allowable depreciation	45,000	
		(65,000)
Taxable loss		(312,000)

1.5 A All three items are taxable temporary differences.

1.6 A The cost or value can be measured reliably.

1.7 A A statement of recognised income and expense may be replaced by a statement of changes in equity.

1.8 A Item (1) is now included as a current liability after the revision of IAS 1.

1.9 C 2 and 4 are distributions to/collections from shareholders, not income or expenses.

1.10 B Capitalised development expenditure should be carried forward to be matched against future revenue.

1.11 C

	$'000
Total contract price	36,000
Total expected costs (10,000 + 20,000)	30,000
Total expected profit	6,000
Profit to date = 6,000,000 × 10/30	2,000
Due to customer:	
Progress billings	24,000
Costs to date	(10,000)
Profit to date	(2,000)
Balance due to customer	12,000

1.12 B

3 Obligations under finance leases due after twelve months will be shown under *non-current* liabilities.

4 An asset held under an operating lease is *not* capitalised by the lessee.

1.13 A

FINANCE LEASE ACCOUNT

	$m		$m
20X1 1 Jan deposit	4,000	Non-current assets	15,400
31 Dec – instalment	4,000	Interest 15% × $11,400	1,710
Balance c/d	9,110		
	17,110		17,110
		Balance b/d	9,110
20X2 31 Dec – instalment	4,000	Interest 15% × 9,110	1,366

31 December 20X1

Current liabilities = 4,000 – 1,366
= $2,634

1.14 C

Theory underlying answer

The decision to close the division was taken after the year end and therefore does not affect the accounts for the year to 30 June 20X6 even though the division was loss-making. Option A confirms the final price of a transaction entered into before the year end and is therefore an adjusting event. Option B provides evidence of a diminution in value of an investment held at the year end and is therefore an adjusting event. Option D provides evidence that the previous estimate of accrued profit was inaccurate and therefore an adjustment should be made.

1.15 C The general requirements of IAS 24 for related party status are that two or more parties are related if:

- one party has control of the other
- the parties are subject to common control
- one party has influence over the financial and operating policies of another party
- the parties are subject to influence from the same source.

An 10% investment in another company does not fall into any of these categories.

1.16 D The currency in which the loan is denominated will have little, if any, effect on the credit risk.

1.17 D Convertible loan stock is a longer term investment, and transaction costs will be too high for a short-term investment.

The minimum term for a local authority deposit (A) is normally overnight, and longer-term arrangements can also be made.

If the company is large enough to lend directly on the money markets (B), it will be able to negotiate overnight, daily or weekly terms.

Treasury bills (C) have a term of 91 days to maturity. No interest as such is paid, but the bills can be sold at any time.

1.18 7.5%

$$\frac{9}{120} \times 100\%$$

1.19 B This is the ratio of current assets to current liabilities. C is wrong as the five year bank loan would not normally be included with current liabilities. A is the quick ratio (excludes inventories).

1.20 C Current ratio = $\frac{\text{Current assets}}{\text{Current liabilities}}$ and total current assets are unchanged.

SECTION B

Question 2

(a) The four main sources are as follows.

- Domestic tax legislation and court rulings
- Domestic tax authority practice
- Supranational bodies
- International tax treaties

Domestic tax legislation and court rulings

The main source of tax rules arises from the domestic tax legislation of the country, eg in the UK, the annual Finance Act. Although the legislators try to think of all possible situations, business is always changing and so the law may have to be interpreted by the courts. This gives rise to court rulings that have the force of law.

Domestic tax authority practice

Every tax authority develops its own practice on how the law is applied. For example, UK tax law states that employees should be taxed on all 'benefits' supplied by the employer. However, in practice, certain benefits are exempted from the rules because it would be too time consuming and yield little in the way of tax.

> **Alternative answers.** You could have chosen to explain any of the four main sources and so would have gained credit for the following.
>
> **Supranational bodies**
>
> Supranational bodies, such as the European Union (EU), can affect tax rules. The EU has a number of rules on value added or sales tax, which have to be applied by all members of the EU.
>
> **International tax treaties**
>
> Some businesses trade in many different countries of the world, so called 'multi-national' companies. This means that their profits will be subject to tax in the local countries they trade in, as well as the country where the company has its headquarters. This could mean that the company pays tax on certain profits twice. In order to avoid this 'double tax', countries enter into tax treaties which set out which country taxes the profits. These treaties also allow relief for local taxes paid, for example withholding taxes.

(b) A conceptual framework provides the theoretical basis upon which financial reporting can be regulated. It establishes generally agreed-upon principles and accounting standards can be developed in accordance with this. Lack of a conceptual framework can lead to the following problems:

(i) Standards being developed in a **firefighting fashion**, in response to problems or abuses as they arise. Standards developed in this way are unlikely to be well thought-out and may need further revision as more problems are identified.

(ii) Because standards are not being developed as part of a consistent whole, there may be **conflicts** and **inconsistencies** between different standards. Also issues may be addressed in more than one standard, leading to duplication of effort and confusion.

(iii) If there is no overall framework to which reference can be made, standard setters will feel the need to cover every eventuality. This can lead to standards becoming very detailed and **prescriptive**. This has already been observed in the USA with the FASB standards.

(iv) A conceptual framework provides some sort of **protection from political pressure** from vested interests. A new standard developed as part of a conceptual framework cannot be amended in a way which will bring it into conflict with the conceptual framework.

(c) INCOME STATEMENT (EXTRACTS)

	$'000
Depreciation charge	
North (($1.2m × 80%)/20 years)	48
Central (($4.8m × 140%)/40 years)	168
South ($2.25m/30 years)	75
	291
Loss on revaluation (20% × $1.2m)	240

BALANCE SHEET (EXTRACTS)

	Cost/ revaluation	*Depreciation*	*NBV*
	$'000	$'000	$'000
North	960	48	912
Central	6,720	168	6,552
South	2,250	75	2,175
	9,930	291	9,639

At 1 January 20X0 the accumulated depreciation of the Central property is $1.2m, which represents 10 years' worth of depreciation, leaving 40 years remaining life. For the South and North properties, the respective lives in these calculations are 30 and 20 years. If there is no previous revaluation surplus on the North property, then the loss in the current year is classed as an impairment, and must be taken to the income statement.

(d) **Adjusting events** are events that provide further evidence of conditions that existed at the balance sheet date.

Examples of adjusting events include:

(i) The subsequent determination of the purchase price or of the proceeds of sale of non-current assets purchased or sold before the year-end

(ii) The renegotiation of amounts owing by customers or the insolvency of a customer

(iii) Amounts received or receivable in respect of insurance claims which were in the course of negotiation at the balance sheet date

Non-adjusting events are indicative of conditions that arose subsequent to the balance sheet date.

Examples of non-adjusting events might be:

(i) Losses of non-current assets or inventories as a result of a catastrophe such as fire or flood
(ii) Closing a significant part of the trading activities if this was not begun before the year-end
(iii) The value of an investment falls between the balance sheet date and the date the accounts are authorised

(e) The spread will be calculated using the formula:

$$\text{Spread} = 3\left(\frac{\frac{3}{4} \times \text{transaction cost} \times \text{variance of cash flows}}{\text{interest rate}}\right)^{\frac{1}{3}}$$

$$\text{This gives: } 3\left(\frac{\frac{3}{4} \times 25 \times 9{,}000{,}000}{0.000236}\right)^{\frac{1}{3}} = 26{,}827$$

(variance of cashflows = standard deviation^2)

With a lower limit of $15,000 and a spread of $26,827, the upper limit of cash will be $41,827.

When the cash balance falls to $15,000 or reaches $41,827, cash will be transferred into or out of the account in order to bring the balance back to the **return point**. This is calculated as:

Lower limit + (spread × $^1/_3$)

This enables calculation of **how much** cash should be transferred. In this case the return point is:

15,000 + (26,827 × $^1/_3$) = $23,942

So, when the balance falls to $15,000, $8,942 will be transferred in to restore the balance to $23,942. When the balance reaches $41,827. $17,885 will be transferred out to bring the balance back down to $23,942.

(f) The main factors to consider are:

(i) **Matching**

The traditional view is that **non-current assets** should be **financed** by **long-term sources** of **finance** and **current assets** by a **mixture of long-term and short-term sources**. Thus a company with a greater proportion of non-current assets and permanent current assets is also likely to have a higher proportion of long-term debt in its capital structure.

(ii) **Cost**

The company will seek to **minimise its cost of capital**. The cost of debt capital will be made up of the interest cost of the debt and the transaction costs incurred in arranging the finance. Short-term debt will need to be renegotiated more frequently and this will give rise to recurring transaction costs.

The **relative interest rates** carried by long-term and short-term debt will **vary over time** according to supply and demand and to market expectations of interest rate changes. Rates are generally higher on long-term loans than on short-term since the level of risk faced by the lender that interest rates may rise before repayment is due is higher.

(iii) **Security**

The company may find it easier to **raise short-term finance** with **low security** than long-term finance. However the cost of such loans is likely to be higher.

(iv) **Risk**

In opting for short-term debt, the company faces the risk that it may **not** be able to **renegotiate the loan** on such good terms, or even at all, when the repayment date is reached. Long-term loans are thus less risky. The fact that a firm is seeking a large amount of short-term debt, and is frequently going back to the market, may lead to a loss of confidence in the firm on the part of investors.

(v) **Flexibility**

Long-term debt may carry **early repayment penalties** if it is found that the loan is no longer needed or a more attractive form of finance becomes available. Short-term debt is **more flexible** since it allows the firm to react to interest rate changes and to avoid being locked into an expensive long-term fixed rate commitment at a time when rates are falling. Many firms use overdraft finance – a form of short-term credit whose amount varies from day to day according to the needs of the company. This avoids the company having to pay interest on funds which it does not actually need.

SECTION C

Question 3

Text references. Cash flow statements are covered in Chapter 8: *IAS 7 Cash flow statements.*

Top tips. This is fairly straightforward, especially the income statement, although the bonus issue may have confused you. If so, leave the more difficult calculation to the end and concentrate on those areas you can do confidently. Be methodical and don't get bogged down in one part of the question. Write out for yourself a reconciliation of the movement on share capital and share premium and you will see that the only cash flow is $60,000 from the share issue.

Easy marks Start with the income statement and then the cash flow proforma and get cash flows from operating activities done. You can get easy marks on all of this. You will need to do a working for property, plant and equipment, but you have done an income statement, so the rest of the cash flow statement is relatively easy. If you have worked out property, plant and equipment, you will also get the marks on investing activities.

(a) YZ

INCOME STATEMENT FOR THE YEAR TO 30 SEPTEMBER 20X3

	$'000	$'000
Sales revenue (2,900 – 23)		2,877
Cost of sales (460 + 1,694 – 420)		(1,734)
Gross profit		1,143
Other income – profit on disposal		23
Other expenses (775 + 87)		(862)
		304
Investment income	5	
Finance cost	(19)	(14)
Profit before tax		290
Income tax expense		(104)
Profit for the period		186

(b) YZ
CASH FLOW STATEMENT
FOR THE YEAR ENDED 30 SEPTEMBER 20X3

	$'000	$'000
Cash flows from operating activities		
Profit before tax	290	
Adjustments for		
Finance cost	14	
Depreciation	87	
Profit on disposal (W1)	(23)	
Operating profit before working capital changes	368	
Decrease in inventory	40	
Increase in receivables	(70)	
Increase in payables	150	
Cash generated from operations	488	
Interest paid (W2)	(46)	
Income taxes paid (W3)	(94)	
Net cash from operating activities		348
Cash flows from investing activities		
Purchase of property, plant and equipment (W1)	(236)	
Proceeds from sale of property, plant and equipment	98	
Interest received (W4)	10	
Net cash used in investing activities		(128)
Cash flows from financing activities		
Proceeds from issuance of share capital (W5)	60	
Repurchase of loan notes	(60)	
Dividends paid	(23)	
Net cash used in financing activities		(23)
Net increase in cash and cash equivalents		197
Cash and cash equivalents at beginning of period		(65)
Cash and cash equivalents at end of period		132

(c) *Analysis of cash and cash equivalents*

	As at 30.9.X3 $'000	As at 30.9.X2 $'000	Change in year $'000
Cash in hand and balances at bank	82	5	77
Bank overdraft	–	(70)	70
Short term investments	50	–	50
	132	(65)	197

Note

The current asset investment qualifies as a cash equivalent since it is short-term (less than 3 months maturity) and highly liquid (being a government bond).

Workings

1 *Property, plant and equipment*

PROPERTY, PLANT AND EQUIPMENT

	$'000		$'000
Bal b/fwd (NBV)	510	Disposals	75
Revaluation	50	Depreciation	87
Additions (bal fig)	236	Balance c/fwd (NBV)	634
	796		796

DISPOSALS

	$'000		$'000
Property, plant and equipment	75	Bank proceeds	98
Income statement (profit on sale)	23		
	98		98

2 *Interest paid*

INTEREST PAYABLE

	$'000		$'000
Paid (bal. fig)	46	Balance b/fwd	33
Balance c/fwd	6	Income statement	19
	52		52

3 *Income taxes paid*

TAXATION

	$'000		$'000
∴ Paid (bal.fig)	94	Balance b/fwd	90
Balance c/fwd	100	Income statement	104
	194		194

4 *Interest received*

INTEREST RECEIVABLE

	$'000		$'000
Balance b/fwd	9	Cash received	10
Income statement	5	Balance c/fwd	4
	14		14

5 *Share capital issue*

	Share capital	*Share premium*
	$'000	$'000
Bal b/f	300	92
Share issue for cash	30	30
Bonus issue ($\frac{1}{10} \times 330$)	33	(33)
	363	89

CIMA

Paper P7 (Managerial) Financial Accounting and Tax Principles

Mock Exam 3 November 2008

Question Paper		
Time allowed:	Reading time Answering question paper	**20 mins** **3 hours**
This paper is divided into three sections		
Section A	**Answer ALL sub-questions in this section**	
Section B	**Answer ALL of the six short answer questions**	
Section C	**Answer this ONE question**	

DO NOT OPEN THIS PAPER UNTIL YOU ARE READY TO START UNDER EXAMINATION CONDITIONS

SECTION A – 40 marks

Answer ALL sub-questions in this section

Question 1

1.1 The OECD Model tax convention defines a permanent establishment.

Which ONE of the following is not specifically listed as a "permanent establishment" by the OECD Model tax convention?

A An office.
B A factory.
C An oil well.
D A site of an 11 month construction project. **(2 marks)**

1.2 In no more than **25** words, explain the meaning of 'overtrading'. **(2 marks)**

1.3 Which ONE of the following would not have the effect of shortening the working capital cycle?

A Reducing raw material inventory holding.
B Increasing credit given to customers.
C Delaying payments to suppliers.
D Increasing the turnover of finished goods inventory. **(2 marks)**

1.4 GD's financial reporting period is 1 September 2007 to 31 August 2008.

Which ONE of the following would be classified as a non-adjusting event according to IAS 10 *Events after the balance sheet date*?

Assume all amounts are material and that GD's financial statements have not yet been approved for publication.

A On 30 October 2008, GD received a communication stating that one of its customers had ceased trading and gone into liquidation. The balance outstanding at 31 August 2008 was unlikely to be paid.

B At 31 August 2008, GD had not provided for an outstanding legal action against the local government administration for losses suffered as a result of incorrect enforcement of local business regulations. On 5 November 2008, the court awarded GD $50,000 damages.

C On 1 October 2008, GD made a rights issue of 1 new share for every 3 shares held at a price of $175. The market price on that date was $200.

D At 31 August 2008, GD had an outstanding insurance claim of $150,000. On 10 October 2008, the insurance company informed GD that it would pay $140,000 as settlement. **(2 marks)**

1.5 The external auditors have completed the audit of GQ for the year ended 30 June 2008 and have several outstanding differences of opinion that they have been unable to resolve with the management of GQ. The senior partner of the external auditors has reviewed these outstanding differences and concluded that individually and in aggregate the differences are not material.

Which ONE of the following audit opinions will the external auditors use for GQ's financial statements for the year ended 30 June 2008?

A An unqualified opinion.
B An adverse opinion.
C An emphasis of matter.
D A qualified opinion.

(2 marks)

1.6 GS forecast its need for financing to be $220,000, comprising:

	$
Non-current assets	100,000
Permanent portion of current assets	70,000
Fluctuating portion of current assets	50,000
	220,000

GS plans to fund this requirement as follows:

	$
Equity share capital	125,000
Seven year bank loan	65,000
Bank overdraft and funding from trade payables	30,000
	220,000

Gs could be said to have a financing of working capital policy that is

A aggressive.
B conservative.
C tactical.
D strategic.

(2 marks)

1.7 GY made a number of changes during the financial year to 30 September 2008.

Which ONE of the following changes would be classified as a change in accounting policy, according to IAS 8 *Accounting policies, changes in accounting estimates and errors*?

A Depreciation of motor vehicles was changed from straight line to reducing balance from 1 October 2007.

B Up to 30 September 2007, GY had been applying the benchmark treatment of IAS 23 *Borrowing costs* and charged all interest paid to its income statement. GY has decided to adopt IAS 23 (revised 2007) early and, from 1 October 2007, will charge interest incurred on the purchase, or construction, of non-current assets to the cost of the asset.

C On 1 March 2008, GY decided to change the method it used to apportion revenue and costs on its construction contracts. From 1 March 2008, GY changed from the cost incurred to date as a percentage of total cost of the contract, to the value of work completed to date as a percentage of total contract revenue.

D On 1 August 2008, GY decided to sell one of its factories and designated the factory and all related facilities as a disposal group as required by IFRS 5 *Disposal of non-current assets held for sale and discontinued operations*. GY revalued the disposal group assets to fair value less costs to sell.

(2 marks)

1.8 Which ONE of the following actions is **most** likely to reduce tax evasion?

A Creating a tax system that is perceived as equitable to all.
B Deducting tax at source whenever possible.
C Simplifying the tax structure as much as possible.
D Reducing penalties for late or incorrect tax returns. **(2 marks)**

1.9 Developed countries generally use three tax bases. One tax base widely used is income.

List the other TWO widely used bases. **(2 marks)**

1.10 An investment account pays interest every quarter. The quarterly interest rate is 3%.

Assuming the interest is reinvested every quarter, calculate the annual yield. **(2 marks)**

1.11 State the TWO concepts of capital referred to in the International Accounting Standards Board's (IASB's) *Framework for the Preparation and Presentation of Financial Statements (Framework).* **(2 marks)**

1.12 The IASB's *Framework* identifies eight categories of users of financial statements. Investors, employees and government are three of the eight categories of users of financial statements.

List TWO of the other categories. **(2 marks)**

1.13 GK purchased a piece of development land on 31 October 2000 for $500,000. GK revalued the land on 31 October 2004 to $700,000. The latest valuation report, dated 31 October 2008, values the land at $450,000.

GK has adjusted the land balance shown in non-current assets at 31 October 2008.

Which ONE of the following shows the correct debit entry in GK's financial statements for the year ended 31 October 2008?

A DR Revaluation reserve $50,000 and DR Income Statement $200,000
B DR Revaluation reserve $250,000
C DR Revaluation reserve $200,000 and DR Income Statement $50,000
D DR Revaluation reverse $250,000 **(2 marks)**

1.14 GL's trade payables days outstanding at 30 September 2008 were 45 days. Purchases for the year to 30 September 2008 were $324,444 accruing evenly throughout the year.

GL is budgeting for an increase in annual purchases to $356,900 for the 12 months to 30 September 2009.

Assume that the accounts payable outstanding balance at 30 September 2009 will be the same amount as at 30 September 2008.

Calculate the budgeted trade payables days outstanding at 30 September 2009. **(3 marks)**

1.15 GF wants to sell an unquoted bond. The bond has a coupon rate of 5% and will repay its face value of $1,000 at the end of four years.

GF estimates that the market requires a yield to maturity of 11% from this type of bond. GF has asked you to recommend a selling price for the bond.

Calculate a selling price for the bond. **(4 marks)**

1.16 Explain briefly THREE major principles of modern taxation. **(3 marks)**

1.17 Country Z has a VAT system where VAT is charged on all goods and services. Registered VAT entities are allowed to recover input VAT paid on their purchases.

VAT operates at three different levels in Z:

- Standard rate 15%
- Luxury rate 22%
- Zero rate 0%

During the last VAT period, an entity, GW, purchased materials and services costing $138,000, including VAT. All materials and services were at standard rate VAT.

GW converted the materials into two products A and B; product A is zero-rated and product B is luxury-rated for VAT purposes.

During the VAT period, GW made the following sales, including VAT:

	$
A	70,000
B	183,000

At the end of the period, GW paid the net VAT due to the tax authorities.

Assume no opening or closing inventory balances.

Assuming GW had no other VAT-related transactions, calculate GW's profit and the amount of VAT that GW paid?

(4 marks)

(Total for Section A = 40 marks)

SECTION B – 30 marks

Answer ALL six sub-questions

Question 2

(a) The International Accounting Standards Committee Foundation (IASCF) oversees a number of other International committees, two of which are the Standards Advisory Council (SAC) and the International Financial Reporting Interpretations Committee (IFRIC).

Required

Explain the role of the SAC and the IFRIC in assisting with developing and implementing International Financial Reporting Standards.

(Total for sub-question (a) = 5 marks)

(b) GC manufactures a range of bicycles and holds an inventory of certain bicycle parts.

Part number 1258 costs GC $800 per unit. GC expects to use 8,000 units of part 1258 per year.

Ordering costs have been calculated at $150 per order and inventory holding costs have been estimated at $275 per unit per year.

The supplier of part number 1258 has offered a 2% discount off the purchase price if each order is for 2,000 units or more.

Required

(i) Calculate the economic order quantity for part 1258, assuming no discount is given.
(ii) State whether GC should accept the discount offered.

(Total for sub-question (b) = 5 marks)

(c) GN is a retailer, selling directly to the public for cash payment and to other entities on credit. GN is preparing a cash forecast for the first three months of 2009. Credit customers are given 30 days to pay. Credit sales are expected to be six times the value of direct sales to the public.

GN's estimate of sales for the first three months of 2009 is as follows:

Month	*January*	*February*	*March*
	$'000	$'000	$'000
Sales value	400	400	500

Actual and estimated sales for the last three months of 2008 are:

Month	*October (actual)*	*November (estimate)*	*December (estimate)*
	$'000	$'000	$'000
Sales value	396	428	550

From past experience, GN expects 10% of credit customers to pay in the same month as the sale is made, a further 25% to pay in the month after the sale, and 63% in the month after that. The outstanding balance is expected to be written off.

Required

Prepare a monthly cash forecast of GN's total receipts for January to March 2009. (Work to the nearest $'000.)

(Total for sub-question (c) = 5 marks)

(d) GJ commenced business on 1 October 2005 and, on that date, it acquired property, plant and equipment for $220,000. GJ uses the straight line method of depreciation. The estimated useful life of the assets was five years and the residual value was estimated at $10,000. GJ's accounting year end is 30 September.

All the assets acquired qualified for a first year tax allowance of 50% and then an annual tax allowance of 25% of the reducing balance.

On 1 October 2007, GJ revalued all of its assets; this led to an increase in asset values of $53,000.

GJ's applicable tax rate for the year is 25%.

Required

Calculate the amount of the deferred tax provision that GJ should include in its balance sheet at 30 September 2008, in accordance with IAS 12 Income Taxes.

(Total for sub-question (d) = 5 marks)

The following data are to be used to answer questions (e) and (f)

The financial statements of GK for the year to 31 October 2008 were as follows:

BALANCE SHEET AT	*31 October 2008*		*31 October 2007*	
	$'000	$'000	$'000	$'000
Assets				
Non-current tangible assets	10,000		10,500	
Property	5,000	15,000	4,550	15,050
Plant and equipment				
Current assets				
Inventory	1,750		1,500	
Trade receivables	1,050		900	
Cash and cash equivalents	310		150	
		3,110		2,550
Total assets		18,110		17,600
Equity and liabilities				
Ordinary shares @ $.050 each	6,000		3,000	
Share premium	2,500		1,000	
Revaluation reserve	3,000		3,000	
Retained earnings	1,701		1,000	
		13,201		8,000
Non-current liabilities				
Interest-bearing borrowings	2,400		7,000	
Deferred tax	540	2,940	450	7,450
Current liabilities				
Trade and other payables	1,060		1,400	
Tax payable	909		750	
		1,969		2,150
		18,110		17,600

INCOME STATEMENT FOR THE YEAR 31 OCTOBER 2008

	$'000	$'000
Revenue		16,000
Cost of sales		10,000
Gross profit		6,000
Administrative expenses	(2,000)	
Distribution costs	(1,200)	(3,200)
		2,800
Finance cost		(600)
Profit		2,200
Income tax expense		(999)
Profit for the period		(1,201)

Additional information:

1. Trade and other payables comprise:

	31 October 2008	*31 October 2007*
	$'000	$'000
Trade payables	730	800
Interest payable	330	600
	1,060	1,400

2. Plant disposed of in the year had a net book value of $35,000; cash received on disposal was $60,000.

3. GK's income statement includes depreciation for the year of $1,110,000 for properties and $882,000 for plant and equipment.

4. Dividends paid during the year were $500,000.

(e) Using the data relating to GK above, calculate the cash generated from operations that would appear in GK's Cash flow statement, using the indirect method, for the year ended 31 October 2008, in accordance with IAS 7 *Cash flow statements*.

(Total for sub-question (e) = 5 marks)

(f) Using the data relating to GK above, calculate the cash flow from investing activities and cash flows from financing activities sections of GK's Cash flow statement for the year ended 31 October 2008, in accordance with IAS 7 *Cash flow statements*.

(Total for sub-question (f) = 5 marks)

(Total for Section B = 30 marks)

SECTION C – 30 marks

Answer this ONE question

Question 3

GZ is a small mining entity which operated a single gold mine for many years. The gold mine ceased operations on 31 October 2007 and was closed on 1 January 2008.

On 1 November 2007, GZ commenced operating a new silver mine.

The trial balance for GZ at 31 October 2008 was as follows:

	$'000	$'000
4% Loan notes (redeemable 1 April 2009)		1,900
Administrative expenses	1,131	
Available for sale investments at market value 31 October 2007	2,177	
Bank & cash	2,025	
Decommissioning and landscaping expenses of gold mine (see note (c))	1,008	
Direct operating expenses (excluding depreciation)	5,245	
Distribution costs	719	
Dividend paid 1 March 2008	550	
Equity shares $1 each, fully paid		5,000
Finance lease payable at 1 November 2007 (see note (i))		900
Government operating license, silver mine at cost (see note (b))	100	
Income tax	13	
Interest paid on loan notes – half year to 30 April 2008	38	
Inventory at 31 October 2008	2,410	
Investment income received		218
Mine properties at cost (see note (d))	6,719	
Plant (finance lease) at 1 November 2007 (see note (i))	900	
Plant and equipment at 31 October 2007 (excluding finance lease)	3,025	
Plant lease rentals paid in year	160	
Provision for decommissioning gold mine at 31 October 2007		950
Provision for deferred tax at 31 October 2007		731
Provision for depreciation at 31 October 2007:		
Mine properties (see note (d))		2,123
Plant and equipment		370
Receipt from sale of plant (see note (c))		2
Retained earnings at 31 October 2007		2,810
Revaluation reserve a 31 October 2007		80
Revenue		9,600
Suspense account (see note (I)		1,820
Trade payables		2,431
Trade receivables	2,715	
	28,935	28,935

Additional information provided:

(a) Each mine requires a government operating licence for 20 years and is expected to be productive for that time. After 20 years, the mine will be closed and decommissioned.

(b) On 1 November 2007, GZ received a government operating licence to operate the new silver mine. The licence cost $100,000 and is for 20 years. Included in the licence is a condition that, on closure of the mine, all above-ground structures must be removed and the ground landscaped. GZ has estimated this cost and discounted it to a present value of $3,230,000 at 31 October 2008. The trial balance excludes this decommissioning provision.

(c) On 1 January 2008, GZ closed its gold mine. The $950,000 shown in the trial balance provision as "provision for decommissioning gold mine" has been charged against profits in the previous year. The removal of buildings and other above ground structures, landscaping and other decommissioning costs was complete at 31 October 2008; the actual cost incurred was $1,008,000. GZ sold old plant and equipment from the gold mine for $2,000 (original cost $200,000, net book value $5,000). The gold mine property is now surplus to GZ's requirements. At 31 October 2008, the gold mine property had a market value of $520,000 with estimated selling and legal costs of $27,000.

(d) The mine property balances in the trial balance comprised:

Mine property	*Gold mine*	*Silver mine*	*Total*
	$'000	$'000	$'000
Cost	2,623	4,096	6,719
Provision for depreciation	2,123	0	2,123
	500	4,096	4,596

(e) The market value of the available for sale investments at 31 October 2008 was $2,311,000.

(f) There were no sales or purchases of available for sale investments during the year ended 31 October 2008 and no acquisitions of other non-current assets, except for those in note (i) below.

(g) Income tax due for the year ended 31 October 2008 is estimated at $375,000. The deferred tax provision needs to be reduced by $60,000.

(h) Depreciation is charged on mining property using the straight-line basis at 5% per annum. Plant and equipment is depreciated using the reducing balance method at 25%. The depreciation policy is to charge a full year's depreciation in the year of acquisition and no depreciation in the year of disposal. Depreciation is regarded as a cost of production.

(i) GZ entered into a non-cancellable seven-year finance lease on 1 November 2007 to acquire mining machinery. Under the terms of the lease, GZ will make annual payments of $160,000 in arrears, the first payment being made on 31 October 2008. The machinery is estimated to have a useful economic life of seven years. The fair value of the machinery at 1 November 2007 was $900,000. GZ allocates finance charges using the sum of digits method.

(j) The 4% loan notes are ten-year loans due for repayment 1 April 2009. GZ incurred no other interest charges in the year to 31 October 2008.

(k) The final dividend for the year to 31 October 2007 was paid on 1 March 2008.

(l) GZ made a new issue of 1,400 equity shares on 31 October 2008 at a premium of 30%. The cash received was debited to the bank account and credited to the suspense account.

Required

(a) Prepare GZ's Property, Plant and Equipment note to the financial statements for the year to 31 October 2008. **(6 marks)**

(b) Prepare GZ's income statement and a statement of changes in equity for the year to 31 October 2008 and a balance sheet at that date, in a form suitable for presentation to the shareholders and in accordance with the requirements of International Financial Reporting Standards. (All workings should be to the nearest $'000).

Notes to the financial statements, except as indicated in part (a) above, are NOT required, but all workings must be clearly shown. Do NOT prepare a statement of accounting policies. **(24 marks)**

(Total for Section C = 30 marks)

[illegible] discounted to a present value of $3,220,000 at 31 October 2008. The trial balance excludes this decommissioning provision.

(c) On 1 January 2008 [illegible] closed its gold mine. The $350,000 shown in the trial balance provision as [illegible] gold mine has been charged against profits in the previous year. The [illegible] of buildings and other above ground structures, landscaping and other decommissioning costs was completed at 31 October 2008; the actual cost incurred was [illegible]. [illegible] old plant and equipment from the gold mine for [illegible] (original cost [illegible], net book value [illegible]). The gold mine property is [illegible] requirements. At 31 October 2008, the gold mine property had a market value of [illegible] and [illegible] costs of [illegible].

[illegible] trial balance [illegible]:

[illegible]	[illegible]	[illegible]	[illegible]
[illegible]	[illegible]	[illegible]	[illegible]
[illegible]	[illegible]	[illegible]	[illegible]
[illegible]	[illegible]	[illegible]	[illegible]
[illegible]	[illegible]	[illegible]	[illegible]

[illegible] at 31 October 2008 was [illegible].

[illegible] of other [illegible] below.

(d) Income tax [illegible] for the year ended 31 October 2008 [illegible]. The deferred tax provision [illegible] by $300,000.

(e) Depreciation is charged on mining property using the straight line basis [illegible]. Plant and equipment is depreciated using the reducing balance method at 25%. [illegible] policy is to charge a full year's depreciation in the year of acquisition and no depreciation in the year of disposal. Depreciation is regarded as a cost of production.

(f) [illegible] entered into a non-cancellable seven-year finance lease [illegible] mining machinery. Under the terms of the lease [illegible] will make annual payments of [illegible] in arrears, the first [illegible] on 31 [illegible] 2008. [illegible] useful economic life of seven years. [illegible] charges using the sum of digits method.

(g) The [illegible] loan notes [illegible]-year loans due for repayment [illegible]. No other [illegible] in the year to 31 October 2008.

(h) The final dividend for the year to 31 October 2007 was paid on [illegible] March 2008.

(i) [illegible] made [illegible] at a premium of [illegible]. The cash received was credited to [illegible].

Required

(a) Prepare [illegible] for the year to 31 October 2008. **(5 marks)**

(b) Prepare [illegible] statement of financial position at 31 October 2008 and [illegible] for the year [illegible] in a form suitable for presentation to the shareholders and in accordance with the requirements of International Financial Reporting Standards. All workings should be to the nearest $000.

[illegible] are NOT required but all workings must be shown. [illegible] NOT required. **(24 marks)**

(Total for Section C = 29 marks)

Answers

DO NOT TURN THIS PAGE UNTIL YOU HAVE COMPLETED MOCK EXAM 3

A plan of attack

This is the third mock exam, so you will now have some feel of what you have to get done in the exam.

Your approach

This paper has three sections. All questions are compulsory. The first section contains 15 multiple choice questions. The second has six short questions. The third is a compulsory 30-mark question.

OTs first again

However you find the paper, chances are you should **start with the objective test questions**. You should be able to do a good number of them and answering them will give you a boost. **Don't even look at the other questions before doing Section A**. Remember how long to allocate to the OTs? That's right, 72 minutes.

You then have a **choice**.

- Read through and answer Section B before moving on to Section C
- Answer the question in Section C, and then go back to Section B

Time spent at the start of each Section B question and the Section C question confirming the requirements and producing a plan for the answers is time well spent.

Doing the exam

Actually doing the exam is a personal experience. There is not a single *right way.* As long as you submit complete answers to the MCQs, question 1, the six Section B questions and the Section C question, your approach obviously works.

One approach

Having done or guessed at the MCQs, I would work straight through Section B. The possible pitfall would be getting sucked too deeply into Section B and leaving insufficient time for Section C.

So lets look at the Section B questions in the paper:

- Question (a) is on the IASB. You needed a good knowledge of the SAC and IFRIC for 5 marks.
- Question (b) is an easy question on EOQ.
- Question (c) is a straightforward question on cash forecasting.
- Question (d) is on deferred tax. As long as you had an understanding of how to do the calculation this was easy.
- Questions (e) and (f) were both on cash flow statements. There was a lot of information presented in the question so you needed to be careful you did not overrun and leave insufficient time for Section C.

Having hacked your way through Section B, taking no more than 9 minutes per question, you should now be left with 54 minutes to do your Section C question.

For the Section C Question you must proceed in a methodical way. Set out your format and then work through the question requirements, doing neat, readable calculations and fill out the figures. Even if you do not finish, you will get marks for what you have done, so do the easy bits first.

Time allocation

Be disciplined. Allocate your time according to the marks available but never go over the time allocation. The last few marks in a question are the hardest to earn.

Be sure to follow the requirements. If four advantages are required, give four. No extra credit will be given for five. Two advantages will only get you half marks.

Answer all of the question. Having a go at every part of all the Section B questions you are required to do will put you in a better position to pass than, say, only doing five questions. However difficult that sixth question seems at first there are marks to be earned.

If you have time left at the end of the exam ensure that you have attempted every part of every question. If you have, then scan through and ensure you complete any part of an answer you left earlier. Use the full three hours working towards a pass.

Marking the exam

Marking the MCQs is not too difficult. You only have 2-4 marks to award. In the longer questions, give yourself credit where you used the correct method, even if your answer was wrong.

Most important, list out all the items you did not know or got wrong, and make sure you revise them.

SECTION A

Question 1

1.1 D A construction project is only a permanent establishment if it lasts more than twelve months.

1.2 **Overtrading** is where a company is over-reliant on short-term finance to support its operations. This is risky because short-term finance may be withdrawn relatively quickly.

1.3 B Reducing the period of credit given to customers and work in progress will also shorten the working capital cycle.

1.4 C Share transactions after the balance sheet date do not require adjustments.

1.5 A The auditor does not report on items that are not material.

1.6 B GS has used long-term funding to finance all permanent assets and part of the fluctuating portion of current assets.

1.7 B This is a change required by the revision of an accounting standard.

1.8 B A will not prevent a dishonest individual evading tax. C reduces tax avoidance rather than tax evasion. B reduces opportunities to manipulate and thus evade tax.

1.9 Assets and consumption

1.10 12.55%

$((1+0.03)^4-1)\times100 = 12.55\%$

1.11
- The **financial** concept of capital
- The **physical** concept of capital

1.12 Any two of the following.

- Suppliers and other trade creditors
- Lenders
- Customers
- The public

1.13 C Land is not depreciated

1.14 49.5 days

September 30 2008
Average daily purchases on credit terms = 324,444/45 = 7,209.87

September 30 2009
Trade payable days = 356,900/7,209.87 = 49.5 days

1.15 $814

	$
Capital at maturity: 1,000 × 0.659*	659
Interest: 50 over 4 years = 50 × 3.102*	155
Market price	814

* discount rate for 4 years at 11%

1.16 **Equity**: the tax burden should be fairly distributed

Efficiency: tax should be easy and cheap to collect

Economic effects: the government must consider the effect of taxation policy on various sectors of the economy

1.17 VAT paid \$15,000

Gross profit \$100,000

	\$
Output VAT (183,000 × 22/122)	33,000
Input VAT (138,000 × 15/115)	(18,000)
Amount paid	15,000
Revenue (183,000 × 100/122) + 70,000	220,000
Cost of sales (138,000 × 100/115)	(120,000)
Gross profit	100,000

SECTION B

Question 2

(a) **Standards Advisory Council (SAC)**

The SAC provides a forum for groups and individuals to give advice to the International Accounting Standards Board (IASB), the board responsible for setting IFRS. The committee members are from diverse geographical and functional backgrounds to allow them to gather opinions from a wide range of representatives.

The committee meets three times a year and advises the IASB on its agenda and priorities for setting new IFRS. Consultation with the SAC continues throughout the development of an IFRS. In particular, the SAC advises the IASB on issues related to the practical application and implementation of new IFRS. It also advises on the advantages and disadvantages of different proposals.

International Financial Reporting Interpretations Committee (IFRIC)

The IFRIC provides timely guidance on the application and interpretation of IFRS. It normally deals with complex accounting issues that could give rise to a diversity of accounting treatments. In this way it assists the IASB in setting and improving IFRS.

IFRIC produces interpretations which, once finalised, are ratified and issued by the IASB. The IASB may choose to add an item to its own agenda if an interpretation is not ratified.

(b) (i)

$$\text{EOQ} = \sqrt{\frac{2C_oD}{C_h}}$$

$$= \sqrt{\frac{2 \times 150 \times 8{,}000}{2.75}}$$

$$= 934 \text{ units}$$

(ii) **Total cost at order quantity of 934 units**

	$
Purchase price 8,000 × $8	64,000
Order costs (8,000/934) × $150	1,285
Holding costs (934/2) × $2.75	1,285
	66,570

Total cost at order quantity of 2,000 units

	$
Purchase price 8,000 × $8 × 0.98	62,720
Order costs (8,000/2,000) × $150	600
Holding costs (2,000/2) × $2.75	2,750
	66,070

GC should accept the offer of the 2% discount as this decreases the total annual inventory cost.

(c) **Cash receipts for January to March 2009**

Month	*January*	*February*	*March*
	$'000	$'000	$'000
Cash receipts	440	474	416

Workings

January receipts	$'000
Cash sales to public 1/7 × 400	57
January credit sales 10% × 6/7 × 400	34
December credit sales 25% × 6/7 × 550	118
November credit sales 63% × 6/7 × 428	231
Total January cash receipts	440

February receipts	$'000
Cash sales to public 1/7 × 400	57
February credit sales 10% × 6/7 × 400	34
January credit sales 25% × 6/7 × 400	86
December credit sales 63% × 6/7 × 550	297
Total February cash receipts	474

March receipts	$'000
Cash sales to public 1/7 × 500	71
March credit sales 10% × 6/7 × 500	43
February credit sales 25% × 6/7 × 400	86
January credit sales 63% × 6/7 × 400	216
Total March cash receipts	416

(d) Deferred tax provision = $21,281.25

Tax written down value:

	$
1 Oct 2005 cost	220,000
2006 tax allowance 50% × 220,000	(110,000)
30 Sept 2006 tax written down value	110,000
2007 tax allowance 25% × 110,000	(27,500)
30 Sept 2007 tax written down value	82,500
2008 tax allowance 25% × 82,500	(20,625)
30 Sept 2008 tax written down value	61,875

Accounting carrying value:

	$
Cost	220,000
Depreciation 3 × (220,000-10,000)/5	(126,000)
30 Sept 2008 accounting carrying value	94,000

Temporary difference = 94,000 – 61,875
= 32,125

	$
Deferred tax provision (25% × 32,125)	8,031.25
Deferred tax provision on revaluation (53,000 × 25%)	13,250
Total deferred tax provision	21,281.25

(e)

	$'000
Net profit before taxation	2,200
Depreciation (1,110 + 882)	1,992
Profit on disposal of plant (60 – 35)	(25)
Finance cost	600
Increase in trade receivables (1,050 – 900)	(150)
Increase in inventories (1,750 – 1,500)	(250)
Decrease in trade payables (730 – 800)	(70)
Cash generated from operations	4,297

(f) *Cash flows from investing activities*

	$'000
Purchase of property, plant and equipment (W)	(1,977)
Proceeds from sale of plant	60
Net cash used in investing activities	(1,917)

Cash flows from financing activities

	$'000
Proceeds from issue of share capital (6,000 – 3,000 + 2,500 – 1,000)	4,500
Dividends paid	(500)
Borrowings repaid (7,000 – 2,400)	(4,600)
Net cash used in financing activities	(600)

Workings

PROPERTY, PLANT AND EQUIPMENT

	$'000		$'000
Balance b/f	15,050	Depreciation (1,110 + 882)	1,992
Additions (bal fig)	1,977	Disposal	35
		Balance c/f	15,000
	17,027		17,027

SECTION C

Question 3

Text references. Chapter 3, 5, 7 and 9.

Top tips. Write out your proformas first making sure you space these out. Next, slot the trial balance figures which are unaffected by any adjustments into your proforma. Then tackle the information in the order you find easiest to complete the requirements.

Note that the gold mine would have been a discontinued operation in the year to 31 October 2007.

Easy marks. Marks were available for including the figures unaffected by the additional information in your proformas. The statement of changes in equity was relatively straightforward for some easy marks.

(a) Property, plant and equipment

	Mine property $'000	*Plant* $'000	*Plant held under finance lease* $'000	*Total* $'000
Balance at 1 November 2007	4,596	2,655	900	8,151
Decommissioning costs	3,230			3,230
Disposals (200 – 195)		(5)		(5)
Depreciation (W2)	(497)	(662)	(129)	(1,288)
Transfer to non-current asset held for sale (W1)	(369)	—	—	(369)
Balance at 31 October 2008	6,960	1,988	771	9,719

(b) GZ

INCOME STATEMENT FOR THE PERIOD ENDING 31 OCTOBER 2008

	$'000
Revenue	9,600
Cost of sales (W3)	(6,599)
Gross profit	3,001
Investment income	218
Distribution costs	(719)
Administrative expenses	(1,131)
Profit from operations	1,369
Finance cost (W4)	(131)
Profit before tax	1,238
Income tax expense (W6)	(328)
Profit for the period	910

GZ

STATEMENT OF CHANGES IN EQUITY FOR THE PERIOD ENDED 31 OCTOBER 2008

	Share capital	*Share premium*	*Revaluation reserve*	*Available for sale investment*	*Retained earnings*	*Total*
	$'000	$'000	$'000	$'000	$'000	$'000
Balance at 1 Nov 2007	5,000	0	80		2,810	7,890
Available for sale investments (W7)				134		134
Profit for the period					910	910
Dividends					(550)	(550)
Issue of share capital (W8)	1,400	420				1,820
Balance at 31 Oct 2008	6,400	420	80	134	3,170	10,204

GZ

BALANCE SHEET AT 31 OCTOBER 2008

	$'000	$000
Assets		
Non-current assets		
Property, plant and equipment (see a)		9,719
Intangible assets (W9)		95
Available for sale investments (W7)		2,311
		12,125
Current assets		
Inventory	2,410	
Trade receivables	2,715	
Cash and cash equivalents	2,025	
Non-current assets classified as held for sale	369	
		7,519
Total assets		19,644
Equity and liabilities		
Equity		
Share capital (W8)		6,400
Share premium account (W8)		420
Revaluation surplus		80
Retained earnings		3,170
Surplus on available for sale investment		134
		10,204
Non-current liabilities		
Deferred tax (731-60)	671	
Finance lease (W5)	682	
Provision (W10)	3,230	
		4,583
Current liabilities		
4% Loan notes	1,900	
Trade payables	2,431	
Tax payable	375	
Finance lease (W5)	113	
Accruals (1900 × 4% × 0.5)	38	
		4,857
Total equity and liabilities		19,644

Workings

1 *Non-current asset held for sale*

	$'000
Carrying amount (500 – (2,623 × 5%))	369
Fair value less costs to sell (520-27)	493
Therefore no write-down required	

2 *Depreciation*

	$'000
Mines ((6,719 + 3,230) × 5%)	497
Property, plant and equipment (excluding finance lease) ((3,025-200-370 + 195) × 25%)	662
Leased plant (900/7)	129
	1,288

3 *Cost of sales*

	$'000
Per trial balance	5,245
Amortisation operating licence (100/20)	5
Depreciation (W2)	1,288
Reverse provision – gold mine	(950)
Decommissioning costs – gold mine	1,008
Loss on sale of plant (5 – 2)	3
	6,599

4 *Finance cost*

	$'000
4% loan notes (1,900 × 4%)	76
Interest payable on finance lease (W5)	55
	131

5 *Finance lease*

	$'000
Total lease payments (7 × 160)	1,120
Fair value of asset	(900)
Total finance charge	220

Using sum of digits method:

31.10.08 220 × 7/28 = 55

	$'000
1 November 2007	900
Finance charge	55
Payment	(160)
Balance at 31 October 2008	795
Finance charge	47
Payment	(160)
Balance at 31 October 2009	682

	$'000
Due within one year (795 – 682)	113
Due after one year	682
	795

6 *Income tax expense*

	$'000
Per trial balance	13
Reduction in deferred tax provision	(60)
Charge for year	375
	328

7 *Surplus on available for sale investments*

	$'000
Market value	2,311
Less amount as per trial balance	(2,177)
	134

8 *Share issue*

	$'000
Share capital (1,400 x 1)	1,400
Share premium ((1,400 x 1.3) -1400)	420
	1,820

Share capital after issue = 5,000 + 1,400 = 6,400

9 *Intangible assets*

	$'000
Licence	100
Amortisation – (100/20)	(5)
Total	95

10 *Provision*

	$'000
As per trial balance	950
Gold mine closed	(950)
Decommissioning costs	3,230
	3,230

Mathematical tables and exam formulae

PRESENT VALUE TABLE

Present value of £1 ie $(1+r)^{-n}$ where r = interest rate, n = number of periods until payment or receipt.

Periods (n)	Interest rates (r) 1%	2%	3%	4%	5%	6%	7%	8%	9%	10%
1	0.990	0.980	0.971	0.962	0.952	0.943	0.935	0.926	0.917	0.909
2	0.980	0.961	0.943	0.925	0.907	0.890	0.873	0.857	0.842	0.826
3	0.971	0.942	0.915	0.889	0.864	0.840	0.816	0.794	0.772	0.751
4	0.961	0.924	0.888	0.855	0.823	0.792	0.763	0.735	0.708	0.683
5	0.951	0.906	0.863	0.822	0.784	0.747	0.713	0.681	0.650	0.621
6	0.942	0.888	0.837	0.790	0.746	0.705	0.666	0.630	0.596	0.564
7	0.933	0.871	0.813	0.760	0.711	0.665	0.623	0.583	0.547	0.513
8	0.923	0.853	0.789	0.731	0.677	0.627	0.582	0.540	0.502	0.467
9	0.914	0.837	0.766	0.703	0.645	0.592	0.544	0.500	0.460	0.424
10	0.905	0.820	0.744	0.676	0.614	0.558	0.508	0.463	0.422	0.386
11	0.896	0.804	0.722	0.650	0.585	0.527	0.475	0.429	0.388	0.350
12	0.887	0.788	0.701	0.625	0.557	0.497	0.444	0.397	0.356	0.319
13	0.879	0.773	0.681	0.601	0.530	0.469	0.415	0.368	0.326	0.290
14	0.870	0.758	0.661	0.577	0.505	0.442	0.388	0.340	0.299	0.263
15	0.861	0.743	0.642	0.555	0.481	0.417	0.362	0.315	0.275	0.239
16	0.853	0.728	0.623	0.534	0.458	0.394	0.339	0.292	0.252	0.218
17	0.844	0.714	0.605	0.513	0.436	0.371	0.317	0.270	0.231	0.198
18	0.836	0.700	0.587	0.494	0.416	0.350	0.296	0.250	0.212	0.180
19	0.828	0.686	0.570	0.475	0.396	0.331	0.277	0.232	0.194	0.164
20	0.820	0.673	0.554	0.456	0.377	0.312	0.258	0.215	0.178	0.149

Periods (n)	Interest rates (r) 11%	12%	13%	14%	15%	16%	17%	18%	19%	20%
1	0.901	0.893	0.885	0.877	0.870	0.862	0.855	0.847	0.840	0.833
2	0.812	0.797	0.783	0.769	0.756	0.743	0.731	0.718	0.706	0.694
3	0.731	0.712	0.693	0.675	0.658	0.641	0.624	0.609	0.593	0.579
4	0.659	0.636	0.613	0.592	0.572	0.552	0.534	0.516	0.499	0.482
5	0.593	0.567	0.543	0.519	0.497	0.476	0.456	0.437	0.419	0.402
6	0.535	0.507	0.480	0.456	0.432	0.410	0.390	0.370	0.352	0.335
7	0.482	0.452	0.425	0.400	0.376	0.354	0.333	0.314	0.296	0.279
8	0.434	0.404	0.376	0.351	0.327	0.305	0.285	0.266	0.249	0.233
9	0.391	0.361	0.333	0.308	0.284	0.263	0.243	0.225	0.209	0.194
10	0.352	0.322	0.295	0.270	0.247	0.227	0.208	0.191	0.176	0.162
11	0.317	0.287	0.261	0.237	0.215	0.195	0.178	0.162	0.148	0.135
12	0.286	0.257	0.231	0.208	0.187	0.168	0.152	0.137	0.124	0.112
13	0.258	0.229	0.204	0.182	0.163	0.145	0.130	0.116	0.104	0.093
14	0.232	0.205	0.181	0.160	0.141	0.125	0.111	0.099	0.088	0.078
15	0.209	0.183	0.160	0.140	0.123	0.108	0.095	0.084	0.074	0.065
16	0.188	0.163	0.141	0.123	0.107	0.093	0.081	0.071	0.062	0.054
17	0.170	0.146	0.125	0.108	0.093	0.080	0.069	0.060	0.052	0.045
18	0.153	0.130	0.111	0.095	0.081	0.069	0.059	0.051	0.044	0.038
19	0.138	0.116	0.098	0.083	0.070	0.060	0.051	0.043	0.037	0.031
20	0.124	0.104	0.087	0.073	0.061	0.051	0.043	0.037	0.031	0.026

CUMULATIVE PRESENT VALUE TABLE

This table shows the present value of £1 per annum, receivable or payable at the end of each year for *n* years $\frac{1-(1+r)^{-n}}{r}$.

Periods (n)	Interest rates (r) 1%	2%	3%	4%	5%	6%	7%	8%	9%	10%
1	0.990	0.980	0.971	0.962	0.952	0.943	0.935	0.926	0.917	0.909
2	1.970	1.942	1.913	1.886	1.859	1.833	1.808	1.783	1.759	1.736
3	2.941	2.884	2.829	2.775	2.723	2.673	2.624	2.577	2.531	2.487
4	3.902	3.808	3.717	3.630	3.546	3.465	3.387	3.312	3.240	3.170
5	4.853	4.713	4.580	4.452	4.329	4.212	4.100	3.993	3.890	3.791
6	5.795	5.601	5.417	5.242	5.076	4.917	4.767	4.623	4.486	4.355
7	6.728	6.472	6.230	6.002	5.786	5.582	5.389	5.206	5.033	4.868
8	7.652	7.325	7.020	6.733	6.463	6.210	5.971	5.747	5.535	5.335
9	8.566	8.162	7.786	7.435	7.108	6.802	6.515	6.247	5.995	5.759
10	9.471	8.983	8.530	8.111	7.722	7.360	7.024	6.710	6.418	6.145
11	10.368	9.787	9.253	8.760	8.306	7.887	7.499	7.139	6.805	6.495
12	11.255	10.575	9.954	9.385	8.863	8.384	7.943	7.536	7.161	6.814
13	12.134	11.348	10.635	9.986	9.394	8.853	8.358	7.904	7.487	7.103
14	13.004	12.106	11.296	10.563	9.899	9.295	8.745	8.244	7.786	7.367
15	13.865	12.849	11.938	11.118	10.380	9.712	9.108	8.559	8.061	7.606
16	14.718	13.578	12.561	11.652	10.838	10.106	9.447	8.851	8.313	7.824
17	15.562	14.292	13.166	12.166	11.274	10.477	9.763	9.122	8.544	8.022
18	16.398	14.992	13.754	12.659	11.690	10.828	10.059	9.372	8.756	8.201
19	17.226	15.679	14.324	13.134	12.085	11.158	10.336	9.604	8.950	8.365
20	18.046	16.351	14.878	13.590	12.462	11.470	10.594	9.818	9.129	8.514

Periods (n)	Interest rates (r) 11%	12%	13%	14%	15%	16%	17%	18%	19%	20%
1	0.901	0.893	0.885	0.877	0.870	0.862	0.855	0.847	0.840	0.833
2	1.713	1.690	1.668	1.647	1.626	1.605	1.585	1.566	1.547	1.528
3	2.444	2.402	2.361	2.322	2.283	2.246	2.210	2.174	2.140	2.106
4	3.102	3.037	2.974	2.914	2.855	2.798	2.743	2.690	2.639	2.589
5	3.696	3.605	3.517	3.433	3.352	3.274	3.199	3.127	3.058	2.991
6	4.231	4.111	3.998	3.889	3.784	3.685	3.589	3.498	3.410	3.326
7	4.712	4.564	4.423	4.288	4.160	4.039	3.922	3.812	3.706	3.605
8	5.146	4.968	4.799	4.639	4.487	4.344	4.207	4.078	3.954	3.837
9	5.537	5.328	5.132	4.946	4.772	4.607	4.451	4.303	4.163	4.031
10	5.889	5.650	5.426	5.216	5.019	4.833	4.659	4.494	4.339	4.192
11	6.207	5.938	5.687	5.453	5.234	5.029	4.836	4.656	4.486	4.327
12	6.492	6.194	5.918	5.660	5.421	5.197	4.988	4.793	4.611	4.439
13	6.750	6.424	6.122	5.842	5.583	5.342	5.118	4.910	4.715	4.533
14	6.982	6.628	6.302	6.002	5.724	5.468	5.229	5.008	4.802	4.611
15	7.191	6.811	6.462	6.142	5.847	5.575	5.324	5.092	4.876	4.675
16	7.379	6.974	6.604	6.265	5.954	5.668	5.405	5.162	4.938	4.730
17	7.549	7.120	6.729	6.373	6.047	5.749	5.475	5.222	4.990	4.775
18	7.702	7.250	6.840	6.467	6.128	5.818	5.534	5.273	5.033	4.812
19	7.839	7.366	6.938	6.550	6.198	5.877	5.584	5.316	5.070	4.843
20	7.963	7.469	7.025	6.623	6.259	5.929	5.628	5.353	5.101	4.870

Exam formulae

Valuation models

(i) Future value of S, of a sum X, invested for n periods, discounted at r% interest per annum:

$$S = X[1 + r]^n$$

(ii) Present value of £1 payable or receivable in n years, discounted at r% per annum:

$$PV = \frac{1}{[1+r]^n}$$

(iii) Present value of an annuity of £1 per annum, receivable or payable for n years, commencing in one year, discounted at r% per annum:

$$PV = \frac{1}{r}\left[1 - \frac{1}{[1+r]^n}\right]$$

(iv) Present value of £1 per annum, payable or receivable in perpetuity, commencing in one year, discounted at r% per annum:

$$PV = \frac{1}{r}$$

(v) Present value of £1 per annum, receivable or payable, commencing in one year, growing in perpetuity at a constant rate of g% per annum, discounted at r% per annum:

$$PV = \frac{1}{r - g}$$

Inventory management

(i) Economic Order Quantity $EOQ = \sqrt{\frac{2C_oD}{C_h}}$

Where C_o = cost of placing an order D = annual demand

C_h = cost of holding one unit in stock for one year

Cash management

(i) Optimal sale of securities, Baumol model:

$$\text{Optimal sale} = \sqrt{\frac{2 \times \text{Annual cash disbursements} \times \text{Cost per sale of securities}}{\text{Interest rate}}}$$

(ii) Spread between upper and lower cash balance limits, Miller-Orr model:

$$\text{Spread} = 3\left[\frac{\frac{3}{4} \times \text{transaction cost} \times \text{variance of cash flows}}{\text{Interest rate}}\right]^{\frac{1}{3}}$$

Notes

Notes

Review Form & Free Prize Draw - Paper P7 Financial Accounting and Tax Principles (1/09)

All original review forms from the entire BPP range, completed with genuine comments, will be entered into one of two draws on 31 July 2009 and 31 January 2010. The names on the first four forms picked out on each occasion will be sent a cheque for £50.

Name: ______________________________ **Address:** ______________________________

____

____

How have you used this Kit?
(Tick one box only)

☐ Home study (book only)
☐ On a course: college ______________________
☐ With 'correspondence' package
☐ Other ______________________

Why did you decide to purchase this Kit?
(Tick one box only)

☐ Have used the complementary Study text
☐ Have used other BPP products in the past
☐ Recommendation by friend/colleague
☐ Recommendation by a lecturer at college
☐ Saw advertising
☐ Other ______________________

During the past six months do you recall seeing/receiving any of the following?
(Tick as many boxes as are relevant)

☐ Our advertisement in *Financial Management*
☐ Our advertisement in *Pass*
☐ Our advertisement in *PQ*
☐ Our brochure with a letter through the post
☐ Our website www.bpp.com

Which (if any) aspects of our advertising do you find useful?
(Tick as many boxes as are relevant)

☐ Prices and publication dates of new editions
☐ Information on product content
☐ Facility to order books off-the-page
☐ None of the above

Which BPP products have you used?

Text	☐	*Success CD*	☐	*Learn Online*	☐
Kit	☑	*i-Learn*	☐	*Home Study Package*	☐
Passcard	☐	*i-Pass*	☐	*Home Study PLUS*	☐

Your ratings, comments and suggestions would be appreciated on the following areas.

	Very useful	*Useful*	*Not useful*
Passing CIMA exams	☐	☐	☐
Passing P7	☐	☐	☐
Planning your question practice	☐	☐	☐
Questions	☐	☐	☐
Top Tips etc in answers	☐	☐	☐
Content and structure of answers	☐	☐	☐
'Plan of attack' in mock exams	☐	☐	☐
Mock exam answers	☐	☐	☐

Overall opinion of this Kit *Excellent* ☐ *Good* ☐ *Adequate* ☐ *Poor* ☐

Do you intend to continue using BPP products? *Yes* ☐ *No* ☐

The BPP author of this edition can be e-mailed at: annabellefton@bpp.com

Please return this form to: Nick Weller, CIMA Publishing Manager, BPP Learning Media Ltd, FREEPOST, London, W12 8BR

Review Form & Free Prize Draw (continued)

TELL US WHAT YOU THINK

Please note any further comments and suggestions/errors below.

Free Prize Draw Rules

1 Closing date for 31 July 2009 draw is 30 June 2009. Closing date for 31 January 2010 draw is 31 December 2009.

2 Restricted to entries with UK and Eire addresses only. BPP employees, their families and business associates are excluded.

3 No purchase necessary. Entry forms are available upon request from BPP Learning Media Ltd. No more than one entry per title, per person. Draw restricted to persons aged 16 and over.

4 Winners will be notified by post and receive their cheques not later than 6 weeks after the relevant draw date.

5 The decision of the promoter in all matters is final and binding. No correspondence will be entered into.